Herndon's
Lincoln

American

History

Landmarks

Edited by

David Freeman Hawke

Herndon's Lincoln:

THE TRUE STORY
OF A
GREAT LIFE

by

William H. Herndon

A SELECTION

The Bobbs-Merrill Company, Inc.
Indianapolis & New York

William H. Herndon: 1818-1891

Contents

Editor's Introduction

1.

One day in 1844 Abraham Lincoln startled the young man who for the past three years had been reading law in his office. "Billy, do you want to enter into partnership with me in the law business?" William H. Herndon, nine years Lincoln's junior, knew the honor that had been offered, for Lincoln already ranked as one of the ablest lawyers in Illinois. Herndon accepted at once. "Billy, I can trust you, if you can trust me," Lincoln said, and with that remark sealed a partnership that lasted sixteen years.

Out of those years came *Herndon's Lincoln*. Soon after it was published in 1889, a friend predicted—correctly, it turned out—that as a portrait of Lincoln "Mr. Herndon's work will never be surpassed." Fuller, more scholarly biographies of Lincoln's years as an Illinois lawyer have been published since, but none is livelier, more vivid, or more readable. Historians over the years have chipped away at the book, uncovering minor errors (a name misspelled, a date incorrect), exposing at least one serious flaw (the Ann Rutledge love affair), and turning up a few major inaccuracies (notably in passages dealing with Lincoln's youth). But the core of the work, that half describing the years Herndon knew Lincoln on a day-to-day basis, continues to resist the scholarly chisel. "When Herndon relates a fact as of his own observation, it may generally be accepted without question," says Paul M. Angle, a close student of the book, adding that even when the points where Herndon erred are totaled together "the value of his work is not seriously impaired." Today, some three quarters of a century after the book was published, anyone writing of Lincoln in Illinois inevitably depends in a large way on Herndon's recollections for his source material.

Few modern writers, however, seek to make the point that Herndon reiterates throughout his book—that Lincoln's

vii

greatness could be seen only when measured against "other men" who had been reared in the "stagnant putrid pool" of the early-nineteenth-century midwest. "Lincoln rose from a lower depth than any of them," Herndon held. In making the point he in effect censured himself: compared to Lincoln, he was born with a silver spoon in his mouth. True, he could remember as a child of five seeing a "savage lift my mother's long hair and threaten to scalp her." But soon afterward his father carried the family out of the forest to the village of Springfield, there to open a tavern that did well; he also speculated successfully in land. He died leaving an estate worth at least $60,000.

Herndon split no rails as a boy. He attended school in Springfield and then went to Illinois College, which had a faculty of five Yale graduates determined to impress the standards of their alma mater on their 64 students. Then, as later, Herndon had trouble settling down to the job at hand. Although a Southerner in upbringing—his father was a Jacksonian Democrat who had emigrated from Kentucky shortly after Billy was born in 1818—he soon got mixed up in the abolition movement, then beginning to stir the people of Illinois, and his studies went by the board. A year after arriving at college he was back home, either because the Depression of 1837, which had just struck the nation, had forced his father to retrench on expenses, or because he failed to pass arithmetic and flunked out, or else, as he later insisted, because his involvement in the antislavery movement distressed his parents. Once back in Springfield Herndon for the time being broke with his father, joined the Whig party, and moved from home to the loft over Joshua F. Speed's store. It was here he met Lincoln, who had recently come from New Salem to study law in Springfield and also used the loft for sleeping.

Herndon began to earn a living as a clerk in Speed's store. The pay was $700 a year, which "was considered good pay then," but with the nation still suffering from the depression, Herndon found "poverty is staring us all in the face." In 1840, when 22 years old, he married a local girl who made him, by all accounts, blissfully happy. The first child of what was to be a large and closely-knit family arrived the following year. Herndon now saw he "had to push and hustle along" if he were adequately to care for his family. At this point Lincoln, now one of Springfield's leading lawyers and a partner of the even better known Stephen T. Logan, suggested he read law in the offices of Logan and Lincoln. Herndon accepted the offer. He worked hard—"too much so," he later said, "studied from 12 to 14 hours a day"—and within a year or so was handling much of the routine office work for the partners. For reasons still not clear, Lincoln and Logan decided sometime in 1844 to dissolve their partnership, and in the fall of that year Lincoln stunned Herndon by asking him to come in as the new partner. Years later when an acquaintance wondered why Lincoln had invited Billy into the firm, he said, "I don't know and no one else does."

2.

Herndon knew the adult Lincoln for a longer consecutive period than any other man, but he never pretended to make more of the friendship than existed in fact. "Probably except in his scrapes, Lincoln never poured out his soul to any mortal creature at any time and on no subject," he once told a friend. "He was the most secretive—reticent—shut-mouthed man that ever existed." But even a "shut-mouthed man" occasionally lets down the bars, and Herndon during the next sixteen years rarely missed a revelation when it came. "He was so good and so odd a man," he once said in an effort to explain his ability to recall the years with Lincoln in such accurate detail, "how in hell could I help study him."

That last remark might have been phrased differently: this man at once "so good and so odd" puzzled and fascinated Herndon partly because he differed so much from him. Herndon enjoyed nature: a tree, for him a thing of beauty, was for Lincoln a symbol of toil and sweat, something out of which log cabins were made and fence rails were split. Lincoln never drank; Billy drank too much and often went on sprees that embarrassed his partner. Herndon was humorless, indiscreet, impetuous, and garrulous. He had no side, opening himself completely to all who came along, where Lincoln exposed only as much of himself or his thought as the moment demanded. A lawyer who knew both men once said: "Mr. Herndon as a rule considered propositions and questions in the abstract, while Mr. Lincoln considered them more in the concrete." That difference carried over into their reading preferences. Herndon's centered on philosophy, history, and science; Lincoln's on daily newspapers. Sometimes, though, Lincoln did look into the books Billy was constantly lugging into the office. In one that contained a speech by Theodore Parker—a particular hero of Herndon's—he underlined a sentence for future use: "Democracy is Direct Self-Government, over all the people, for all the people, by all the people."

Altogether their differences in character, coupled with Herndon's occasional indiscretions, bulked so large that friends often urged Lincoln to drop his partner. He always refused. "I know my business, I reckon," he would say. "I know Billy Herndon better than anybody and . . . I intend to stick by him."

What Lincoln knew about Billy Herndon was this: first, he excelled as a lawyer, and to the extent that he was better read in the law, he surpassed Lincoln. Herndon always handled the work when it came to researching precedents in a complex case. "I made out his best briefs in the largest law cases," he once said in a rare boasting mood, adding, "Lincoln would argue his case from those briefs and get the credit for them while I was the power behind them." Herndon proved his worth in 1847–48 during the years Lincoln spent in Washington as a congressman, for the firm continued to do a good share of the business in Sangamon County. By the mid-1850's the partners handled one out of every four cases in the county and led the bar in their share of business.

Lincoln always called Herndon "Billy"; Herndon, on the other hand, always addressed his senior partner as "Mr. Lincoln." Billy's youth—he was twenty-six when the partnership began—gave Lincoln further reason for satisfaction. Lincoln's two previous partners had been older, more eminent men who turned over to the junior partner the drudgery involved in running a law office. Also, their political ambitions had tended to put a damper on Lincoln's activities. Herndon loved politics but had no ambitions for himself in that arena, and he accepted the role of junior partner with equanimity. Lincoln, he said, "was the great big man of our firm and I was the little one."

Herndon had further qualities that were valuable to Lincoln. His youth gave him ties with an upcoming generation of voters, and those ties persisted into middle age. "I am the young man's friend," he said, "and am not without influence among them." He had a way with the "wild boys," many of them present or former drinking companions—Herndon periodically swore off liquor and joined the temperance movement, but it was not until old age he finally gave it up for good—that Lincoln never hesitated to use. "Form a 'Rough and Ready Club,'" he wrote from Washington on the eve of the campaign for Zachary Taylor, "and have regular meetings and speeches. . . . Gather up all the shrewd, wild boys about town, whether just of age or a little under age. . . . Let every one play the part he can play best— some speak, some sing, and all 'holler.'" When there was hackwork to be done, Herndon often saw it through. Lincoln "does not know the details of how we get along," he told a friend during the campaign against Douglas in 1858. "I do, but he does not. That kind of thing does not suit his tastes, nor does it suit me, yet I am compelled to do it—do it because I cannot get rid of it."

Herndon's political usefulness went to seed, as did Lincoln's interest in politics, for several years after 1849, when Lincoln returned from Washington after being defeated for re-election to Congress. Both men concentrated on earning what was for an Illinois lawyer of that day a substantial living. The passage in 1854 of Stephen A. Douglas's Kansas-Nebraska Act carried both men back into politics. That act, by repealing the Missouri Compromise and substituting in its stead the doctrine of popular sovereignty, made it possible for slavery to expand into a western territory hitherto closed to it. "I commenced early in 1854 in our county and spoke on every stump and every church and schoolhouse therein," said Herndon, "and thus carried our county by a larger majority than ever before." Lincoln lost out on a bid for the Senate, but Herndon, without really seeking the post, was elected mayor of Springfield. He came in as a reform candidate, eager, among other things, to inaugurate a public school system and determined, now that he was again on the wagon, to enforce an ordinance that forbade the sale of liquor within the town limits. By all accounts he was a forceful, effective mayor. The free schools the town eventually established stemmed largely from Herndon's work during his year in office. He came so close to drying up the town's liquor supply that the parched voters complained about their mayor's "peculiar hobby," and Herndon's name did not appear on the ballot at the next election.

The disgruntlement of his fellow citizens bothered Herndon little. By the end of his term the mayor had become involved in the affairs of the newly created Republican Party, and in 1856 both he and Lincoln were engrossed in getting its first national candidate, John Charles Frémont, elected to the presidency "Wake up and shake off that *timidity—sensitiveness* or what not," he admonished a friend, "*roll up your sleeves* and get into the fight like a tiger." The offices of Lincoln and Herndon were turned "into a kind of war-office," and Herndon "took the young, active, vigorous honest men there and talked to them— got them to take an interest that they would not otherwise have done in favor of human liberty—human rights." For the first time he felt himself involved in a great crusade, and to advance it he spoke "in almost every part of our wide extended state." Never before had he enjoyed a campaign so much, and not even Frémont's defeat diminished the pleasure of the fight. "I shall ever hold the year 1856 the crown of my life," he said after the votes had been counted.

During the campaign of 1856 the issue of slavery began to swallow up Herndon's interest in the other reforms—civic improvements, women's rights, temperance, free schools—that had engaged his energy. His biographer, David Donald, believes that from this point on he became, at least publicly, a different man. "The antislavery agitation had an unfortunate effect on Herndon's personality," says Donald. "He lost something of [his] exuberance and versatility . . . Now all his emotions were squeezed through one wine press and the juice was bitter." Deprived of Lincoln's "genial tolerance," he became "obsessed by the notion of a mission to be performed."

Be that as it may, Herndon still remained politically useful to Lincoln: it was in the campaign against Douglas in 1858 that he performed his greatest service. While Lincoln debated with Douglas before audiences numbering in the thousands, Herndon again visited "the schoolhouses and the village churches, where good can be done and where the 'big bugs' do not go," as he put it. "There are no great crowds at these crossroads places, yet they are really the places where good can be done." One wonders at Herndon's eagerness to give so much of himself to Lincoln's career, especially considering Lincoln's treatment of him after Douglas's victory in 1858. But for Herndon there was no puzzle why he acted as he did. "He moved me by a shrug of a shoulder," he once said. It was as simple as that.

3.

After the defeat in 1858, Lincoln said: "I expect everyone to desert me except Billy." Actually, it was Lincoln who all but deserted Billy, whose political usefulness had by now virtually come to an end. Herndon's obsession with slavery offended many who had been attracted into the Republican Party for other reasons—its views on the tariff, on the dispensation of western lands, and so on. Where Lincoln, now a national figure, had to tread carefully when commenting on John Brown's raid on Harper's Ferry, Herndon saw no reason for not regarding Brown as one of "the world's gods and heroes." And there were other embarrassing indiscretions, these tied to Illinois politics. Herndon once, for example, accused the state party chairman of a "misapplication of funds," which led that gentleman to demand that Lincoln "set him right."

Herndon, curiously, did not number among the original supporters of Lincoln for president, and his role at the nominating convention in Chicago was so slight as to pass unnoticed by the key figures there. During the campaign Herndon, of course, stumped the state for Lincoln and as usual touched the spots where he was most effective—the hamlets and crossroad villages—but he had no hand in shaping strategy on the national or even local level. After the election, Billy slipped beyond the pale, and from him Lincoln "took no advice, and sought no counsel," according to a mutual friend. If Herndon resented the treatment, he never, then or ever after, so far as is known, voiced any bitterness.

The last day in Springfield before setting out for Washington

Lincoln came round to the office to visit Herndon. The sun was setting as they talked over pending business matters; then, that done, they began to reminisce.

"Billy," Lincoln asked, "how long have we been together?"

"Over sixteen years."

"We've never had a cross word during all that time, have we?"

"No, indeed, we have not."

"Billy, there's one thing I have, for some time, wanted you to tell me, but I reckon I ought to apologize for my nerve and curiosity in asking it even now."

"What is it?"

"I want you to tell me how many times you have been drunk."

Herndon, stunned—Lincoln had never before alluded to his drinking—answered "as promply and definitely" as he could, then waited for a moral lecture. None came. Lincoln went on to tell how many times he had been urged to drop Billy from the partnership and that "despite my shortcomings, he believed in me and therefore would not desert me."

It is hard to resist the thought that Lincoln, who was the subtlest of men and who could also be ruthless, was at this moment saying, in effect: "Billy, your drinking forbids me from carrying you with me to Washington to serve in my administration." Regardless of why he had asked the blunt question, Lincoln at no time during his presidency went out of the way to reward a friend whose service and devotion to him few had equaled and none exceeded. After their last encounter in Springfield the two men met only once more, when Herndon paid a brief visit to Washington to ask a small favor for an acquaintance, his single imposition during Lincoln's years as president.

4.

Within a month after Lincoln's death Herndon began to collect material on this man "so good and so odd," about whom he had puzzled so long. He traveled through Indiana and Illinois talking to those who had known the young Lincoln and his family and then, back in Springfield, sent out a stream of letters with further questions. "Friend Hall," goes one letter:

Please *write to me at any time you may think of anything that is* good or bad *of Mr. Lincoln, truthfully just as it happened and took place. Were any of you boys applicants for any office made to Mr. Lincoln while he was President?*

Hall—What is your honest opinion—Come, honest *opinion— in reference to Mr. Lincoln's love for his kin and relations generally.* Please—*friend*—*accommodate me.*

Affection for Lincoln prohibited Herndon becoming a muckraker or debunker of the man, but as the letter to "Friend Hall" shows, neither did he plan to present him as a paragon of virtue. He aimed to write about Lincoln for those who "love the truth for its own sake," he said 35 years later, when the biography had at last been published; "and sooner or later the life of L. will find them. I drew the picture of Mr. Lincoln as I saw and knew him. I told the naked God's truth, and I'll stand by it, let the consequences be what they may be."

Herndon completed the bulk of his research within a year after Lincoln's death. In the winter of 1865–1866 he skimmed off some of the material and delivered it in three lectures which were generally well received. The cream of the research was used in a fourth lecture given in November, 1866, in which he revealed to the world the great love with Ann Rutledge, which for Herndon explained the deep streak of melancholy he had observed in Lincoln. The storm that greeted this talk, especially from Mrs. Lincoln and her friends, gave Herndon an inkling how few people wanted to hear "the naked God's truth." Thereafter he said little more publicly about his friend.

Herndon continued to reminisce with anyone who would listen to his tales about Lincoln, but the effort to organize the recollections into a book proved too much, as did just about everything else during the next decade or so. He continued to practice law, but a lingering distaste for a profession he had never especially liked increased steadily. "*I hate the law;* it cramps me; it seems to me priestly and barbaric," he had once said, and finally one day he snapped shut the tome in hand and said: "Damn the law." With that he left the office and never returned, determined to live out his life on a farm inherited from his father.

Herndon proved to be not much of a farmer, for all his love of the soil. "He could tell anyone how to plant seeds to produce the best results," a neighbor remarked, "but he could not raise anything but Hell." He took to drinking again, and the farm deteriorated as his alcoholic intake rose. The "considerable property" he had inherited or had purchased during prosperous years gave him few financial worries until he "lost much of it in the crash and consequent crisis of 1873," and from that time on he lived uncomfortably close to poverty. Early in the 1880's he got hold of himself, stopped drinking for good, and inspired by a young man named Jesse W. Weik, who had begun to correspond with him about Lincoln, thought once again of his biography. Pressure from Weik, and a loan or two in cash to carry the Herndon family through thin periods, led to a formal agreement in 1885 to collaborate on the work that came forth four years later as *Herndon's Lincoln.* Herndon confessed he "was as poor as a church mouse" when it was published. He expected to pull in a fortune from it, but once again the world gave less than he expected or deserved. He died on March 18, 1891, without having received sufficient royalties to pay off his modest debt to Jesse Weik.

Note on the Text

Careful readers gave Herndon's book the praise it deserved, but those who preferred that Lincoln be treated as a god condemned it outright. The work did not sell well, yet it refused to die. Professor Donald found in 1948 that by then it had gone through at least 25 various editions, issues, and printings. The freshness of its literary style did much to keep it alive, and for this virtue the unsung Jesse Weik rates praise. Herndon wrote as he talked, "in a gallop—with a whoop." Weik with considerable skill took his rambling, unconnnected thoughts, and polished them into sentences, paragraphs, and chapters without destroying the informal, conversational tone of Herndon's style. Few nonwriters have been better served.

The book's attitude toward Lincoln, as much as the style, has also contributed to its longevity. Herndon was the first to attempt a balanced portrait of Lincoln, to present him as a man whose "ambition was a little engine that knew no rest" and yet at the same time a man of greatness. But to show Lincoln as great during the years in Illinois gave Herndon trouble, for it was only during the tortuous years of the presidency that his stature manifested itself. He sought to resolve the difficulty by introducing his three mediocre chapters on the presidency with the remark: "Lincoln, the President, did not differ greatly from Lincoln the lawyer and politician," a view no student today would accept. For all its virtues, Herndon's version of Abraham Lincoln had a built-in flaw he could do nothing about. "It is," as David Donald so well puts it, "a statue without a head."

However, there were flaws in the book that Herndon could have done something about if he had proceeded with more care. The major points on which he has been censured are these, as summarized by Professor Donald: (1) The illegitimacy of Lincoln's mother, Nancy Hanks: "There seems to be a slight preponderance of testimony favoring the Herndon theory of illegitimacy." (2) Lincoln's illegitimacy: Herndon's insinuation of "is utterly groundless." (3) The picture of Lincoln's father as a shiftless wretch: "definitely incorrect." (4) The Ann Rutledge love affair: "Of reliable evidence touching upon the romance itself, there is not the slightest particle," says Paul M. Angle. (5) The account of Lincoln as a defaulting bridegroom: "unsupported by facts." (6) The "domestic hell" of Lincoln's married life: "distorted" and exaggerated. (7) Lincoln's religion: Herndon's effort to make Lincoln resemble the village atheist overstates the case.

Herndon once aptly called his life of Lincoln "a limited one—kind of subjective—inner life, with a mere thread of history running along." This edition seeks to preserve that quality of the work. It centers on those years that Herndon knew and worked with Lincoln. The excisions have been heaviest where Herndon drew on the recollections of others, notably in the early chapters dealing with Lincoln's youth and the later ones dealing with his presidency. For most readers the most obvious omission will be the debatable Ann Rutledge story. The occasional spots where Herndon gets a date wrong or misspells a name have been silently corrected. This abridgement has been drawn from a copy in the New-York Historical Society of the original three-volume edition published in 1889. All chapter headings in this edition have been supplied.

For those who wish to collate the present edition with the original, the pagination is as follows. The material in Chapter 1 is taken from pages 1-13, 18-21, 23-25, 27-30, 32, 34, 36-40, 42-44, and 59-68 of the 1889 work; that in Chapter 2, from pages 69-76, 78-81, 84-85, 92-95, and 97-127; Chapter 3, from pages 162-167, 169-199; Chapter 4, pages 205-231; Chapter 6, pages 295-299, 307-331; Chapter 7, pages 332-359; Chapter 8, pages 361-389; Chapter 9, pages 390-418; Chapter 10, pages 423-445; Chapter 11, pages 447-468; and Chapter 12, pages 469-474, 477-487.

Herndon's

Lincoln

1

Youth

Beyond the fact that he was born on the 12th day of February, 1809, in Hardin County, Kentucky, Mr. Lincoln usually had but little to say of himself, the lives of his parents, or the history of the family before their removal to Indiana. If he mentioned the subject at all, it was with great reluctance and significant reserve. There was something about his origin he never cared to dwell upon. His nomination for the Presidency in 1860, however, made the publication of his life a necessity, and attracted to Springfield an army of campaign biographers and newspaper men. They met him in his office, stopped him in his walks, and followed him to his house. Artists came to paint his picture, and sculptors to make his bust. His autographs were in demand, and people came long distances to shake him by the hand. This sudden elevation to national prominence found Mr. Lincoln unprepared in a great measure for the unaccustomed demonstrations that awaited him. While he was easy of approach and equally courteous to all, yet, as he said to me one evening after a long day of hand-shaking, he could not understand why people should make so much over him.

Among the earliest newspaper men to arrive in Springfield after the Chicago convention was the late J. L. Scripps of the Chicago *Tribune*, who proposed to prepare a history of his life. Mr. Lincoln deprecated the idea of writing even a campaign biography. "Why, Scripps," said he, "it is a great piece of folly to attempt to make anything out of me or my early life. It can all be condensed into a single sentence, and that sentence you will find in Gray's Elegy.

> *'The short and simple annals of the poor.'*

"That's my life, and that's all you or anyone else can make out of it."

On the subject of his ancestry and origin I only remember one time when Mr. Lincoln ever referred to it. It was about 1850, when he and I were driving in his one-horse buggy to the court in Menard County, Illinois. The suit we were going to try was one in which we were likely, either directly or collaterally, to touch upon the subject of hereditary traits. During the ride he spoke, for the first time in my hearing, of his mother, dwelling on her characteristics, and mentioning and enumerating what qualities he inherited from her. He said, among other things, that she was the illegitimate daughter of Lucy Hanks and a well-bred Virginia farmer or planter; and he argued that from this last source came his power of analysis, his logic, his mental activity, and all the qualities that distinguished him from the other members and descendants of the Hanks family. His theory in discussing the matter of hereditary traits had been, that, for certain reasons, illegitimate children are oftentimes sturdier and brighter than those born in lawful wedlock; and in his case, he believed that his better nature and finer qualities came from this broad-minded, unknown Virginian. The revelation—painful as it was—called up the recollection of his mother, and, as the buggy jolted over the road, he added ruefully, "God bless my mother; all that I am or ever hope to be I owe to her," and immediately lapsed into silence. Our interchange of ideas ceased, and we rode on for some time without exchanging a word. He was sad and absorbed. Burying himself in thought, and musing no doubt over the disclosure he had just made, he drew round him a barrier which I feared to penetrate. His words and melancholy tone made a deep impression on me. It was an experience I can never forget. As we neared the town of Petersburg we were overtaken by an old man who rode beside us for awhile, and entertained us with reminiscences of days on the frontier. Lincoln was reminded of several Indiana stories, and by the time we had reached the unpretentious courthouse at our destination, his sadness had passed away.

After Mr. Lincoln had attained some prominence in the world, persons who knew both himself and his father were constantly pointing to the want of resemblance between the two. Thomas, roving and shiftless, to whom was "reserved the honor of an illustrious paternity," was, we are told, five feet ten inches high, weighed 195 pounds, had a well-rounded face, dark hazel eyes, coarse black hair, and was slightly stoop-shouldered. His build was so compact that Dennis Hanks used to say that he could not find the point of separation between his ribs. He was proverbially slow of movement, mentally and physically; was careless, inert, and dull; was sinewy, and gifted with great strength; was inoffensively quiet and peaceable, but when roused to resistance a dangerous antagonist. He had a liking for jokes and stories, which was one of the few traits he transmitted to his illustrious son; was fond of the chase, and had no marked aversion for the bottle, though in the latter case he indulged no more freely than the average Kentuckian of his day. At the time of his marriage to Nancy Hanks he could neither read nor write; but his wife, who was gifted with more education, and was otherwise his mental superior, taught him, it is said, to write his name and to read—at least, he was able in later years to spell his way slowly through the Bible. In his religious belief he first affiliated with the Free-Will Baptists. After his removal to Indiana he changed his adherence to the Presbyterians—or Predestinarians, as they were then called—and later united with the Christian—vulgarly called Campbellite—Church, in which latter faith he is supposed to have died. He was a carpenter by trade, and essaged farming too.

Nancy Hanks, the mother of the President, at a very early age was taken from her mother Lucy—afterwards married to Henry Sparrow—and sent to live with her aunt and uncle, Thomas and Betsy Sparrow. Under this same roof the irrepressible and cheerful waif, Dennis Hanks—whose name will be frequently seen in these pages—also found a shelter. At the time of her marriage to Thomas Lincoln, Nancy was in her twenty-third year. She was above the ordinary height in stature, weighed about 130 pounds, was slenderly built, and had much the appearance of one inclined to consumption. Her skin was dark; hair dark brown; eyes gray and small; forehead prominent; face sharp and angular, with a marked expression of melancholy which fixed itself in the memory of everyone who ever saw or knew her. Though her life was seemingly beclouded by a spirit of sadness, she was in disposition amiable and generally cheerful. Mr. Lincoln himself said to me in 1851, on receiving the news of his father's death, that whatever might be said of his parents, and however unpromising the early surroundings of his mother may have been, she was highly intellectual by nature, had a strong memory, acute judgment, and was cool and heroic.

Kentucky, at that day, afforded few if any privileges, and possessed fewer advantages to allure the poor man; and no doubt so it seemed to Thomas Lincoln. The land he occupied was sterile and broken. A mere barren glade, and destitute of timber, it required a persistent effort to coax a living out of it; and to one of his easy going disposition, life there was a never ending struggle. Stories of vast stretches of rich and unoccupied land in Indiana reaching his ears, and despairing of the prospect of any betterment in his condition so long as he remained in Kentucky, he resolved, at last, to leave the State and seek a more inviting lodgement beyond the Ohio. The assertion made by some of Mr. Lincoln's biographers, and so often repeated by sentimental writers, that his father left Kentucky to aviod the sight of or contact with slavery, lacks confirmation. In all Hardin County— at that time a large area of territory—there were not over fifty slaves; and it is doubtful if he saw enough of slavery to fill him with the righteous opposition to the institution with which he has so frequently been credited. Moreover, he never in later years manifested any especial aversion to it.

Having determined on emigrating to Indiana, he began preparations for removal in the fall of 1816 by building for his use a flatboat. Loading it with his tools and other personal effects, including in the invoice, as we are told, four hundred gallons of whiskey, he launched his "crazy craft" on a tributary of Salt Creek known as the Rolling Fork. Along with the current he floated down to the Ohio River, but his rudely made vessel, either from the want of experience in the navigator, or because of its ill adaption to withstand the force and caprices of the currents in the great river, capsized one day, and boat and cargo went to the bottom. The luckless boatman set to work however, and by dint of great patience and labor succeeded in recovering the tools and the bulk of the whiskey. Righting his boat, he continued down the river, landing at a point called Tompson's Ferry, in Perry County, on the Indiana side. Here he disposed of his vessel, and placing his goods in the care of a settler named Posey, he struck out through the interior in search of a location for his new home. Sixteen miles back from the river he found one that pleased his fancy, and he marked it off for himself. Having secured a place for his home he trudged back to Kentucky—walking all the way—for his family. Two horses brought them and all their effects to the Indiana shore. Posey kindly gave or hired them the use of a wagon, into which they packed not only their furniture and carpenter tools, but the liquor, which it is presumed had lain undisturbed in the former's cellar. Slowly and carefully picking their way through the dense woods, they at last reached their destination on the banks of Little Pigeon Creek. There were some detentions on the way, but no serious mishaps.

The head of the household now set resolutely to work to build a shelter for his family.

The structure, when completed, was fourteen feet square, and was built of small unhewn logs. In the language of the day, it was called a "half-faced camp," being enclosed on all sides but one. It had neither floor, door, nor windows. In this forbidding hovel these doughty emigrants braved the exposure of the varying elements for an entire year. At the end of that time Thomas and Betsy Sparrow followed, bringing with them Dennis Hanks; and to them Thomas Lincoln surrendered the "half-faced camp," while he moved into a more pretentious structure—a cabin enclosed on all sides.

The cabin was of hewed logs, and was eighteen feet square. It was high enough to admit of a loft, where Abe slept, and to which he ascended each night by means of pegs driven in the wall. The rude furniture was in keeping with the surroundings. Three-legged stools answered for chairs. The bedstead, made of poles fastened in the cracks on one side, and supported by a crotched stick driven in the ground on the other, was covered with skins, leaves, and old clothes. A table of the same finish as the stools, a few pewter dishes, a Dutch oven, and a skillet completed the household outfit. In this uninviting frontier structure the future President was destined to pass the greater part of his boyhood.

The dull routine of chores and household errands in the boy's everyday life was brightened now and then by a visit to the mill. I often in later years heard Mr. Lincoln say that going to the mill gave him the greatest pleasure of his boyhood days.

"We had to go seven miles to mill," relates David Turnham,

the friend of his youth, "and then it was a handmill that would only grind from fifteen to twenty bushels of corn in a day. There was but little wheat grown at that time, and when we did have wheat we had to grind it in the mill described and use it without bolting, as there were no bolts in the country. Abe and I had to do the milling, frequently going twice to get one grist."

In his eleventh year he began that marvelous and rapid growth in stature for which he was so widely noted in the Pigeon Creek settlement. "As he shot up," says Turnham, "he seemed to change in appearance and action. Although quick-witted and ready with an answer, he began to exhibit deep thoughtfulness, and was so often lost in studied reflection we could not help noticing the strange turn in his actions. He disclosed rare timidity and sensitiveness, especially in the presence of men and women, and although cheerful enough in the presence of the boys, he did not appear to seek our company as earnestly as before." It was only the development we find in the history of every boy. Nature was a little abrupt in the case of Abraham Lincoln; she tossed him from the nimbleness of boyhood to the gravity of manhood in a single night.

In the fall of 1818, the scantily settled region in the vicinity of Pigeon Creek—where the Lincolns were then living—suffered a visitation of that dread disease common in the West in early days, and known in the vernacular of the frontier as "the milk-sick." Thomas and Betsy Sparrow fell ill of the disease and died within a few days of each other. Thomas Lincoln performed the services of undertaker. With his whipsaw he cut out the lumber, and with commendable promptness he nailed together the rude coffins to enclose the forms of the dead. The bodies were borne to a scantily cleared knoll in the midst of the forest, and there, without ceremony, quietly let down into the grave. Meanwhile Abe's mother had also fallen a victim to the insidious disease. Her sufferings, however, were destined to be of brief duration. Within a week she too rested from her labors. "She struggled on, day by day," says one of the household, "a good Christian woman, and died on the seventh day after she was taken sick. Abe and his sister Sarah waited on their mother, and did the lit-tle jobs and errands required of them. There was no physician nearer than thirty-five miles. The mother knew she was going to die, and called the children to her bedside. She was very weak, and the children leaned over while she gave her last message. Placing her feeble hand on little Abe's head she told him to be kind and good to his father and sister; to both she said, 'Be good to one another,' expressing a hope that they might live, as they had been taught by her, to love their kindred and worship God."

Thomas Lincoln's widowerhood was brief. He had scarcely mourned the death of his first wife a year until he reappeared in Kentucky at Elizabethtown in search of another. His admiration centred on Sally Bush, the widow of Daniel Johnston, the jailer of Hardin County, who had died several years before of a disease known as the "cold plague." "He made a very short courtship," wrote Samuel Haycraft to me in a letter, December 7, 1866. "He came to see her on the first day of December, 1819, and in a straightforward manner told her that they had known each other from childhood. '*Miss* Johnston,' said he, 'I have no wife and you no husband. I came a-purpose to marry you. I knowed you from a gal and you knowed me from a boy. I've no time to lose; and if you're willin' let it be done straight off.' She replied that she could not marry him right off, as she had some little debts which she wanted to pay first. He replied, 'Give me a list of them.' He got the list and paid them that evening. Next morning I issued the license, and they were married within sixty yards of my house."

Lincoln's brother-in-law, Ralph Krume, and his four horses and spacious wagon were again brought into requisition. With commendable generosity he transported the newly married pair and their household effects to their home in Indiana. The new Mrs. Lincoln was accompanied by her three children, John, Sarah, and Matilda. Her social status is fixed by the comparison of a neighbor, who observed that "life among the Hankses, the Lincolns, and the Enlows was a long ways below life among the Bushes."

The two sets of children in the Lincoln household—to their credit be it said—lived together in perfect accord. Abe was in his tenth year, and his stepmother, awake to the importance of an education, made a way for him to attend school. To her he seemed full of promise; and although not so quick of comprehension as other boys, yet she believed in encouraging his every effort. He had had a few weeks of schooling in Kentucky, but it is hardly probable that he could read; he certainly could not write.

Hazel Dorsey was Abe's first teacher in Indiana. He held forth a mile and a half from the Lincoln farm. The schoolhouse was built of round logs, and was just high enough for a man to stand erect under the loft. The floor was of split logs, or what were called puncheons. The chimney was made of poles and clay; and the windows were made by cutting out parts of two logs, placing pieces of split boards a proper distance apart, and over the aperture thus formed pasting pieces of greased paper to admit light.

At Dorsey's school Abe was ten years old; at the next one, Andrew Crawford's, he was about fourteen; and at Swaney's he was in his seventeenth year. The last school required a walk of over four miles, and on account of the distance his attendance was not only irregular but brief. Schoolmaster Crawford introduced a new feature in his school, and we can imagine its effect on his pupils, whose training had been limited to the social requirements of the backwoods settlement. It was instruction in manners. One scholar was required to go outside, and re-enter the room as a lady or gentleman would enter a drawing room or parlor. Another scholar would receive the first party at the door, and escort him or her about the room, making polite introductions to each person in the room. How the gaunt and clumsy Abe went through this performance we shall probably never know. If his awkward movements gave rise to any amusement, his schoolmates never revealed it.

The books used at school were Webster's Spelling Book and the American speller. All the scholars learned to cipher, and afterwards used Pike's Arithmetic. Mr. Lincoln told me in later years that Murray's English Reader was the best schoolbook ever put into the hands of an American youth. I conclude, therefore, he must have used that also.

He was now over six feet high and was growing at a tremendous rate, for he added two inches more before the close of his seventeenth year, thus reaching the limit of his stature. He weighed in the region of a hundred and sixty pounds; was wiry, vigorous, and strong. His feet and hands were large, arms and legs long and in striking contrast with his slender trunk and small head. "His skin was shriveled and yellow," declares one of the girls who attended Crawford's school. "His shoes, when he had any, were low. He wore buckskin breeches, linsey-woolsey shirt, and a cap made of the skin of a squirrel or coon. His breeches were baggy and lacked by several inches meeting the tops of his shoes, thereby exposing his shinbone, 'sharp, blue, and narrow.' " In one branch of school learning he was a great success; that was spelling. We are indebted to Kate Roby, a pretty miss of fifteen, for an incident which illustrates alike his proficiency in orthography and his natural inclination to help another out of the mire. The word "defied" had been given out by Schoolmaster Crawford, but had been misspelled several times when it came Miss Roby's turn. "Abe stood on the opposite side of the room" (related Miss Roby to me in 1865) "and was watching me. I began d-e-f—and then I stopped, hesitating whether to proceed with an 'i' or a 'y'. Looking up I beheld Abe, a grin covering his face, and pointing with his index finger to his eye. I took the hint, spelled the word with an 'i', and it went through all right." There was more or less of an attachment between Miss Roby and Abe, although the lady took pains to assure me that they were never in love. She described with self-evident pleasure, however, the delightful experience of an evening's stroll down to the river with him, where they were wont to sit on the bank and watch the moon as it slowly rose over the neighboring hills. Dangling their youthful feet in the water, they gazed on the pale orb of night, as many a fond pair before them had done and will continue to do until the end of the world. One evening, when thus engaged, their conversation and thoughts turned on the movement of the planets. "I did not suppose that Abe, who had seen so little of the world, would know anything about it, but he proved to my satisfaction that the moon did not go down at all; that it only seemed to; that the earth, revolving from west to east, carried us under, as it were. 'We do the sinking,' he explained; 'while to us the moon is comparatively still. The moon's sinking is only an illusion.' I at once dubbed him a fool, but later developments convinced me that I was the fool, not he. He was well acquainted with the general laws of astronomy and the movements of the heavenly bodies, but where he could have learned so much, or how to put it so plainly, I never could understand."

Absalom Roby is authority for the statement that even at that early day Abe was a patient reader of a Louisville newspaper, which some one at Gentryville kindly furnished him. Among the books he read were the Bible, *Æsop's Fables*, *Robinson Crusoe*, Bunyan's *Pilgrim's Progress*, a *History of the United States*, and Weems' *Life of Washington*. A little circumstance attended the reading of the last-named book, which only within recent years found its way into public print. The book was borrowed from a closefisted neighbor, Josiah Crawford, and one night, while lying on a little shelf near a crack between two logs in the Lincoln cabin during a storm, the covers were damaged by rain. Crawford—not the schoolmaster, but old Blue Nose, as Abe and others called him—assessed the damage to his book at seventy-five cents, and the unfortunate borrower was required to pull fodder for three days at twenty-five cents a day in settlement of the account. While at school it is doubtful if he was able to own an arithmetic. His stepmother was unable to remember his ever having owned one. She gave me, however, a few leaves from a book made and bound by Abe, in which he had entered, in a large, bold hand, the tables of weights and measures, and the "sums" to be worked out in illustration of each table. Where the arithmetic was obtained I could not learn. On one of the pages which the old lady gave me, and just underneath the table which tells how many pints there are in a bushel, the facetious young student had scrawled these four lines of schoolboy doggerel:

> *Abraham Lincoln,*
> *His hand and pen,*
> *He will be good,*
> *But God knows when.*

His chief delight during the day, if unmolested, was to lie down under the shade of some inviting tree to read and study. At night, lying on his stomach in front of the open fireplace, with a piece of charcoal he would cipher on a broad, wooden shovel. When the latter was covered on both sides he would take his father's drawing knife or plane and shave it off clean, ready for a fresh supply of inscriptions the next day. He often moved about the cabin with a piece of chalk, writing and ciphering on boards and the flat sides of hewn logs. When every bare wooden surface had been filled with his letters and ciphers he would erase them and begin anew. His stepmother told me he devoured everything in the book line within his reach. If in his reading he came across anything that pleased his fancy, he entered it down in a copybook—a sort of repository, in which he was wont to store everything worthy of preservation. "Frequently," related his stepmother, "he had no paper to write his pieces down on. Then he would put them with chalk on a board or plank, sometimes only making a few signs of what he intended to write. When he got paper he would copy them, always bringing them to me and reading them. He would ask my opinion of what he had read, and often explained things to me in his plain and simple language." How he contrived at the age of fourteen to absorb information is thus told by John Hanks: "When Abe and I returned to the house from work he would go to the cupboard, snatch a piece of corn bread, sit down, take a book, cock his legs up as high as his head, and read. We grubbed, plowed, mowed, and worked together barefooted in the field. Whenever Abe had a chance in the field while at work, or at the house, he would stop and read." He kept the Bible and *Æsop's Fables* always within reach, and read them over and over again.

No feature of his backwoods life pleased Abe so well as going to mill. It released him from a day's work in the woods, besides affording him a much desired opportunity to watch the movement of the mill's primitive and cumbersome machinery. In later years Mr. Lincoln related the following reminiscence of his experience as a miller in Indiana: One day, taking a bag of corn, he mounted the old flea-bitten gray mare and rode leisurely to Gordon's mill. Arriving somewhat late, his turn did not come till almost sundown. In obedience to the custom requiring each man to furnish his own power he hitched the old mare to the arm, and as the animal moved round, the machinery responded with equal speed. Abe was mounted on the arm, and at frequent intervals made use of his whip to urge the animal on to better speed. With a careless "Get up, you old hussy," he applied the lash at each revolution of the arm. In the midst of the exclamation, or just as half of it had escaped through his teeth, the old jade, resenting the continued use of the goad, elevated her shoeless hoofs and striking the young engineer in the forehead, sent him sprawling to the earth. Miller Gordon hurried in, picked up the bleeding, senseless boy, whom he took for dead, and at once sent for his father. Old Thomas Lincoln came—came as soon as embodied listlessness could move—loaded the lifeless boy in a wagon and drove home. Abe lay unconscious all night, but towards break of day the attendants noticed signs of returning consciousness. The blood beginning to flow normally, his tongue struggled to loosen itself, his frame jerked for an instant, and he awoke, blurting out the words "you old hussy," or the latter half of the sentence interrupted by the mare's heel at the mill.

Mr. Lincoln considered this one of the remarkable incidents of his life. He often referred to it, and we had many discussions in our law office over the psychological phenomena involved in the operation. Without expressing my own views I may say that his idea was that the latter half of the expression, "Get up, you old hussy," was cut off by a suspension of the normal flow of his mental energy, and that as soon as life's forces returned he unconsciously ended the sentence; or, as he in a plainer figure put it: "Just before I struck the old mare my will through the mind had set the muscles of my tongue to utter the expression, and when her heels came in contact with my head the whole thing stopped half-cocked, as it were, and was only fired off when mental energy or force returned."

By the time he had reached his seventeenth year he had attained the physical proportions of a full-grown man. He was employed to assist James Taylor in the management of a ferryboat across the Ohio River near the mouth of Anderson's Creek, but was not allowed a man's wages for the work. He received thirty-seven cents a day for what he afterwards told me was the roughest work a young man could be made to do. In the midst of whatever work he was engaged on he still found time to utilize his pen. He prepared a composition on the American Government, calling attention to the necessity of preserving the Constitution and perpetuating the Union, which with characteristic modesty he turned over to his friend and patron, William Woods, for safekeeping and perusal. Through the instrumentality of Woods it attracted the attention of many persons, among them one Pitcher, a lawyer at Rockport, who with faintly concealed enthusiasm declared "the world couldn't beat it." An article on Temperance was shown under similar circum-

stances to Aaron Farmer, a Baptist preacher of local renown, and
by him furnished to an Ohio newspaper for publication. The
thing, however, which gave him such prominence—a prominence too which could have been attained in no other way—was
his remarkable physical strength, for he was becoming not only
one of the longest, but one of the strongest men around Gentryville. He enjoyed the brief distinction his exhibitions of
strength gave him more than the admiration of his friends for
his literary or forensic efforts. Some of the feats attributed to
him almost surpass belief. One witness declares he was equal to
three men, having on a certain occasion carried a load of six
hundred pounds. At another time he walked away with a pair of
logs which three robust men were skeptical of their ability to
carry. "He could strike with a maul a heavier blow—could sink
an axe deeper into wood than any man I ever saw," is the testimony of another witness.

After he had passed his nineteenth year and was nearing his
majority he began to chafe and grow restless under the restraints
of home rule. Seeing no prospect of betterment in his condition,
so long as his fortune was interwoven with that of his father, he
at last endeavored to strike out into the broad world for himself.
Having great faith in the judgment and influence of his fast
friend Woods, he solicited from him a recommendation to the
officers of some one of the boats plying up and down the river,
hoping thereby to obtain employment more congenial than the
dull, fatiguing work of the farm. To this project the judicious
Woods was much opposed, and therefore suggested to the
would-be boatman the moral duty that rested on him to remain
with his father till the law released him from that obligation.
With deep regret he retraced his steps to the paternal mansion,
seriously determined not to evade the claim from which in a few
weary months he would be finally released. Meanwhile occurred
his first opportunity to see the world. In March, 1828, James
Gentry, for whom he had been at work, had fitted out a boat
with a stock of grain and meat for a trading expedition to New
Orleans, and placed his son Allen in charge of the cargo for the
voyage. Abe's desire to make a river trip was at last satisfied,
and he accompanied the proprietor's son, serving as "bow
hand." His pay was eight dollars a month and board. The only

occurrence of interest they could relate of the voyage was the encounter with a party of marauding negroes at the plantation of
Madame Duchesne, a few miles below Baton Rouge. Abe and
Gentry, having tied up for the night, were fast asleep on their
boat when aroused by the arrival of a crowd of negroes bent on
plunder. They set to work with clubs, and not only drove off the
intruders, but pursued them inland, then hastily returning to
their quarters they cut loose their craft and floated downstream
till daylight.

Before passing on further it may not be amiss to glance for a
moment at the social side of life as it existed in Gentryville in
Abe's day. "We thought nothing," said an old lady whom I in-
terviewed when in Indiana, "of going eight or ten miles to
church. The ladies did not stop for the want of a shawl, cloak, or
riding dress in winter time, but would put on their husbands'
old overcoats and wrap up their little ones and take one or two
of them on their beasts. Their husbands would walk, and thus
they would go to church, frequently remaining till the second
day before they returned home."

The old men starting from the fields and out of the woods
would carry their guns on their shoulders and go also. They
dressed in deerskin pants, moccasins, and coarse hunting
shirts—the latter usually fastened with a rope or leather strap.
Arriving at the house where services were to be held they would
recite to each other thrilling stories of their hunting exploits,
and smoke their pipes with the old ladies. They were treated,
and treated each other, with the utmost kindness. A bottle of
liquor, a pitcher of water, sugar, and glasses were set out for
them; also a basket of apples or turnips, with, now and then, a
pie or cakes. Thus they regaled themselves till the preacher
found himself in a condition to begin. The latter, having also
partaken freely of the refreshments provided, would "take his
stand, draw his coat, open his shirt collar, read his text, and
preach and pound till the sweat, produced alike by his exertions
and the exhilarating effects of the toddy, rolled from his face in
great drops. Shaking hands and singing ended the service."

The houses were scattered far apart, but the people traveled
great distances to participate in the frolic and coarse fun of a
logrolling and sometimes a wedding. Unless in midwinter the

young ladies carried their shoes in their hands, and only put them on when the scene of the festivities was reached. The ladies of maturer years drank whiskey toddy, while the men took the whiskey straight. They all danced merrily, many of them barefooted, to the tune of a cracked fiddle the night through. We can imagine the gleeful and more hilarious swaggering home at daybreak to the tune of Dennis Hanks' festive lines:

> *Hail Columbia, happy land,*
> *If you ain't drunk I will be damned.*

Although gay, prosperous, and lighthearted, these people were brimming over with superstition. It was at once their food and drink. They believed in the baneful influence of witches, pinned their faith to the curative powers of wizards in dealing with sick animals, and shot the image of a witch with a silver ball to break the spell she was supposed to have over human beings. They followed with religious minuteness the directions of the water wizard, with his magic divining rod, and the faith doctor who wrought miraculous cures by strange sounds and signals to some mysterious agency. The flight of a bird in at the window, the breath of a horse on a child's head, the crossing by a dog of a hunter's path, all betokened evil luck in store for someone. The moon exercised greater influence on the actions of the people and the growth of vegetation than the sun and all the planetary system combined. Fence rails could only be cut in the light of the moon, and potatoes planted in the dark of the moon. Trees and plants which bore their fruit above ground could be planted when the moon shone full. Soap could only be made in the light of the moon, and it must only be stirred in one way and by one person. They had the horror of Friday which with many exists to this day. Nothing was to be begun on that unlucky day, for if the rule were violated an endless train of disasters was sure to follow.

Surrounded by people who believed in these things, Lincoln grew to manhood. With them he walked, talked, and labored, and from them he also absorbed whatever of superstition showed itself in him thereafter. His early Baptist training made him a fatalist up to the day of his death, and, listening in boyish wonder to the legends of some toothless old dame led him to believe in the significance of dreams and visions. His surroundings helped to create that unique character which in the eyes of a great portion of the American people was only less curious and amusing than it was august and noble.

The winter of 1829 was marked by another visitation of that dreaded disease, "the milk-sick." It was making the usual ravages among the cattle. Human victims were falling before it every day, and it caused the usual stampede in southern Indiana. Dennis Hanks, discouraged by the prospect and grieving over the loss of his stock, proposed a move further westward. Returning emigrants had brought encouraging news of the newly developed state of Illinois. Vast stretches of rich alluvial lands were to be had there on the easiest of terms.

Besides this, Indiana no longer afforded any inducements to the poor man. The proposition of Dennis met with the general assent of the Lincoln family, and especially suited the roving and migratory spirit of Thomas Lincoln. He had been induced to leave Kentucky for the hills of Indiana by the same rosy and alluring reports. He had moved four times since his marriage and in point of worldly goods was not better off than when he started in life. Having disposed of his land to James Gentry, and his grain and stock to young David Turnham, he loaded his household effects into a wagon drawn by two yoke of oxen, and in March, 1830, started for Illinois. The two daughters of Mrs. Lincoln had meanwhile married Dennis Hanks and Levi Hall, and with these additions the party numbered thirteen in all. Abe had just passed his twenty-first birthday.

The journey was a long and tedious one; the streams were swollen and the roads were muddy almost to the point of impassability. The rude, heavy wagon, with its primitive wheels, creaked and groaned as it crawled through the woods and now and then stalled in the mud. Many were the delays, but none ever disturbed the equanimity of its passengers. They were cheerful in the face of all adversity, and some of them determined; but none of them more so than the tall, ungainly youth in buckskin breeches and coonskin cap who wielded the gad and urged the patient oxen forward.

As these humble emigrants entered the new State little did the curious people in the towns through which they passed dream that the obscure and penniless driver who yelled commands to the oxen would yet become Chief Magistrate of the greatest nation of modern times.[1]

[1]Mr. Lincoln once described this journey to me. He said the ground had not yet yielded up the frosts to winter; that during the day the roads would thaw out on the surface and at night freeze over again, thus making traveling, especially with oxen, painfully slow and tiresome. There were, of course, no bridges, and the party were consequently driven to ford the streams, unless by a circuitous route they could avoid them. In the latter part of the day the latter were also frozen slightly, and the oxen would break through a square yard of thin ice at every step. Among other things which the party brought with them was a pet dog, which trotted along after the wagon. One day the little fellow fell behind and failed to catch up till after they had crossed the stream. Missing him they looked back, and there, on the opposite bank, he stood, whining and jumping about in great distress. The water was running over the broken edges of the ice, and the poor animal was afraid to cross. It would not pay to turn the oxen and wagon back and ford the stream again in order to recover a dog, and so the majority, in their anxiety to move forward, decided to go on without him. "But I could not endure the idea of abandoning even a dog," related Lincoln. "Pulling off shoes and socks I waded across the stream and triumphantly returned with the shivering animal under my arm. His frantic leaps of joy and other evidences of a dog's gratitude amply repaid me for all the exposure I had undergone."

2

New Salem

After a fortnight of rough and fatiguing travel the colony of
Indiana emigrants reached a point in Illinois five miles northwest of the town of Decatur in Macon County. John Hanks, son
of that Joseph Hanks in whose shop at Elizabethtown Thomas
Lincoln had learned what he knew of the carpenter's art, met
and sheltered them until they were safely housed on a piece of
land which he had selected for them five miles further westward.
He had preceded them over a year, and had in the meantime
hewed out a few timbers to be used in the construction of their
cabin. The place he had selected was on a bluff overlooking the
Sangamon River—for these early settlers must always be in
sight of a running stream—well supplied with timber. It was a
charming and picturesque site, and all hands set resolutely to
work to prepare the new abode. One felled the trees; one hewed
the timbers for the cabin; while another cleared the ground of its
accumulated growth of underbrush. All was bustle and activity.
Even old Thomas Lincoln, infused with the spirit of the hour,
was spurred to unwonted exertion. What part of the work fell to
his lot our only chronicler, John Hanks, fails to note; but it is
conjectured from the old gentleman's experience in the art of
building that his services corresponded to those of the more
modern supervising architect. With the aid of the oxen and a
plow John and Abe broke up fifteen acres of sod, and "Abe and
myself," observes Hanks in a matter-of-fact way, "split rails
enough to fence the place in."

Abe had now attained his majority and began to throw from
his shoulders the vexations of parental restraint. He had done
his duty to his father, and felt able to begin life on his own account. As he steps out into the broad and inviting world we
take him up for consideration as a man. At the same time we
dispense with further notice of his father, Thomas Lincoln. In
the son are we alone interested. The remaining years of his life
marked no change in the old gentleman's nature. He still listened to the glowing descriptions of prosperity in the adjoining

21

counties, and before his death moved three times in search of better times and a healthy location. In 1851 we find him living on forty acres of land on Goose Nest prairie, in Coles County, Illinois. The land bore the usual incumbrance—a mortgage for two hundred dollars, which his son afterwards paid. On the 17th of January, after suffering for many weeks from a disorder of the kidneys, he passed away at the ripe old age—as his son tells us—of "seventy-three years and eleven days."

For a long time after beginning life on his own account Abe remained in sight of the parental abode. He worked at odd jobs in the neighborhood, or wherever the demand for his services called him. As late as 1831 he was still in the same parts, and John Hanks is authority for the statement that he "made three thousand rails for Major Warnick" walking daily three miles to his work. During the intervals of leisure he read the few books obtainable, and continued the practice of extemporaneous speaking to the usual audience of undemonstrative stumps and voiceless trees. His first attempt at public speaking after landing in Illinois is thus described to me by John Hanks, whose language I incorporate: "After Abe got to Decatur, or rather to Macon County, a man by the name of Posey came into our neighborhood and made a speech. It was a bad one, and I said Abe could beat it. I turned down a box and Abe made his speech. The other man was a candidate—Abe wasn't. Abe beat him to death, his subject being the navigation of the Sangamon River. The man, after Abe's speech was through, took him aside and asked him where he had learned so much and how he could do so well. Abe replied, stating his manner and method of reading, and what he had read. The man encouraged him to persevere."

For the first time we are now favored with the appearance on the scene of a very important personage—one destined to exert no little influence in shaping Lincoln's fortunes. It is Denton Offut, a brisk and venturesome business man, whose operations extended up and down the Sangamon River for many miles. Having heard glowing reports of John Hanks' successful experience as a boatman in Kentucky he had come down the river to engage the latter's services to take a boatload of stock and provisions to New Orleans. "He wanted me to go badly," observes Hanks, "but I waited awhile before answering. I hunted up Abe, and I introduced him and John Johnston, his stepbrother, to Offut. After some talk we at last made an engagement with Offut at fifty cents a day and sixty dollars to make the trip to New Orleans. Abe and I came down the Sangamon River in a canoe in March, 1831; landed at what is now called Jamestown, five miles east of Springfield, then known as Judy's Ferry." Here Johnston joined them, and, leaving their canoe in charge of one Uriah Mann, they walked to Springfield, where after some inquiry they found the genial and enterprising Offut regaling himself with the good cheer dispensed at "The Buckhorn" inn. Offut had agreed with Hanks to have a boat ready for him and his two companions at the mouth of Spring Creek on their arrival, but too many deep potations with the newcomers who daily thronged about the "Buckhorn" had interfered with the execution of his plans, and the boat still remained in the womb of the future. Offut met the three expectant navigators on their arrival, and deep were his regrets over his failure to provide the boat. The interview resulted in the trio engaging to make the boat themselves. From what was known as "Congress land" they obtained an abundance of timber, and by the aid of the machinery at Kirkpatrick's mill they soon had the requisite material for their vessel. While the work of construction was going on a shanty was built in which they were lodged. Lincoln was elected cook, a distinction he never underestimated for a moment. Within four weeks the boat was ready to launch. Offut was sent for, and was present when she slid into the water. It was the occasion of much political chat and buncombe, in which the Whig party and Jackson alike were, strangely enough, lauded to the skies. It is difficult to account for the unanimous approval of such strikingly antagonistic ideas, unless it be admitted that Offut must have brought with him some substantial reminder of the hospitality on draught at the "Buckhorn" inn. Many disputes arose, we are told, in which Lincoln took part and found a good field for practice and debate.

A traveling juggler halted long enough in Sangamontown, where the boat was launched, to give an exhibition of his art and dexterity in the loft of Jacob Carman's house. In Lincoln's low-crowned, broad-brimmed hat the magician cooked eggs. As explanatory of the delay in passing up his hat Lincoln drolly observed, "It was out of respect for the eggs, not care for my hat."

Having loaded the vessel with pork in barrels, corn, and hogs,

these sturdy boatmen swung out into the stream. On April 19
they reached the town of New Salem, a place destined to be an
important spot in the career of Lincoln. There they met with
their first serious delay. The boat stranded on Rutledge's mill-
dam and hung helplessly over it a day and a night. "We unload-
ed the boat," narrated one of the crew to explain how they obtained relief from their embarrassing situation; "that is, we
transferred the goods from our boat to a borrowed one. We then
rolled the barrels forward; Lincoln bored a hole in the end
[projecting] over the dam; the water which had leaked in ran
out and we slid over." Offut was profoundly impressed with this
exhibition of Lincoln's ingenuity. In his enthusiasm he declared
to the crowd who covered the hill and who had been watching
Lincoln's operation that he would build a steamboat to plow up
and down the Sangamon, and that Lincoln should be her Captain. She would have rollers for shoals and dams, runners for
ice, and with Lincoln in charge, "By thunder, she'd have to go!"

After release from their embarrassing, not to say perilous,
position the boat and her crew floated away from New Salem
and passed on to a point known as Blue Banks, where as the historian of the voyage says: "We had to load some hogs bought of
Squire Godbey. We tried to drive them aboard, but could not.
They would run back past us. Lincoln then suggested that we
sew their eyes shut. Thinking to try it, we caught them, Abe
holding their heads and I their tails while Offut sewed up their
eyes. Still they wouldn't drive. At last, becoming tired, we
carried them to the boat. Abe received them and cut open their
eyes, Johnston and I handing them to him." After thus disposing
of the hog problem they again swung loose and floated downstream. From the Sangamon they passed to the Illinois. At
Beardstown their unique craft, with its "sails made of planks
and cloth," excited the amusement and laughter of those who
saw them from the shore. Once on the bosom of the broad Mississippi they glided past Alton, St. Louis, and Cairo in rapid succession, tied up for a day at Memphis, and made brief stops at
Vicksburg and Natchez. Early in May they reached New
Orleans, where they lingered a month, disposing of their cargo
and viewing the sights which the Crescent City afforded.

In New Orleans, for the first time Lincoln beheld the true horrors of human slavery. He saw "negroes in chains—whipped and scourged." Against this inhumanity his sense of right and justice rebelled, and his mind and conscience were awakened to a realization of what he had often heard and read. No doubt, as one of his companions has said, "Slavery ran the iron into him then and there." One morning in their rambles over the city the trio passed a slave auction. A vigorous and comely mulatto girl was being sold. She underwent a thorough examination at the hands of the bidders; they pinched her flesh and made her trot up and down the room like a horse, to show how she moved, and in order, as the auctioneer said, that "bidders might satisfy themselves" whether the article they were offering to buy was sound or not. The whole thing was so revolting that Lincoln moved away from the scene with a deep feeling of "unconquerable hate." Bidding his companions follow him he said, "By God, boys, let's get away from this. If ever I get a chance to hit that thing [meaning slavery], I'll hit it hard." This incident was furnished me in 1865, by John Hanks. I have also heard Mr. Lincoln refer to it himself.

In June the entire party, including Offut, boarded a steamboat going up the river. At St. Louis they disembarked, Offut remaining behind while Lincoln, Hanks, and Johnston started across Illinois on foot. At Edwardsville they separated, Hanks going to Springfield, while Lincoln and his stepbrother followed the road to Coles County, to which point old Thomas Lincoln had meanwhile removed. Here Abe did not tarry long, probably not over a month, but long enough to dispose most effectually of one Daniel Needham, a famous wrestler who had challenged the returned boatman to a test of strength. The contest took place at a locality known as "Wabash Point." Abe threw his antagonist twice with comparative ease, and thereby demonstrated such strength and agility as to render him forever popular with the boys of that neighborhood.

In August the waters of the Sangamon River washed Lincoln in to New Salem. The village, which once stood on the ridge, was laid out in 1828; it became a trading place, and in 1836 contained twenty houses and a hundred inhabitants. In the days of land offices and stagecoaches it was a sprightly village with a busy market. Its people were progressive and industrious. Propitious

winds filled the sails of its commerce, prosperity smiled
graciously on its every enterprise, and the outside world encouraged its social pretensions. It had its day of glory, but,
singularly enough, contemporaneous with the departure of Lincoln from its midst it went into a rapid decline. A few crumbling
stones here and there are all that attest its former existence.
"How it vanished," observes one writer, "like a mist in the
morning, to what distant places its inhabitants dispersed, and
what became of the abodes they left behind, shall be questions
for the local historian."

Lincoln's return to New Salem in August, 1831, was, within a
few days, contemporaneous with the reappearance of Offut, who
made the gratifying announcement that he had purchased a
stock of goods which were to follow him from Beardstown. He
had again retained the services of Lincoln to assist him when his
merchandise should come to hand. The tall stranger—destined
to be a stranger in New Salem no longer—pending the arrival of
his employer's goods, lounged about the village with nothing to
do. Leisure never sat heavily on him. To him there was nothing
uncongenial in it, and he might very properly have been dubbed
at the time a "loafer." He assured those with whom he came in
contact that he was a piece of floating driftwood; that after the
winter of deep snow, he had come down the river with the
freshet; borne along by the swelling waters, and aimlessly floating about, he had accidentally lodged at New Salem. Looking
back over his history we are forced to conclude that Providence
or chance, or whatever power is responsible for it, could not
have assigned him to a more favorable refuge.

His introduction to the citizens of New Salem, as Mentor
Graham the schoolteacher tells us, was in the capacity of clerk of
an election board. Graham furnishes ample testimony of the fa-
cility, fairness, and honesty which characterized the new clerk's
work, and both teacher and clerk were soon bound together by
the warmest of ties. During the day, when votes were coming in
slowly, Lincoln began to entertain the crowd at the polls with a
few attempts at storytelling. My cousin, J. R. Herndon, was
present and enjoyed this feature of the election with the keenest
relish. He never forgot some of Lincoln's yarns and was fond of
repeating them in after years. The recital of a few stories by Lin-

coln easily established him in the good graces of all New Salem. Perhaps he did not know it at the time, but he had used the weapon nearest at hand and had won.

A few days after the election Lincoln found employment with one Dr. Nelson, who after the style of dignitaries of later days started with his family and effects in his "private" conveyance—which in this instance was a flatboat—for Texas. Lincoln was hired to pilot the vessel through to the Illinois River. Arriving at Beardstown the pilot was discharged, and returned on foot across the sand and hills to New Salem. In the meantime Offut's long expected goods had arrived, and Lincoln was placed in charge. Offut relied in no slight degree on the business capacity of his clerk. In his effusive way he praised him beyond reason. He boasted of his skill as a business man and his wonderful intellectual acquirements. As for physical strength and fearlessness of danger, he challenged New Salem and the entire world to produce his equal. In keeping with his widely known spirit of enterprise Offut rented the Rutledge and Cameron mill, which stood at the foot of the hill, and thus added another iron to keep company with the half-dozen already in the fire as a further test of his business ability Lincoln was placed in charge of this also. William G. Greene was hired to assist him, and between the two a lifelong friendship sprang up. They slept in the store, and so strong was the intimacy between them that "when one turned over the other had to do likewise."

The business done over Offut's counter gave his clerk frequent intervals of rest, so that, if so inclined, an abundance of time for study was always at his disposal. Lincoln had long before realized the deficiencies of his education, and resolved, now that the conditions were favorable, to atone for early neglect by a course of study. Nothing was more apparent to him than his limited knowledge of language, and the proper way of expressing his ideas. Moreover, it may be said that he appreciated his inefficiency in a rhetorical sense, and therefore determined to overcome all these obstacles by mastering the intricacies of grammatical construction. Acting on the advice of Mentor Graham he hunted up one Vaner, who was the reputed owner of Kirkham's *Grammar*, and after a walk of several miles returned to the store with the coveted volume under his arm.

With zealous perseverance he at once applied himself to the book. Sometimes he would stretch out at full length on the counter, his head propped up on a stack of calico prints, studying it; or he would steal away to the shade of some inviting tree, and there spend hours at a time in a determined effort to fix in his mind the arbitrary rule that "adverbs qualify verbs, adjectives, and other adverbs." From the vapidity of grammar it was now and then a great relaxation to turn to the more agreeable subject of mathematics; and he might often have been seen lying face downwards, stretched out over six feet of grass, figuring out on scraps of paper some problems given for solution by a quizzical store lounger, or endeavoring to prove that, "multiplying the denominator of a fraction divides it, while dividing the denominator multiplies it." Rather a poor prospect one is forced to admit for a successful man of business.

At this point in my narrative I am pained to drop from further notice our buoyant and effusive friend Offut. His business ventures failing to yield the extensive returns he predicted, and too many of his obligations maturing at the same time, he was forced to pay the penalty of commercial deliquency and went to the wall. He soon disappeared from the village, and the inhabitants thereof never knew whither he went. In the significant language of Lincoln he "petered out."

The downfall of Denton Offut's varied enterprises and his disappearance from New Salem followed in rapid succession, and before the spring of 1832 had merged into summer Lincoln found himself a piece of "floating driftwood" again. Where he might have lodged had not the Black Hawk war intervened can only be a matter of conjecture. A glance at this novel period in his life may not be out of keeping with the purpose of this book. The great Indian chief, Black Hawk, who on the 30th of June, 1831, had entered into an agreement, having all the solemnity of a treaty, with Governor Reynolds and General Gaines that none of his tribe should ever cross the Mississippi "to their usual place of residence, nor any part of their old hunting grounds east of the Mississippi, without permission of the President of the United States or the governor of the State of Illinois," had openly broken the compact. On the 6th of April, 1832, he recrossed the Mississippi and marched up Rock River Valley, accompanied by about five hundred warriors on horseback; while his women and children went up the river in canoes. The great chief was now sixty-seven years old, and believed that his plots were all ripe and his allies fast and true. Although warned by General Atkinson, then in command of Fort Armstrong, against this aggression, and ordered to return, he proudly refused, claiming that he had "come to plant corn." On being informed of the movement of Black Hawk Governor Reynolds called for a thousand mounted volunteers to cooperate with the United States forces under command of General Atkinson, and drive the wily Indian back across the Mississippi. The response to the governor's call was prompt and energetic. In the company from Sangamon County Lincoln enlisted, and now for the first time entered on the vicissitudinous and dangerous life of a soldier. That he in fact regarded the campaign after the Indians as a sort of holiday affair and chicken-stealing expedition is clearly shown in a speech he afterwards made in Congress in exposure of the military pretensions of General Cass. However, in grim, soldierly severity he marched with the Sangamon County contingent to Rushville, in Schuyler County, where, much to his surprise, he was elected captain of the company over William Kirkpatrick.

On being elected captain, Lincoln replied in a brief response of modest and thankful acceptance. It was the first official trust ever turned over to his keeping, and he prized it and the distinction it gave him more than any which in after years fell to his lot. His company savored strongly of the Clary's Grove order, and though daring enough in the presence of danger, were difficult to bring down to the inflexibilities of military discipline. Each one seemed perfectly able and willing to care for himself, and while the captain's authority was respectfully observed, yet, as some have said, they were nonetheless a crowd of "generous ruffians." I heard Mr. Lincoln say once on the subject of his career as captain in this company and the discipline he exercised over his men, that to the first order given one of them he received the response, "Go to the devil, sir!" Not withstanding the interchange of many such unsoldierlike civilities between the officer and his men, a strong bond of affection united them together, and if a contest had arisen over the conflict of orders between the United States authorities and those emanating from Captain Lincoln or some other Illinois officer—as at one time was threatened—we need not be told to which side the Sangamon County company to a man would have gone. A general order forbidding the discharge of firearms within fifty yards of the camp was disobeyed by Captain Lincoln himself. For this violation of rule he was placed under arrest and deprived of his sword for a day. But this and other punishments in no way humiliated him in the esteem of his men; if anything, they only clung the closer, and when Clary's Grove friendship asserted itself it meant that firm and generous attachment found alone on the frontier—that bond, closer than the affinity of blood, which becomes stronger as danger approaches death.

At times the soldiers were hard pressed for food, but by a combination of ingenuity and labor in proportions known only to a volunteer soldier, they managed to avoid the unpleasant results of long-continued and unsatisfied hunger. "At an old Winnebago town called Turtle Village," narrates a member of the company, "after stretching our rations over nearly four days, one of our mess, an old acquaintance of Lincoln, G. B. Fanchier, shot a dove, and having a gill of flour left we made a gallon and a half of delicious soup in an old tin bucket that had been lost by Indians. This soup we divided among several messes that were hungrier than we were and our own mess by pouring in each man's cup a portion of the esculent. Once more, at another time, in the extreme northern part of Illinois, we had been very hungry for two days, but suddenly came upon a new cabin at the edge of the prairie that the pioneer sovereign squatter family had vacated and 'skedaddled' from for fear of losing their scalps. There were plenty of chickens about the cabin, much hungrier than we ourselves were, if poverty is to test the matter, and the boys heard a voice saying 'Slay and eat.' They at once went to running, clubbing, and shooting them as long as they could be found. Whilst the killing was going on I climbed to the ridgepole of the smoke-house to see distinctly what I saw obscurely from the ground and behold! the cleanest, sweetest jole I ever saw—alone, half hid by boards and ridgepole, stuck up no doubt for future use. By this time many of the chickens were on the fire, broiling, for want of grease or gravy to fry them in. Some practical fellow proposed to throw in with the fowls enough bacon to convert broiling into frying; the proposition was adopted, and they were soon fried. We began to eat the tough, dry chickens with alternating mouthfuls of the jole, when Lincoln came to the repast with the query, 'Eating chicken, boys?' 'Not much, sir,' I responded, for we had operated principally on the jole, it being sweeter and more palatable than the chickens. 'It is much like eating saddlebags,' he responded; 'but I think the stomach can accomplish much today; but what have you got there with the skeletons, George?' 'We did have a sweet jole of a hog, sir,' I answered, 'but you are nearly too late for your share,' at the same time making room for him to approach the elmbark dish. He ate the bacon a moment, then commenced dividing by mouthfuls to the boys from other messes, who came to 'see what Abe was at,' and saying many quaint and funny things suited to the time and the jole." The captain, it will be seen, by his "freedom without familiarity" and his "courtesy without condescension," was fast making inroads on the respect of his rude but appreciative men. He was doubtless looking a long way ahead, when both their friendship and respect would be of avail, for as the chronicler last quoted from continues: "He was acquainted with everybody, and he had determined, as he told me, to become a candidate for the next Legislature. The mess immediately pitched on him as our standard-bearer, and he accepted."

The term for which the volunteers had enlisted had now expired, and the majority, tiring of the service, the novelty of which had worn off, and longing for the comforts and good cheer of their homes, refused either to reenlist or render further service. They turned their faces homeward, each with his appetite for military glory well satiated. But the war was not over, and the mighty Black Hawk was still east of the Mississippi. A few remained and reenlisted. Among them was Lincoln. This time, eschewing the responsibility of a captaincy, and to avoid the possible embarrassment of dragging about camp a wooden sword, he entered the company of Elijah Iles as a dignified private. It has pleased some of Mr. Lincoln's biographers to attribute this reenlistment to pure patriotism on his part and a conscientious desire to serve his country. From the standpoint of sentiment that is a comfortable view to take of it; but I have strong reason to believe that Mr. Lincoln never entertained such serious notions of the campaign. In fact, I may say that my information comes from the best authority to be had in the matter—the soldier himself. Mr. Lincoln had no home; he had cut loose from his parents, from the Hankses and the Johnstons; he left behind him no anxious wife and children; and no chair before a warm fireplace remained vacant for him. "I was out of work," he said to me once, "and there being no danger of more fighting, I could do nothing better than enlist again." After his discharge from this last and brief period of service, along with the remainder of the Sangamon County soldiers, he departed from the scenes of recent hostilities for New Salem again. His soldier days had ended, and he returned now to enter upon a far different career. However much in later years he may have pretended to ridicule the disasters of the Black Hawk war, or the part he took in it, yet I believe he was rather proud of it after all. When Congress, along in the fifties, granted him a land warrant he was greatly pleased. He located it on some land in Iowa, and declared to me one day that he would die seized of that land, and although the tract never yielded him anything, he never, so far as my knowledge extends, parted with his ownership.

The return of the Black Hawk warriors to New Salem occurred in the month of August, but a short time before the general election. A new Legislature was to be chosen, and as Lincoln had declared to his comrades in the army he would, and in obedience to the effusive declaration of principles which he had issued over his signature in March, before he went to the war, he presented himself to the people of his newly adopted county as a candidate for the Legislature. It is not necessary to enter into an account of the political conditions in Illinois at that time, or the effect had on the same by those who had in charge the governmental machinery. Lincoln's course is all that interests us. Though he may not have distinctly avowed himself a Whig, yet, as one of his friends asserted, "he stood openly on Whig principles." He favored a national bank, a liberal system of internal improvements, and a high protective tariff.

The election being near at hand only a few days remained for his canvass. One who was with him at the time, describing his appearance, says: "He wore a mixed jeans coat, clawhammer style, short in the sleeves and bobtail—in fact it was so short in the tail he could not sit on it; flax and towlinen pantaloons, and a straw hat. I think he wore a vest, but do not remember how it looked. He wore potmetal boots." His maiden effort on the stump was a speech on the occasion of a public sale at Papps-ville, a village eleven miles west of Springfield. After the sale was over and speechmaking had begun, a fight—a "general fight," as one of the bystanders relates—ensued, and Lincoln, noticing one of his friends about to succumb to the energetic at-tack of an infuriated ruffian, interposed to prevent it. He did so most effectually. Hastily descending from the rude platform he edged his way through the crowd, and seizing the bully by the neck and seat of his trousers, threw him by means of his strength and long arms, as one witness stoutly insists, "twelve feet away." Returning to the stand and throwing aside his hat he inaugurated his campaign with the following brief but juicy declaration:

"Fellow Citizens, I presume you all know who I am. I am humble Abraham Lincoln. I have been solicited by many friends to become a candidate for the Legislature. My politics are short and sweet, like the old woman's dance. I am in favor of a na-tional bank. I am in favor of the internal improvement system and a high protective tariff. These are my sentiments and politi-cal principles. If elected I shall be thankful; if not it will be all the same."

The election, as he had predicted, resulted in his defeat—the only defeat, as he himself afterward stated, that he ever suffered at the hands of the people. The most gratifying feature of it all was the hearty support of his neighbors at New Salem. Of the entire 277 votes in the precinct he received every one save seven.

It may not be amiss to explain the cause of this remarkable endorsement of Lincoln by the voters in New Salem. It arose chiefly from his advocacy of the improvement of the Sangamon River. He proposed the digging of a canal a few miles east of the point where the Sangamon enters the Illinois River, thereby giv-ing the former two mouths. This, he explained to the farmers, would prevent the accumulation of backwater and consequent overflow of their rich alluvial bottom lands in the spring. It would also avert the sickness and evil results of stagnant pools, which formed in low places after the high waters receded. His scheme—that is the name by which it would be known today—commended itself to the judgment of his neighbors, and the flattering vote he received shows how they endorsed it.

The unsuccessful result of the election did not dampen his hopes nor sour his ambition. The extensive acquaintance, the practice in public speaking, the confidence gained with the people, together with what was augmented in himself, made a surplus of capital on which he was free to draw and of which he afterwards frequently availed himself. The election being over, however, he found himself without money, though with a goodly supply of experience, drifting again. His political experience had forever weaned him from the dull routine of common labor. Labor afforded him no time for study and no incentive to profitable reflection. What he seemed to want was some lighter work, employment in a store or tavern where he could meet the village celebrities, exchange views with strangers, discuss politics, horseraces, cockfights, and narrate to listening loafers his striking and significant stories. In the communities where he had lived, the village storekeeper held undisturbed sway. He took the only newspaper, owned the only collection of books and half the property in the village; and in general was the social, and oftentimes the political head of the community. Naturally, therefore the prominence the store gave the merchant attracted Lincoln. But there seemed no favorable opening for him—clerks in New Salem were not in demand just then.

My cousins, Rowan and James Herndon, were at that time operating a store, and tiring of their investment and the confinement it necessitated, James sold his interest to an idle, shiftless fellow named William Berry. Soon after Rowan disposed of his to Lincoln. That the latter, who was without means and in search of work, could succeed to the ownership of even a half interest in a concern where but a few days before he would in all probability gladly have exchanged his services for his board, doubtless seems strange to the average young business man of today. I once asked Rowan Herndon what induced him to make such liberal terms in dealing with Lincoln, whom he had known for so short a time.

"I believed he was thoroughly honest," was the reply, "and that impression was so strong in me I accepted his note in payment of the whole. He had no money, but I would have advanced him still more had he asked for it."

A few weeks only were sufficient to render apparent Lincoln's ill adaptation to the requirements of a successful business career. Once installed behind the counter he gave himself up to reading and study, depending for the practical management of the business on his partner. A more unfortunate selection than Berry could not have been found; for, while Lincoln at one end of the store was dispensing political information, Berry at the other was disposing of the firm's liquors, being the best customer for that article of merchandise himself. To put it more plainly, Lincoln's application to Shakespeare and Burns was only equalled by Berry's attention to spigot and barrel. That the latter in the end succeeded in squandering a good portion of their joint assets, besides wrecking his own health, is not to be wondered at. By the spring of 1833 they, like their predecessors, were ready to retire. Two brothers named Trent coming along, they sold to them on the liberal terms then prevalent the business and the goodwill; but before the latter's notes fell due, they in turn had failed and fled. The death of Berry following soon after, released him from the payment of any notes or debts and thus Lincoln was left to meet the unhonored obligations of the ill-fated partnership, or avoid their payment by dividing the responsibility and pleading the failure of the business. That he assumed all the liability and set resolutely to work to pay everything, was strictly in keeping with his fine sense of honor and justice. He was a long time meeting these claims, even as late as 1848 sending to me from Washington portions of his salary as Congressman to be applied on the unpaid remnant of the Berry & Lincoln indebtedness—but in time he extinguished it all, even to the last penny.

Conscious of his many shortcomings as a merchant, and undaunted by the unfortunate complications from which he had just been released, Lincoln returned to his books. Rowan Herndon, with whom he had been living, having removed to the country, he became for the first time a sojourner at the tavern, as it was then called—a public house kept by Rutledge, Onstott, and Alley in succession. "It was a small log house," he explained to me in later years," covered with clapboards, and contained four rooms." It was second only in importance to the store, for there he had the opportunity of meeting passing strangers—lawyers and others from the county seat, whom he frequently impressed with his knowledge as well as wit. He had, doubtless, long before determined to prepare himself for the law; in fact, had begun to read Blackstone while in the store, and now went at it with renewed zeal. He borrowed law books of his former comrade in the Black Hawk war, John T. Stuart, who was practicing law in Springfield, frequently walking there to return one and borrow another. His determination to master any subject he undertook and his application to study were of the most intense order. On the road to and from Springfield he would read and recite from the book he carried open in his hand, and claimed to have mastered forty pages of Blackstone during the first day after his return from Stuart's office. At New Salem he frequently sat barefooted under the shade of a tree near the store, poring over a volume of Chitty or Blackstone, sometimes lying on his back, putting his feet up the tree, which provokes one of his biographers to denote the latter posture as one which might have been "unfavorable to mental application, in the case of a man with shorter extremities."

That Lincoln's attempt to make a lawyer of himself under such adverse and unpromising circumstances excited comment is not to be wondered at. Russell Godby, an old man who still survives, told me in 1865, that he had often employed Lincoln to do farm work for him, and was surprised to find him one day sitting barefoot on the summit of a woodpile and attentively reading a book. "This being an unusual thing for farm hands in that early day to do, I asked him," relates Godby, "what he was reading. 'I'm not reading,' he answered. 'I'm studying.' 'Studying what?' I enquired. 'Law, sir,' was the emphatic response. It was really too much for me, as I looked at him sitting there proud as Cicero. 'Great God Almighty!' I exclaimed, and passed on."

But Lincoln kept on at his studies. Wherever he was and

whenever he could do so the book was brought into use. He carried it with him in his rambles through the woods and his walks to the river. When night came he read it by the aid of any friendly light he could find. Frequently he went down to the cooper's shop and kindled a fire out of the waste material lying about, and by the light afforded read until far into the night.

One of his companions at this time relates that, "while clerking in the store or serving as postmaster he would apply himself as opportunity offered to his studies, if it was but five minutes time—would open his book which he always kept at hand, study it, reciting to himself; then entertain the company present or wait on a customer without apparent annoyance from the interruption. Have frequently seen him reading while walking along the streets. Occasionally he would become absorbed with his book; would stop and stand for a few moments, then walk on, or pass from one house to another or from one crowd or squad of men to another. He was apparently seeking amusement, and with his thoughtful face and ill-fitting clothes was the last man one would have singled out for a student. If the company he was in was unappreciative, or their conversation at all irksome, he would open his book and commune with it for a time, until a happy thought suggested itself and then the book would again return to its wonted resting-place under his arm. He never appeared to be a hard student, as he seemed to master his studies with little effort, until he commenced the study of the law. In that he became wholly engrossed, and began for the first time to avoid the society of men, in order that he might have more time for study. He was not what is usually termed a quick-minded man, although he would arrive at his conclusions very readily. He seemed invariably to reflect and deliberate, and never acted from impulse so far as to force a wrong conclusion on a subject of any moment."

It was not long until he was able to draw up deeds, contracts, mortgages, and other legal papers for his neighbors. He figured conspicuously as a pettifogger before the justice of the peace, but regarding it merely as a kind of preliminary practice, seldom made any charge for his services. Meanwhile he was reading not only law books but natural philosophy and other scientific subjects. He was a careful and patient reader of newspapers, the

Sangamon Journal—published at Springfield—*Louisville Journal, St. Louis Republican,* and *Cincinnati Gazette* being usually within his reach. He paid a less degree of attention to historical works, although he read Rollin and Gibbon while in business with Berry.

It has been denied as often as charged that Lincoln narrated vulgar stories; but the truth is he loved a story however extravagant or vulgar, if it had a good point. If it was merely a ribald recital and had no sting in the end, that is, if it exposed no weakness or pointed no moral, he had no use for it either in conversation or public speech; but if it had the necessary ingredients of mirth and moral no one could use it with more telling effect. As a mimic he was unequalled, and with his characteristic gestures, he built up a reputation for storytelling—although fully as many of his narratives were borrowed as original—which followed him through life. One who listened to his early stories in New Salem says: "His laugh was striking. Such awkward gestures belonged to no other man. They attracted universal attention, from the old sedate down to the schoolboy. Then in a few moments he was as calm and thoughtful as a judge on the bench, and as ready to give advice on the most important matters; fun and gravity grew on him alike."

As a salesman, Lincoln was lamentably deficient. He was too prone to lead off into a discussion of politics or morality, leaving someone else to finish the trade which he had undertaken. One of his employers says: "He always disliked to wait on the ladies, preferring, he said, to wait on the men and boys. I also remember he used to sleep on the store counter when they had too much company at the tavern. He wore flax and towlinen pantaloons— I thought about five inches too short in the legs— and frequently had but one suspender, no vest or coat. He wore a calico shirt, such as he had in the Black Hawk war; coarse brogans, tan color; blue yarn socks and straw hat, old style, and without a band." His friend Ellis attributed his shyness in the presence of ladies to the consciousness of his awkward appearance and the unpretentious condition of his wearing apparel. It was more than likely due to pure bashfulness. "On one occasion," continues Ellis, "while we boarded at the tavern, there came a family consisting of an old lady, her son, and three stylish daughters, from the State of Virginia, who stopped there for two or three weeks, and during their stay I do not remember of Mr. Lincoln's ever appearing at the same table with them."

As a society man, Lincoln was singularly deficient while he lived in New Salem, and even during the remainder of his life. He never indulged in gossip about the ladies, nor aided in the circulation of village scandal. For women he had a high regard, and I can testify that during my long acquaintance with him his conversation was free from injurious comment in individual cases—freer from unpleasant allusions than that of most men. At one time Major Hill charged him with making defamatory remarks regarding his wife. Hill was insulting in his language to Lincoln who never lost his temper. When he saw a chance to edge a word in, Lincoln denied emphatically using the language or anything like that attributed to him. He entertained, he insisted, a high regard for Mrs. Hill, and the only thing he knew to her discredit was the fact that she was Major Hill's wife.

At this time in its brief history New Salem was what in the parlance of large cities would be called a fast place; and it was difficult for a young man of ordinary moral courage to resist the temptations that beset him on every hand. It remains a matter of surprise that Lincoln was able to retain his popularity with the hosts of young men of his own age, and still not join them in their drinking bouts and carousals. "I am certain," contends one of his companions, "that he never drank any intoxicating liquors—he did not even in those days smoke or chew tobacco." In sports requiring either muscle or skill he took no little interest. He indulged in all the games of the day, even to a horserace or cockfight.

While wooing that jealous-eyed mistress, the law, Lincoln was earning no money. As another has said, "he had a running board bill to pay, and nothing to pay it with." By dint of sundry jobs here and there, helping Ellis in his store today, splitting rails for James Short tomorrow, he managed to keep his head above the waves. His friends were firm—no young man ever had truer or better ones—but he was of too independent a turn to appeal to them or complain of his condition. He never at any time abandoned the idea of becoming a lawyer. That was always a spirit which beckoned him on in the darkest hour of his adversity. Someone, probably a Democrat who voted for him in the preceding fall, recommended him to John Calhoun, then surveyor of the county, as suitable material for an assistant. This office, in view of the prevailing speculation in lands and town lots, was the most important and possibly the most profitable in the county. Calhoun, the incumbent, was a Yankee and a typical gentleman. He was brave, intellectual, self-possessed, and cultivated. He had been educated for the law, but never practiced much after coming to Illinois—taught school in preference. As an instructor he was the popular one of his day and age. I attended the school he taught when I was a boy, in Springfield, and was in later years clerk of the city under his administration as Mayor. Lincoln, I know, respected and admired him. After Lincoln's removal to Springfield they frequently held joint debates on political questions. At one time I remember they discussed the tariff question in the court house, using up the better part of two evenings in the contest. Calhoun was polite, affable, and an honest debater, never dodging any question. This made him a formidable antagonist in argumentative controversy. I have heard Lincoln say that Calhoun gave him more trouble in his debates than Douglas ever did, because he was more captivating in his manner and a more learned man than Douglas.

But to resume. The recommendation of Lincoln's friends was sufficient to induce Calhoun to appoint him one of his deputies. At the time he received notice of his selection by Calhoun, Lincoln was out in the woods near New Salem splitting rails. A friend named Pollard Simmons, who still survives and has related the incident to me, walked out to the point where he was working with the cheering news. Lincoln, being a Whig and knowing Calhoun's pronounced Democratic tendencies, inquired if he had to sacrifice any principle in accepting the position. "If I can be perfectly free in my political action I will take the office," he remarked; "but if my sentiments or even expression of them is to be abridged in any way I would not have it or any other office." A young man hampered by poverty as Lincoln was at this time, who had the courage to deal with public office as he did, was certainly made of unalloyed material. No wonder in after years when he was defeated by Douglas he could inspire his friends by the admonition not to "give up after one nor one hundred defeats."

After taking service with Calhoun, Lincoln found he had but little if any practical knowledge of surveying—all that had to be learned. Calhoun furnished him with books, directing him to study them till he felt competent to begin work. He again invoked the assistance of Mentor Graham, the schoolmaster, who aided him in his efforts at calculating the results of surveys and measurements. Lincoln was not a mathematician by nature, and hence, with him, learning meant labor. Graham's daughter is authority for the statement that her father and Lincoln frequently sat up till midnight engrossed in calculations, and only ceased when her mother drove them out after a fresh supply of wood for the fire. Meanwhile Lincoln was keeping up his law studies. "He studied to see the subject matter clearly," says Graham, "and to express it truly and strongly. I have known him to study for hours the best way of three to express an idea." He was so studious and absorbed in his application at one time, that his friends, according to a statement made by one of them, "noticed that he was so emaciated we feared he might bring on mental derangement." It was not long, however, until he had mastered surveying as a study, and then he was sent out to work by his superior—Calhoun. It has never been denied that his surveys were exact and just, and he was so manifestly fair that he was often chosen to settle disputed questions of corners and measurements.

As surveyor under Calhoun he was sent for at one time to decide or locate a disputed corner for some persons in the northern part of the county. Among others interested was his friend and admirer Henry McHenry. "After a good deal of disputing we agreed," says the latter, "to send for Lincoln and to abide by his decision. He came with compass, flagstaff, and chain. He stopped with me three or four days and surveyed the whole section. When in the neighborhood of the disputed corner by actual survey he called for his staff and driving it in the ground at a certain spot said, 'Gentlemen, here is the corner.' We dug down into the ground at the point indicated and, lo! there we found about six or eight inches of the original stake sharpened at the end, and beneath which was the usual piece of charcoal placed there by Rector, the surveyor who laid the ground off for the government many years before." So fairly and well had the young surveyor done his duty that all parties went away completely satisfied. As late as 1865 the corner was preserved by a mark and pointed out to strangers as an evidence of the young surveyor's skill. Russell Godby, mentioned in the earlier pages of this chapter, presented to me a certificate of survey given to him by Lincoln. It was written January 14, 1834, and is signed "J. Calhoun, S. S. C., by A. Lincoln." "The survey was made by Lincoln," says Godby, "and I gave him as pay for his work two buckskins, which Hannah Armstrong 'foxed' on his pants so that the briers would not wear them out."

Honors were now crowding thick and fast upon him. On May 7, 1833, he was commissioned postmaster at New Salem, the first office he ever held under the Federal Government. The salary was proportionate to the amount of business done. Whether Lincoln solicited the appointment himself, or whether it was given him without the asking, I do not know; but certain it is his "administration" gave general satisfaction. The mail arrived once a week, and we can imagine the extent of time and labor required to distribute it, when it is known that "he carried the office around in his hat." Mr. Lincoln used to tell me that when he had a call to go to the country to survey a piece of land, he placed inside his hat all the letters belonging to people in the neighborhood and distributed them along the way. He made headquarters in Samuel Hill's store, and there the office may be said to have been located, as Hill himself had been postmaster before Lincoln. Between the revenue derived from the post office and his income from land surveys Lincoln was, in the expressive language of the day, "getting along well enough." Suddenly, however, smooth sailing ceased and all his prospects of easy times ahead were again brought to naught. One Van Bergen brought suit against him and obtained judgment on one of the notes given in payment of the store debt—a relic of the unfortunate partnership with Berry. His personal effects were levied on and sold, his horse and surveying instruments going with the rest. But again a friend, one James Short, whose favor he had gained interposed; bought in the property and restored it to the hopeless young surveyor. It will be seen now what kind of friends Lincoln was gaining. The bonds he was thus making were destined to stand the severest of tests. His case never became so desperate but a friend came out of the darkness to relieve him.

There was always something about Lincoln in his earlier days to encourage his friends. He was not only grateful for whatever aid was given him, but he always longed to help someone else. He had an unfailing disposition to succor the weak and the unfortunate, and always, in his sympathy, struggling with the under dog in the fight. He was once overtaken when about fourteen miles from Springfield by one Chandler, whom he knew slightly, and who, having already driven twenty miles, was hastening to reach the land office before a certain other man who had gone by a different road. Chandler explained to Lincoln that he was poor and wanted to enter a small tract of land which adjoined his, that another man of considerable wealth had also determined to have it, and had mounted his horse and started for Springfield. "Meanwhile, my neighbors," continued Chandler, "collected and advanced me the necessary one hundred dollars, and now, if I can reach the land office first, I can secure the land." Lincoln noticed that Chandler's horse was too much fatigued to stand fourteen miles more of a forced march, and he therefore dismounted from his own and turned him over to Chandler, saying, "Here's my horse—he is fresh and full of grit; there's no time to be lost; mount him and put through. When you reach Springfield put him up at Herndon's tavern and I'll call and get him." Thus encouraged Chandler moved on, leaving Lincoln to follow on the jaded animal. He reached Springfield over an hour in advance of his rival and thus secured the coveted tract of land. By nightfall Lincoln rode leisurely into town and was met by the now radiant Chandler, jubilant over his success. Between the two a friendship sprang up which all the political discords of twenty-five years never shattered nor strained.

No little of Lincoln's influence with the men of New Salem can be attributed to his extraordinary feats of strength. By an arrangement of ropes and straps, harnessed about his hips, he was enabled one day at the mill to astonish a crowd of village celebrities by lifting a box of stones weighing near a thousand pounds. There is no fiction either, as suggested by some of his biographers, in the story that he lifted a barrel of whiskey from the ground and drank from the bung; but in performing this latter almost incredible feat he did not stand erect and elevate the barrel, but squatted down and lifted it to his knees, rolling it over until his mouth came opposite the bung. His strength, kindness of manner, love of fairness and justice, his original and unique sayings, his power of mimicry, his perseverance—all made a combination rarely met with on the frontier. Nature had burnt him in her holy fire, and stamped him with the seal of her greatness.

In the summer of 1834 Lincoln determined to make another race for the legislature; but this time he ran distinctly as a Whig. He made, it is presumed, the usual number of speeches, but as the art of newspaper reporting had not reached the perfection it has since attained, we are not favored with even the substance of his efforts on the stump. I have Lincoln's word for it that it was more of a hand-shaking campaign than anything else. Rowan Herndon relates that he came to his house during harvest, when there were a large number of men at work in the field. He was introduced to them, but they did not hesitate to apprize him of their esteem for a man who could labor; and their admiration for a candidate for office was gauged somewhat by the amount of work he could do. Learning these facts, Lincoln took hold of a cradle, and handling it with ease and remarkable speed, soon distanced those who undertook to follow him. The men were satisfied, and it is presumed he lost no votes in that crowd. One Dr. Barrett, seeing Lincoln, inquired of the latter's friends: "Can't the party raise any better material than that?" but after hearing his speech the doctor's opinion was considerably altered, for he declared that Lincoln filled him with amazement; "that he knew more than all of the other candidates put together." The election took place in August. Lincoln's friend, John T. Stuart, was also a candidate on the legislative ticket. He encouraged Lincoln's canvass in every way, even at the risk of sacrificing his own chances. But both were elected. The four successful candidates were Dawson, who received 1390 votes, Lincoln 1376, Carpenter 1170, and Stuart 1164.

At last Lincoln had been elected to the legislature, and by a very flattering majority. In order, as he himself said, "to make a decent appearance in the legislature," he had to borrow money to buy suitable clothing and to maintain his new dignity. Coleman Smoot, one of his friends, advanced him "two hundred dollars, which he returned, relates the generous Smoot, according to promise." Here we leave our rising young statesman, to take up a different but very interesting period of his history.

3

State Legislator

In December, 1834, Lincoln prepared himself for the Legislature to which he had been elected by such a complimentary majority. Through the generosity of his friend Smoot he purchased
a new suit of clothes, and entering the stage at New Salem, rode
through to Vandalia, the seat of government. He appreciated the
dignity of his new position, and instead of walking to the capital, as some of his biographers have contended, availed himself
of the usual mode of travel. At this session of the Legislature he
was anything but conspicuous. In reality he was very modest,
but shrewd enough to impress the force of his character on those
persons whose influence might some day be of advantage to him.
He made but little stir, if we are to believe the record, during the
whole of this first session. Made a member of the committee on
Public Accounts and Expenditures, his name appears so seldom
in the reports of the proceedings that we are prone to conclude
that he must have contented himself with listening to the flashes
of border oratory and absorbing his due proportion of parlia-
mentary law. He was reserved in manner, but very observant;
said little, but learned much; made the acquaintance of all the
members and many influential persons on the outside. The lobby
at that day contained the representative men of the state—men
of acknowledged prominence and respectability, many of them
able lawyers, drawn thither in advocacy of some pet bill.
Schemes of vast internal improvements attracted a retinue of
logrollers, who in later days seem to have been an indispensable
necessity in the movement of complicated legislative machinery.
Men of capital and brains were there. He early realized the importance of knowing all these, trusting to the inspiration of
some future hour to impress them with his skill as an organizer
or his power as an orator. Among the members of the outside or
"third body" was Stephen A. Douglas, whom Lincoln then saw
for the first time. Douglas had come from Vermont only the year
before, but was already undertaking to supplant John J. Hardin
in the office of States Attorney for the district in which both

lived. What impression he made on Lincoln, what opinions each
formed of the other, or what the extent of their acquaintance
then was, we do not know. It is said that Lincoln afterwards in
mentioning their first meeting observed of the newly arrived
Vermonter that he was the "least man he had ever seen."

The society of Vandalia and the people attracted thither by
the Legislature made it, for that early day, a gay place indeed.
Compared to Lincoln's former environments, it had no lack of
refinement and polish. That he absorbed a good deal of this by
contact with the men and women who surrounded him there can
be no doubt. The "drift of sentiment and the sweep of civilization" at this time can best be measured by the character of the
legislation. There were acts to incorporate banks, turnpikes,
bridges, insurance companies, towns, railroads, and female
academies. The vigor and enterprise of New England fusing with
the illusory prestige of Kentucky and Virginia was fast forming
a new civilization to spread over the prairies! At this session
Lincoln remained quietly in the background, and contented himself with the introduction of a resolution in favor of securing to
the State a part of the proceeds of sales of public lands within its
limits.

The brief taste of public office which he had just enjoyed, and
the distinction it gave him only whetted his appetite for further
honors. Accordingly, in 1836 we find him a candidate for the
Legislature again. I well remember this campaign and the election which followed, for my father, Archer G. Herndon, was also
a candidate, aspiring to a seat in the State Senate. The legislature at the session previous had in its apportionment bill
increased the delegation from Sangamon County to seven
Representatives and two Senators. Party conventions had not
yet been invented, and there being no nominating machinery to
interfere, the field was open for any and all to run. Lincoln again
resorted, in opening his canvass, to the medium of the political
handbill. Although it had not operated with the most satisfactory results in his first campaign, yet he felt willing to risk it
again. Candidates of that day evinced far more willingness to
announce their position than political aspirants do now.
Without waiting for a convention to construct a platform, or
some great political leader to "sound the keynote of the cam-

paign," they stepped to the forefront and blew the bugle themselves. This custom will account for the boldness of Lincoln's utterances and the unequivocal tone of his declarations. His card—a sort of political fulmination—was as follows:

New Salem, June 13, 1836.

To the Editor of The Journal:

In your paper of last Saturday I see a communication over the signature of 'Many Voters' in which the candidates who are announced in the Journal *are called upon to 'show their hands.' Agreed. Here's mine:*

I go for all sharing the privileges of the government who assist in bearing its burdens. Consequently, I go for admitting all whites to the right of suffrage who pay taxes or bear arms (by no means excluding females).

If elected I shall consider the whole people of Sangamon my constituents, as well those that oppose as those that support me.

While acting as their Representative, I shall be governed by their will on all subjects upon which I have the means of knowing what their will is; and upon all others I shall do what my own judgment teaches me will best advance their interests. Whether elected or not, I go for distributing the proceeds of the sales of public lands to the several States to enable our State, in common with others, to dig canals and construct railroads without borrowing money and paying the interest on it.

If alive on the first Monday in November, I shall vote for Hugh L. White for President.

Very Respectfully,
A. Lincoln

It is generally admitted that the bold and decided stand Lincoln took—though too audacious and emphatic for statesmen of a later day—suited the temper of the times. Leaving out of sight his expressed preference for White of Tennessee,—on whom all the anti-Jackson forces were disposed to concentrate, and which was but a mere question of men—there is much food for thought in the second paragraph. His broad plan for universal suffrage certainly commends itself to the ladies, and we need no further evidence to satisfy our minds of his position on the subject of "Woman's Rights," had he lived. In fact, I cannot refrain from

noting here what views he in after years held with reference to
the great questions of moral and social reforms, under which he
classed universal suffrage, temperance, and slavery. "All such
questions," he observed one day, as we were discussing temperance in the office, "must first find lodgment with the most
enlightened souls who stamp them with their approval. In God's
own time they will be organized into law and thus woven into
the fabric of our institutions."

The canvass which followed this public avowal of creed was
more exciting than any which had preceded it. There were joint
discussions, and, at times, much feeling was exhibited. Each candidate had his friends freely distributed through the crowd, and
it needed but a few angry interruptions or insinuating rejoinders
from one speaker to another to bring on a conflict between their
friends. Frequently the speakers led in the battle themselves, as
in the case of Ninian W. Edwards—afterwards a brother-in-law
of Lincoln—who, in debate, drew a pistol on his opponent
Achilles Morris, a prominent Democrat.

A joint debate in which all the candidates participated, took
place on the Saturday preceding the election. "The speaking
began in the forenoon," says one of the participants, "the candidates speaking alternately until everyone who could speak had
had his turn, generally consuming the whole afternoon." Dr.
Early, a Democratic candidate, in his speech took issue with
Ninian W. Edwards, stigmatizing some of the latter's statements
as untrue. This brought Edwards to his feet with a similar retort.
His angry tone and menacing manner, as he mounted a table
and with clenched fist hurled defiance at his challenger, forebod-
ed a tumultuous scene. "The excitement that followed," relates
another one of the candidates, R. L. Wilson, "was intense—so
much so that fighting men thought a duel must settle the difficulty. Mr. Lincoln by the programme followed Early. Taking
up the subject in dispute, he handled it so fairly and with such
ability, all were astonished and pleased." The turbulent spirits
were quieted and the difficulty was easily overcome.

Lincoln's friend Joshua F. Speed relates that during this campaign he made a speech in Springfield a few days before the election. "The crowd was large," says Speed, "and great numbers of
his friends and admirers had come in from the country. I

remember that his speech was a very able one, using with great power and originality all the arguments used to sustain the principles of the Whig party as against its great rival, the Democratic party of that day. The speech produced a profound impression—the crowd was with him. George Forquer, an old citizen, a man of recognized prominence and ability as a lawyer, was present. Forquer had been a Whig—one of the champions of the party—but had then recently joined the Democratic party, and almost simultaneous with the change had been appointed Register of the Land Office, which office he then held. Just about that time Mr. Forquer had completed a neat frame house—the best house then in Springfield—and over it had erected a lightning rod, the only one in the place and the first one Mr. Lincoln had ever seen. He afterwards told me that seeing Forquer's lightning rod had led him to the study of the properties of electricity and the utility of the rod as a conductor. At the conclusion of Lincoln's speech the crowd was about dispersing, when Forquer rose and asked to be heard. He commenced by saying that the young man would have to be taken down, and was sorry the task devolved on him. He then proceeded to answer Lincoln's speech in a style which, while it was able and fair, in his whole manner asserted and claimed superiority." Lincoln stood a few steps away with arms folded, carefully watching the speaker and taking in everything he said. He was laboring under a good deal of suppressed excitement. Forquer's sting had roused the lion within him. At length Forquer concluded, and he mounted the stand to reply.

"I have heard him often since," continued Speed, "in the courts and before the people, but never saw him appear and acquit himself so well as upon that occasion. His reply to Forquer was characterized by great dignity and force. I shall never forget the conclusion of that speech: 'Mr. Forquer commenced his speech by announcing that the young man would have to be taken down. It is for you, fellow citizens, not for me to say whether I am up or down. The gentleman has seen fit to allude to my being a young man; but he forgets that I am older in years than I am in the tricks and trades of politicians. I desire to live, and I desire place and distinction; but I would rather die now than, like the gentleman, live to see the day that I would

change my politics for an office worth three thousand dollars a
year, and then feel compelled to erect a lightning rod to protect a
guilty conscience from an offended God.' " The effect of this
rejoinder was wonderful, and gave Forquer and his lightning rod
a notoriety the extent of which no one envied him.

In the election which followed, Sangamon County in a political sense was entirely turned over. Hitherto the Democrats had
always carried it, but now the Whigs gained control by an
average majority of four hundred. This time Lincoln led his ticket. The nine elected were, Abraham Lincoln, Ninian W. Edwards, John Dawson, Andrew McCormic, Dan Stone, Wm. F.
Elkin, Robert L. Wilson, Job Fletcher, and Archer G. Herndon.
The last two were Senators. On assembling at Vandalia they
were at once, on account of their stature, dubbed the "Long
Nine." In height they averaged over six feet, and in weight over
two hundred pounds. "We were not only noted," says one of
them, Robert L. Wilson, "for our number and length, but for our
combined influence. All the bad or objectional laws passed at
that session of the Legislature and for many years afterwards
were chargeable to the management and influence of the 'Long
Nine.' "

The Legislature of which Mr. Lincoln thus became a member
was one that will never be forgotten in Illinois. Its legislation in
aid of the so-called internal improvement system was significantly reckless and unwise. The gigantic and stupendous
operations of the scheme dazzled the eyes of nearly everybody,
but in the end it rolled up a debt so enormous as to impede the
otherwise marvelous progress of Illinois. The burdens imposed
by this Legislature under the guise of improvements became so
monumental in size it is little wonder that at intervals for years
afterward the monster of repudiation often showed its hideous
face above the waves of popular indignation. These attempts at a
settlement of the debt brought about a condition of things which
it is said led the Little Giant, in one of his efforts on the stump,
to suggest that "Illinois ought to be honest if she never paid a
cent." However much we may regret that Lincoln took part and
aided in this reckless legislation, we must not forget that his
party and all his constituents gave him their united endorsement. They gave evidence of their approval of his course by two

subsequent elections to the same office. It has never surprised me in the least that Lincoln fell so harmoniously in with the great system of improvement. He never had what some people call "money sense." By reason of his peculiar nature and construction he was endowed with none of the elements of a political economist. He was enthusiastic and theoretical up to a certain degree; could take hold of, and wrap himself up in, a great moral question; but in dealing with the financial and commercial interests of a community or government he was equally as inadequate as he was ineffectual in managing the economy of his own household. In this respect alone I always regarded Mr. Lincoln as a weak man.

The representatives in the Legislature from Sangamon County had been instructed by a mass convention of their constituents to vote "for a general system of internal improvements." Another convention of delegates from all the counties in the State met at Vandalia and made a similar recommendation to the members of the Legislature, specifying that it should be "commensurate with the wants of the people." Provision was made for a gridiron of railroads. The extreme points of the State, east and west, north and south, were to be brought together by thirteen hundred miles of iron rails. Every river and stream of the least importance was to be widened, deepened, and made navigable. A canal to connect the Illinois River and Lake Michigan was to be dug, and thus the great system was to be made "commensurate with the wants of the people." To effect all these great ends, a loan of twelve million dollars was authorized before the session closed. Work on all these gigantic enterprises was to begin at the earliest practicable moment; cities were to spring up everywhere; capital from abroad was to come pouring in; attracted by the glowing reports of marvelous progress and great internal wealth, people were to come swarming in by colonies, until in the end Illinois was to outstrip all the others, and herself become the Empire State of the Union.

Lincoln served on the Committee on Finance, and zealously labored for the success of the great measures proposed, believing they would ultimately enrich the State, and redound to the glory of all who aided in their passage. In advocating these extensive and far-reaching plans he was not alone. Stephen A. Douglas,

John A. McClernand, James Shields, and others prominent in
the subsequent history of the State, were equally as earnest in
espousing the cause of improvement, and sharing with him the
glory that attended it. Next in importance came the bill to
remove the seat of government from Vandalia. Springfield, of
course, wanted it. So also did Alton, Decatur, Peoria, Jacksonville, and Illiopolis. But the Long Nine by their adroitness and influence, were too much for their contestants. They made a bold
fight for Springfield, intrusting the management of the bill to
Lincoln. The friends of other cities fought Springfield bitterly,
but under Lincoln's leadership the Long Nine contested with
them every inch of the way. The struggle was warm and protracted. "Its enemies," relates one of Lincoln's colleagues, "laid
it on the table twice. In those darkest hours when our bill to all
appearances was beyond resuscitation, and all our opponents
were jubilant over our defeat, and when friends could see no
hope, Mr. Lincoln never for one moment despaired; but collecting his colleagues to his room for consultation, his *practical
common sense,* his thorough knowledge of human nature, then
made him an overmatch for his compeers and for any man that I
have ever known." The friends of the bill at last surmounted all
obstacles, and only a day or two before the close of the session
secured its passage by a joint vote of both houses.

Meanwhile the great agitation against human slavery, which
like a rare plant had flourished amid the hills of New England in
luxuriant growth, began to make its appearance in the West.
Missionaries in the great cause of human liberty were settling
everywhere. Taunts, jeers, ridicule, persecution, assassination
even, were destined to prove ineffectual in the effort to suppress
or exterminate these pioneers of Abolitionism. These brave but
derided apostles carried with them the seed of a great reform.
Perhaps, as was then said of them, they were somewhat in advance of their season, and perhaps too, some of the seed might
be sown in sterile ground and never come to life, but they com-
forted themselves with the assurance that it would not all die. A
little here and there was destined to grow to life and beauty.

It is not surprising, I think, that Lincoln should have viewed
this New England importation with mingled suspicion and
alarm. Abstractly, and from the standpoint of conscience, he

abhorred slavery. But born in Kentucky, and surrounded as he was by slave-holding influences, absorbing their prejudices and following in their line of thought, it is not strange, I repeat, that he should fail to estimate properly the righteous indignation and unrestrained zeal of a Yankee Abolitionist. On the last day but one of the session, he solicited his colleagues to sign with him a mild and carefully worded protest against certain resolutions on the subject of domestic slavery, which had been passed by both houses of the Legislature.[1]

They all declined, however, save one, Dan Stone, who with his associate will probably be known long after mention of all other members of the Long Nine has dropped from history. The language and sentiment are clearly Lincolnian, and over twenty years afterward, when it was charged that Lincoln was an Abolitionist, and this protest was cited as proof, it was only necessary to call for a careful reading of the paper for an unqualified and overwhelming refutation of the charge. The records of the Legislature for March 3, 1837, contain this entry:

Resolutions upon the subject of domestic slavery having passed both branches of the General Assembly at its present session, the undersigned hereby protest against the passage of the same.

They believe that the institution of slavery is founded on both injustice and bad policy, but that the promulgation of abolition doctrines tends rather to increase than abate its evils.

They believe that the Congress of the United States has no power under the Constitution to interfere with the institution of slavery in the different States.

[1] Following are the resolutions:
"Resolved by the General Assembly of the State of Illinois:
"That we highly disapprove of the formation of Abolition societies and of the doctrines promulgated by them,
"That the right of property in slaves is sacred to the slave-holding States by the Federal Constitution, and that they cannot be deprived of that right without their consent,
"That the General Government cannot abolish slavery in the District of Columbia without the consent of the citizens of said District, without a manifest breach of good faith,
"That the Governor be requested to transmit to the States of Virginia, Alabama, Mississippi, New York, and Connecticut, a copy of the foregoing report and resolutions."

They believe that the Congress of the United States has the power under the Constitution to abolish slavery in the District of Columbia, but that the power ought not to be exercised unless at the request of the people of the District.

The difference between these opinions and those contained in the above resolutions is their reason for entering this protest.

Dan Stone,
A. Lincoln,

Representatives from the County of Sangamon.

This document so adroitly drawn and worded this protest pruned of any offensive allusions, and cautiously framed so as to suit the temper of the times, stripped of its verbal foliage, reveals in naked grandeur the solemn truth that "the institution of slavery is founded on both injustice and bad policy." A quarter of a century later finds one of these protesters righting the injustice and correcting the bad policy of the inhuman and diabolical institution.

After his return from the Legislature, Lincoln determined to remove to Springfield, the county seat, and begin the practice of the law. Having been so instrumental in securing the removal of the State capital from Vandalia, and having received such encouraging assurances from Major John T. Stuart and other leading citizens, he felt confident of a good start. He had little, if any, money, but hoped to find in Springfield, as he had in New Salem, good and influential friends, who, recognizing alike his honesty and his nobility of character would aid him whenever a crisis and their help was needed. In this hope he was by no means in error, for his subsequent history shows that he indeed united his friends to himeslf with hooks of steel. I had up to this time frequently seen Mr. Lincoln—had often, while visiting my cousins, James and Rowan Herndon, at New Salem, met him at their house—but became warmly attached to him soon after his removal to Springfield. There was something in his tall and angular frame, his ill-fitting garments, honest face, and lively humor that imprinted his individuality on my affection and regard. What impression I made on him I had no means of knowing till many years afterward. He was my senior by nine years, and I looked up to him, naturally enough, as my superior in everything—a thing I continued to do till the end of his days.

In March, 1837, he was licensed to practice law. His name appears for the first time as attorney for the plaintiff in the case of Hawthorne vs. Woolridge. He entered the office and became the partner of his comrade in the Black Hawk war, John T. Stuart, who had gained rather an extensive practice, and who, by the loan of sundry textbooks several years before, had encouraged Lincoln to continue in the study of law. Stuart had emigrated from Kentucky in 1828, and on account of his nativity, if for no other reason, had great influence with the leading people in Springfield. He used to relate that on the next morning after his arrival in Springfield he was standing in front of the village store, leaning against a post in the sidewalk and wondering how to introduce himself to the community, when he was approached by a well-dressed old gentleman, who, interesting himself in the newcomer's welfare, enquired after his history and business. "I'm from Kentucky," answered Stuart, "and my profession is that of a lawyer, sir. What is the prospect here?" Throwing his head back and closing his left eye the old gentleman reflected a moment. "Young man, d——d slim chance for that kind of combination here," was the response.

At the time of Lincoln's entry into the office, Stuart was just recovering from the effects of a congressional race in which he had been the loser. He was still deeply absorbed in politics, and was preparing for the next canvass, in which he was finally successful—defeating the wily and ambitious Stephen A. Douglas. In consequence of the political allurements, Stuart did not give to the law his undivided time or the full force of his energy and intellect. Thus more or less responsibility in the management of business and the conduct of cases soon devolved on Lincoln. The entries in the account books of the firm are all in the handwriting of Lincoln. Most of the declarations and pleas were written by him also. This sort of exercise was never congenial to him, and it was the only time, save a brief period under Judge Logan, that he served as junior partner and performed the labor required of one who serves in that rather subordinate capacity. He had not yet learned to love work. The office of the firm was in the upper story of a building opposite the northwest corner of the present Courthouse Square. In the room underneath, the county court was held. The furniture was in keeping with the pretensions of the firm—a small lounge or bed, a chair containing a buffalo robe, in which the junior member was wont to sit and study, a hard wooden bench, a feeble attempt at a bookcase, and a table which answered for a desk. Lincoln's first attempt at settlement in Springfield, which preceded a few days his partnership with Stuart, has been graphically described by his friend, Joshua F. Speed, who generously offered to share his quarters with the young legal aspirant. Speed, who was a prosperous young merchant, reports that Lincoln's personal effects consisted of a pair of saddlebags containing two or three law books and a few pieces of clothing. "He had ridden into town on a borrowed horse," relates Speed, "and engaged from the only cabinetmaker in the village a single bedstead. He came into my store, set his saddlebags on the counter, and inquired what the furniture for a single bedstead would cost. I took slate and pencil, made a calculation, and found the sum for furniture complete would amount to seventeen dollars in all. Said he: 'It is probably cheap enough; but I want to say that, cheap as it is, I have not the money to pay. But if you will credit me until Christmas, and my experiment here as a lawyer is a success, I will pay you then. If I fail in that I will probably never pay you at all.' The tone of his voice was so melancholy that I felt for him. I looked up at him and I thought then, as I think now, that I never saw so gloomy and melancholy a face in my life. I said to him, 'So small a debt seems to affect you so deeply, I think I can suggest a plan by which you will be able to attain your end without incurring any debt. I have a very large room and a very large double bed in it, which you are perfectly welcome to share with me if you choose.' 'Where is your room?' he asked. 'Upstairs,' said I, pointing to the stairs leading from the store to my room. Without saying a word he took his saddlebags on his arm, went upstairs, set them down on the floor, came down again, and with a face beaming with pleasure and smiles, exclaimed, 'Well, Speed, I'm moved.' "

William Butler who was prominent in the removal of the capital from Vandalia to Springfield, took no little interest in Lincoln, while a member of the Legislature. After his removal to

Springfield, Lincoln boarded at Butler's house for several years. He became warmly attached to the family, and it is probable the matter of pay never entered Butler's mind. He was not only able but willing to befriend the young lawyer in this and many other ways.

Stephen T. Logan was judge of the Circuit Court, and Stephen A. Douglas was prosecuting attorney. Among the attorneys we find many promising spirits. Edward D. Baker, John T. Stuart, Cyrus Walker, Samuel H. Treat, Jesse B. Thomas, George Forquer, Dan Stone, Ninian W. Edwards, John J. Hardin, Schuyler Strong, A. T. Bledsoe, and Josiah Lamborn—a galaxy of names, each destined to shed more or less lustre on the history of the State. While I am inclined to believe that Lincoln did not, after entering Stuart's office, do as much deep and assiduous studying as people generally credit him with, yet I am confident he absorbed not a little learning by contact with the great minds who thronged about the courts and State Capitol. The books of Stuart and Lincoln, during 1837, show a practice more extensive than lucrative, for while they received a number of fees, only two or three of them reached fifty dollars; and one of these has a credit of: "Coat to Stuart, $15.00," showing that they were compelled, now and then, even to "trade out" their earnings. The litigation was as limited in importance as in extent. There were no great corporations, as in this progressive day, retaining for counsel the brains of the bar in every county seat, but the greatest as well as the least had to join the general scramble for practice. The court consumed as much time deciding who had committed an assault or a trespass on a neighbor's ground, as it spent in the solution of questions arising on contracts, or unraveling similar legal complications. Lawyers depended for success, not on their knowledge of the law or their familiarity with its underlying principles, but placed their reliance rather on their frontier oratory and the influence of their personal bearing before the jury.

Lincoln made Speed's store headquarters. There politics, religion, and all other subjects were discussed. There also public sentiment was made. The store had a large fireplace in the rear, and around it the lights of the town collected every evening. As the sparks flew from the crackling logs, another and more

brilliant fire flashed when these great minds came into collision.
Here were wont to gather Lincoln, Douglas, Baker, Calhoun,
Browning, Lamborn, Jesse B. Thomas and others. Only those
who were present and listened to these embryonic statesmen and
budding orators will ever be able to recall their brilliant
thoughts and appreciate their youthful enthusiasm. In the fall
and winter of 1837, while I was attending college at
Jacksonville, the persecution and death of Elijah P. Lovejoy at
Alton took place. This cruel and uncalled for murder had
aroused the antislavery sentiment everywhere. It penetrated the
college, and both faculty and students were loud and unrestrained in their denunciation of the crime. My father, who was
thoroughly proslavery in his ideas, believing that the college was
too strongly permeated with the virus of Abolitionism, forced
me to withdraw from the institution and return home. But it was
too late. My soul had absorbed too much of what my father
believed was rank poison. The murder of Lovejoy filled me with
more desperation than the slave scene in New Orleans did Lincoln; for awhile he believed in noninterference with slavery, so
long as the Constitution permitted and authorized its existence,
I, although acting nominally with the Whig party up to 1853,
struck out for Abolitionism pure and simple.

On my return to Springfield from college, I hired to Joshua F.
Speed as clerk in his store. My salary, seven hundred dollars per
annum, was considered good pay then. Speed, Lincoln, Charles
R. Hurst, and I slept in the room upstairs over the store. I had
worked for Speed before going to college, and after hiring to him
this time again, continued in his employ for several years. The
young men who congregated about the store formed a society
for the encouragement of debate and literary efforts. Sometimes
we would meet in a lawyer's office and often in Speed's room.
Besides the debates, poems and other original productions were
read. Unfortunately we ruled out the ladies. I am free to admit I
would not encourage a similar thing nowadays; but in that early
day the young men had not the comforts of books and newspapers which are within the reach of every boy now. Some allow-
ance therefore should be made for us. I have forgotten the name
of the society—if it had any—and can only recall a few of its
leading spirits. Lincoln, James Matheny, Noah Rickard, Evan

Butler, Milton Hay, and Newton Francis were members. I joined also. Matheny was secretary. We were favored with all sorts of literary productions. Lincoln himself entertained us with a few lines of rhyme intended to illustrate some weakness in woman— her frailty, perhaps. Matheny was able several years ago to repeat the one stanza which follows, and that was all he could recall—perhaps it was best he could remember no more:

> *Whatever spiteful fools may say,*
> *Each jealous, ranting yelper,*
> *No woman ever went astray*
> *Without a man to help her.*

Besides this organization we had a society in Springfield, which contained and commanded all the culture and talent of the place. Unlike the other one its meetings were public, and reflected great credit on the community. We called it the "Young Men's Lyceum." Late in 1837, Lincoln delivered before the society a carefully prepared address on the "Perpetuation of Our Free Institutions." The inspiration and burthen of it was law and order. It has been printed in full so often and is always to be found in the list of Lincoln's public speeches, that I presume I need not reproduce it here. It was highly sophomoric in character and abounded in striking and lofty metaphor. In point of rhetorical effort it excels anything he ever afterward attempted. Probably it was the thing people expect from a young man of twenty-eight. The address was published in the *Sangamon Journal* and created for the young orator a reputation which soon extended beyond the limits of the locality in which he lived. As illustrative of his style of oratory, I beg to introduce the concluding paragraph of the address. Having characterized the surviving soldiers of the Revolution as "living histories," he closes with this thrilling flourish:

But these histories are gone. They can be read no more forever. They were a fortress of strength; but what invading foeman never could do, the silent artillery of time has—the levelling of its walls. They are gone. They were a forest of giant oaks; but the all-resistless hurricane has swept over them, and left only here and there a lonely trunk, despoiled of its verdure, shorn of

*its foliage, unshading and unshaded, to murmur in a few more
gentle breezes, and to combat with its mutilated limbs a few
more rude storms, then to sink and be no more. They were
pillars of the temple of liberty, and now that they have crumbled
away, that temple must fall, unless we, their descendants, supply
their places with other pillars hewn from the same solid quarry
of sober reason. Passion has helped us, but can do so no more. It
will in future be our enemy. Reason—cold, calculating, unim-
passioned reason—must furnish all the materials for our further
support and defense. Let these materials be moulded into general
intelligence, sound morality, and in particular, a reverence for
the Constitution and the laws. . . . Upon these let the proud fabric of freedom rest as the rock of its basis, and as truly as has
been said of the only greater institution, "The gates of hell shall
not prevail against it."*

In time Lincoln's style changed: he became more eloquent but
with less gaudy ornamentation. He grew in oratorical power,
dropping gradually the alliteration and rosy metaphor of youth,
until he was able at last to deliver that grandest of all orations—
the Gettysburg address.

One evening, while the usual throng of loungers surrounded
the inviting fireplace in Speed's store, the conversation turned
on political matters. The disputants waxed warm and
acrimonious as the discussion proceeded. Business being over for
the day, I strolled back and seating myself on a keg listened with
eager interest to the battle going on among these would-be statesmen. Douglas, I recollect, was leading on the Democratic side.
He had already learned the art of dodging in debate, but
still he was subtle, fiery, and impetuous. He charged the Whigs
with every blunder and political crime he could imagine. No vul-
nerable spot seemed to have escaped him. At last, with great
vehemence, he sprang up and abruptly made a challenge to
those who differed with him to discuss the whole matter publicly, remarking that, "This store is no place to talk politics." In
answer to Douglas's challenge the contest was entered into. It
took place in the Presbyterian Church. Douglas, Calhoun, Lamborn, and Thomas represented the Democrats; and Logan,
Baker, Browning, and Lincoln, in the order named, presented the
Whig side of the question. One evening was given to each man,

and it therefore required over a week to complete the tournament. Lincoln occupied the last evening, and although the people by that time had necessarily grown a little tired of the monotony and well-worn repetition, yet Lincoln's manner of presenting his thoughts and· answering his Democratic opponents excited renewed interest. So deep was the impression he created that he was asked to furnish his speech to the *Sangamon Journal* for publication and it afterwards appeared in the columns of that organ.

Meanwhile Mr. Lincoln had attended one special session of the Legislature in July, 1837. The session was called to take some action with regard to the financial condition of the State. The Bank of the United States and the New York and Philadelphia Banks had suspended specie payments. This action had precipitated general ruin among business men and interests over the entire country. The called session of the Legislature was intended to save the Illinois banks from impending dissolution. Lincoln retained his position on the Committee on Finance, and had lost none of his enthusiasm over the glorious prospects of internal improvements. The Legislature, instead of abridging, only extended the already colossal proportions of the great system. In this they paid no heed to the governor, whose head seems to have been significantly clear on the folly of the enterprise.

In 1838 Mr. Lincoln was again elected to the Legislature. At this session, as the nominee of the Whig party, he received thirty-eight votes for Speaker. Wm. L. D. Ewing, his successful competitor, the Democratic candidate, received forty-three votes, and was elected. Besides retaining his place on the Finance Committee, Lincoln was assigned to the Committee on Counties. The enthusiasm and zeal of the friends of internal improvements began to flag now in view of the fact that the bonds issued were beginning to find their true level in point of value. Lincoln, together with others of kindred views, tried to bolster the "system" up; but soon the discouraging fact became apparent that no more money could be obtained, and the Legislature began to descant on what part of the debt was lawful and what unlawful. Repudiation seemed not far off. Mr. Lincoln despaired now of ever becoming the "DeWitt Clinton of Illinois." We find him admitting "his share of the responsibility in the present crisis," and finally concluding that he was "no financier" after all. No sooner had the Legislature adjourned than Lincoln decided—if he had not already so determined—to run for the same place again. He probably wanted it for a vindication. He was pursued now more fiercely than ever, and he was better able to endure the vilification of a political campaign than when he first offered himself to the voters in New Salem.

Among the Democratic orators who stumped the county at this time was one Taylor—commonly known as Colonel Dick Taylor. He was a showy, bombastic man, with a weakness for fine clothes and other personal adornments. Frequently he was pitted against Lincoln, and indulged in many bitter flings at the lordly ways and aristocratic pretensions of the Whigs. He had a way of appealing to "his horny-handed neighbors," and resorted to many other artful tricks of a demagogue. When he was one day expatiating in his accustomed style, Lincoln, in a spirit of mischief and, as he expressed it, "to take the wind out of his sails," slipped up to the speaker's side, and catching his vest by the lower edge gave it a sharp pull. The latter instantly opened and revealed to his astonished hearers a ruffled shirt-front glittering with watchchain, seals, and other golden jewels. The effect was startling. The speaker stood confused and dumbfounded, while the audience roared with laughter. When it came Lincoln's turn to answer he covered the gallant colonel over in this style: "While Colonel Taylor was making these charges against the Whigs over the country, riding in fine carriages, wearing ruffled shirts, kid gloves, massive gold watchchains with large gold seals, and flourishing a heavy gold-headed cane, I was a poor boy, hired on a flatboat at eight dollars a month, and had only one pair of breeches to my back, and they were buckskin. Now if you know the nature of buckskin when wet and dried by the sun, it will shrink; and my breeches kept shrinking until they left several inches of my legs bare between the tops of my socks and the lower part of my breeches; and whilst I was growing taller they were becoming shorter, and so much tighter that they left a blue streak around my legs that can be seen to this day. If you call this aristocracy I plead guilty to the charge."

It was during this same canvass that Lincoln by his manly interference protected his friend E. D. Baker from the anger of an infuriated crowd. Baker was a brilliant and effective speaker, and quite as full too of courage as invective. He was addressing a crowd in the court room, which was immediately underneath Stuart and Lincoln's office. Just above the platform on which the speaker stood was a trap door in the floor, which opened into Lincoln's office. Lincoln at the time, as was often his habit, was lying on the floor looking down through the door at the speaker. I was in the body of the crowd. Baker was hotheaded and impulsive, but brave as a lion. Growing warm in his arraignment of the Democratic party, he charged that "wherever there was a land office there was a Democratic newspaper to defend its corruptions." This angered the brother of the editor of our town paper, who was present, and who cried out, "Pull him down," at the same time advancing from the crowd as if to perform the task himself. Baker, his face pale with excitement, squared himself for resistance. A shuffling of feet, a forward movement of the crowd, and great confusion followed. Just then a long pair of legs was seen dangling from the aperture above, and instantly the figure of Lincoln dropped on the platform. Motioning with his hands for silence and not succeeding, he seized a stone water pitcher standing near by, threatening to break it over the head of the first man who laid hands on Baker. "Hold on, gentlemen," he shouted, "this is the land of free speech. Mr. Baker has a right to speak and ought to be heard. I am here to protect him, and no man shall take him from this stand if I can prevent it." His interference had the desired effect. Quiet was soon restored, and the valiant Baker was allowed to proceed. I was in the back part of the crowd that night and an enthusiastic Baker man myself. I knew he was a brave man, and even if Lincoln had not interposed, I felt sure he wouldn't have been pulled from the platform without a bitter struggle.

This canvass—1840—was Mr. Lincoln's last campaign for the Legislature. Feeling that he had had enough honor out of the office he probably aspired for a place of more distinction. Jesse B. Thomas, one of the men who had represented the Democratic side in the great debate in the Presbyterian Church, in a speech at the courthouse during this campaign, indulged in some fun at the expense of the "Long Nine," reflecting somewhat more on Lincoln than the rest. The latter was not present, but being apprised by his friends of what had been said, hastened to the meeting, and soon after Thomas closed, stepped upon the platform and responded. The substance of his speech on this occasion was not so memorable as the manner of its delivery. He felt the sting of Thomas's allusions, and for the first time, on the stump or in public, resorted to mimicry for effect. In this, as will be seen later along, he was without a rival. He imitated Thomas in gesture and voice, at times caricaturing his walk and the very motion of his body. Thomas, like everybody else, had some peculiarities of expression and gesture, and these Lincoln succeeded in rendering more prominent than ever. The crowd yelled and cheered as he continued. Encouraged by these demonstrations, the ludicrous features of the speaker's performance gave way to intense and scathing ridicule. Thomas, who was obliged to sit near by and endure the pain of this unique ordeal, was ordinarily sensitive; but the exhibition goaded him to desperation. He was so thoroughly wrought up with suppressed emotion that he actually gave way to tears. I was not a witness of this scene, but the next day it was the talk of the town, and for years afterwards it was called the "skinning" of Thomas. Speed was there, so were A. Y. Ellis, Ninian W. Edwards, and David Davis, who was just then coming into prominence. The whole thing was so unlike Lincoln, it was not soon forgotten either by his friends or enemies. I heard him afterwards say that the recollection of his conduct that evening filled him with the deepest chagrin. He felt that he had gone too far, and to rid his good-nature of a load, hunted up Thomas and made ample apology. The incident and its sequel proved that Lincoln could not only be vindictive but manly as well.

He was selected as an Elector on the Harrison ticket for President in 1840, and as such stumped over a good portion of the State. In debate he frequently met Douglas, who had already become the standard-bearer and exponent of Democratic principles. These joint meetings were spirited affairs sometimes; but at no time did he find the Little Giant averse to a conflict. "He was very sensitive," relates one of his colleagues on the stump, "where he thought he had failed to meet the expectations of his friends. I remember a case. He was pitted by the Whigs in 1840 to debate with Mr. Douglas, the Democratic champion. Lincoln did not come up to the requirements of the occasion. He was conscious of his failure, and I never saw any man so much distressed. He begged to be permitted to try it again, and was reluctantly indulged; and in the next effort he transcended our highest expectations. I never heard and never expect to hear such a triumphant vindication as he then gave of Whig measures or policy. He never after, to my knowledge, fell below himself."

The campaign ended in his election to the Legislature. He was again the caucus nominee of the Whigs for Speaker, receiving thirty-six votes; but his former antagonist, William L. D. Ewing, was elected by a majority of ten votes over him. The proceedings of, and laws enacted by, this Legislature are so much a matter of history and so generally known that it seems a needless task on my part to enter into details. It is proper to note, however, in passing, that Mr. Lincoln was neither prompt nor constant in his attendance during the session. He had been to a certain extent "upset" by another love affair, the particulars of which must be assigned to a future chapter.

4

Marriage

The year 1840 finds Mr. Lincoln entering his thirty-second year and still unmarried. "I have come to the conclusion," he suggests in a facetious letter, two years before, "never again to think of marrying." But meanwhile he had seen more of the world. The State Captial had been removed to Springfield, and he soon observed the power and influence one can exert with high family and social surroundings to draw upon. The sober truth is that Lincoln was inordinately ambitious. He had already succeeded in obtaining no inconsiderable political recognition, and numbered among his party friends men of wealth and reputation; but he himself was poor, besides lacking the graces and ease of bearing obtained through mingling in polite society—in fact, to use the expressive language of Mary Owens, he was "deficient in those little links which make up the chain of woman's happiness." Conscious, therefore, of his humble rank in the social scale, how natural that he should seek by marriage in an influential family to establish strong connections and at the same time foster his political fortunes! This may seem an audacious thing to insinuate, but on no other basis can we reconcile the strange course of his courtship and the tempestuous chapters in his married life. It is a curious history, and the facts, long chained down, are gradually coming to the surface. When all is at last known, the world I believe will divide its censure between Lincoln and his wife.

Mary Todd, who afterwards became the wife of Mr. Lincoln, was born in Lexington, Kentucky, December 13, 1818. "My mother," related Mrs. Lincoln to me in 1865, "died when I was still young. I was educated by Madame Mentelle, a lady who lived opposite Mr. Clay's, and who was an accomplished French scholar. Our conversation at school was carried on entirely in French—in fact we were allowed to speak nothing else. I finished my education at Mrs. Ward's Academy, an institution to which many people from the North sent their daughters. In 1837 I visited Springfield, Illinois, remaining three months. I re-

turned to Kentucky, remaining till 1839, when I again set out
for Illinois, which State finally became my home."

When Mary Todd came to her sister's house in Springfield in
1839, she was in her twenty-first year. She was a young woman
of strong, passionate nature and quick temper, and had "left her
home in Kentucky to avoid living under the same roof with a
stepmother." She came to live with her oldest sister, Elizabeth,
who was the wife of Lincoln's colleague in the Legislature,
Ninian W. Edwards. She was of the average height, weighing
when I first saw her about a hundred and thirty pounds. She
was rather compactly built, had a well-rounded face, rich dark
brown hair, and bluish gray eyes. In her bearing she was proud,
but handsome and vivacious. Her education had been in no wise
defective; she was a good conversationalist, using with equal
fluency the French and English languages. When she used a pen,
its point was sure to be sharp, and she wrote with wit and
ability. She not only had a quick intellect but an intuitive judgment of men and their motives. Ordinarily she was affable and
even charming in her manners; but when offended or antago-
nized, her agreeable qualities instantly disappeared beneath a
wave of stinging satire or sarcastic bitterness, and her entire better nature was submerged. In her figure and physical proportions, in education, bearing, temperament, history—in everything she was the exact reverse of Lincoln.

On her return to Springfield she immediately entered society,
and soon became one of the belles, leading the young men of the
town a merry dance. She was a very shrewd observer, and
discreetly and without apparent effort kept back all the unattrac-
tive elements in her unfortunate organization. Her trenchant
wit, affability, and candor pleased the young men not less than
her culture and varied accomplishments impressed the older
ones with whom she came in contact. The first time I met her
was at a dance at the residence of Colonel Robert Allen, a gentleman mentioned in the preceding chapter. I engaged her for a
waltz, and as we glided through it I fancied I never before had
danced with a young lady who moved with such grace and ease.
A few moments later, as we were promenading through the hall,
I thought to compliment her graceful dancing by telling her that
while I was conscious of my own awkward movements, she

seemed to glide through the waltz with the ease of a serpent. The strange comparison was as unfortunate as it was hideous. I saw it in an instant, but too late to recall it. She halted for a moment, drew back, and her eyes flashed as she retorted: "Mr. Herndon, comparison to a serpent is rather severe irony, especially to a newcomer."

Through the influence of Joshua F. Speed, who was a warm friend of the Edwardses, Lincoln was led to call on Miss Todd. He was charmed with her wit and beauty, no less than by her excellent social qualities and profound knowledge of the strong and weak points in individual character. One visit succeeded another. It was the old story. Lincoln had again fallen in love. "I have often happened in the room where they were sitting," relates Mrs. Edwards, describing this courtship, "and Mary invaribly led the conversation. Mr. Lincoln would sit at her side and listen. He scarcely said a word, but gazed on her as if irresistibly drawn towards her by some superior and unseen power. He could not maintain himself in a continued conversation with a lady reared as Mary was. He was not educated and equipped mentally to make himself either interesting or attractive to the ladies. He was a good, honest, and sincere young man whose rugged, manly qualities I admired; but to me he somehow seemed ill-constituted by nature and education to please such a woman as my sister. Mary was quick, gay, and in the social world somewhat brilliant. She loved show and power, and was the most ambitious woman I ever knew. She used to contend when a girl, to her friends in Kentucky, that she was destined to marry a President. I have heard her say that myself, and after mingling in society in Springfield she repeated the seemingly absurd and idle boast. Although Mr. Lincoln seemed to be attached to Mary, and fascinated by her wit and sagacity, yet I soon began to doubt whether they could always be so congenial. In a short time I told Mary my impression that they were not suited, or, as some persons who believe matches are made in heaven would say, not intended for each other."

But Mrs. Edwards' advice was seed sown on rocky soil. The courtship ran on smoothly to the point of engagement, when a new and disturbing element loomed up ahead in their paths. It was no less than the dashing and handsome Stephen A.

Douglas, who now appeared on the scene in the guise of a rival. As a society man Douglas was infinitely more accomplished, more attractive and influential than Lincoln, and that he should supplant the latter in the affections of the proud and aristocratic Miss Todd is not to be marveled at. He was unremitting in his attentions to the lady, promenaded the streets arm-in-arm with her—frequently passing Lincoln—and in every way made plain his intention to become the latter's rival. There are those who believe this warm reciprocation of young Douglas' affection was a mere flirtation on Mary Todd's part, intended to spur Lincoln up, to make him more demonstrative, and manifest his love more positively and with greater fervor. But a lady relative who lived with Lincoln and his wife for two years after their marriage is authority for the statement coming from Mrs. Lincoln herself that "she loved Douglas, and but for her promise to marry Lincoln would have accepted him. The unfortunate attitude she felt bound to maintain between these two young men ended in a spell of sickness. Douglas, still hopeful, was warm in the race, but the lady's physician—her brother-in-law—Dr. William Wallace, to whom she confided the real cause of her illness, saw Douglas and induced him to end his pursuit, which he did with great reluctance.

If Miss Todd intended by her flirtation with Douglas to test Lincoln's devotion, she committed a grievous error. If she believed, because he was ordinarily so undemonstrative, that he was without willpower and incapable of being aroused, she certainly did not comprehend the man. Lincoln began now to feel the sting. Miss Todd's spur had certainly operated and with awakening effect. One evening Lincoln came into our store and called for his warm friend Speed. Together they walked back to the fireplace, where Lincoln, drawing from his pocket a letter, asked Speed to read it. "The letter," relates Speed, "was addressed to Mary Todd, and in it he made a plain statement of his feelings, telling her that he had thought the matter over calmly and with great deliberation, and now felt that he did not love her sufficiently to warrant her in marrying him. This letter he desired me to deliver. Upon my declining to do so he threatened to intrust it to some other person's hand. I reminded him that the moment he placed the letter in Miss Todd's hand, she would have the advantage over him. 'Words are forgotten,' I said, 'misunderstood, unnoticed in a private conversation, but once put your words in writing and they stand a living and eternal monument against you.' Thereupon I threw the unfortunate letter in the fire. 'Now,' I continued, 'if you have the courage of manhood, go see Mary yourself; tell her, if you do not love her, the facts, and that you will not marry her. Be careful not to say too much, and then leave at your earliest opportunity.' Thus admonished, he buttoned his coat, and with a rather determined look started out to perform the serious duty for which I had just given him explicit directions."

That night Speed did not go upstairs to bed with us, but under pretense of wanting to read, remained in the store below. He was waiting for Lincoln's return. Ten o'clock passed, and still the interview with Miss Todd had not ended. At length, shortly after eleven, he came stalking in. Speed was satisfied, from the length of Lincoln's stay, that his directions had not been followed.

"Well, old fellow, did you do as I told you and as you promised?" were Speed's first words.

"Yes, I did," responded Lincoln, thoughtfully, "and when I told Mary I did not love her, she burst into tears and almost springing from her chair and wringing her hands as if in agony, said something about the deceiver being himself deceived." Then he stopped.

"What else did you say?" inquired Speed, drawing the facts from him.

"To tell you the truth, Speed, it was too much for me. I found the tears trickling down my own cheeks. I caught her in my arms and kissed her."

"And that's how you broke the engagement," sneered Speed. "You not only acted the fool, but your conduct was tantamount to a renewal of the engagement, and in decency you cannot back down now."

"Well," drawled Lincoln, "if I am in again, so be it. It's done, and I shall abide by it."

Convinced now that Miss Todd regarded the engagement ratified—instead of broken, as her tall suitor had at first intended—Lincoln continued his visits, and things moved on smoothly as before. Douglas had dropped out of the race, and everything pointed to an early marriage. It was probably at this time that Mr. and Mrs. Edwards began to doubt the wisdom of the marriage, and now and then to intimate the same to the lady; but they went no farther in their opposition and placed no obstacle in their paths.

The time fixed for the marriage was the first day in January, 1841. Careful preparations for the happy occasion were made at the Edwards mansion. The house underwent the customary renovation; the furniture was properly arranged, the rooms neatly decorated, the supper prepared, and the guests invited. The latter assembled on the evening in question, and awaited in expectant pleasure the interesting ceremony of marriage. The bride, bedecked in veil and silken gown, and nervously toying with the flowers in her hair, sat in the adjoining room. Nothing was lacking but the groom. For some strange reason he had been delayed. An hour passed, and the guests as well as the bride were becoming restless. But they were all doomed to disappointment. Another hour passed; messengers were sent out over town, and each returning with the same report, it became apparent that Lincoln, the principal in this little drama, had purposely failed to appear! The bride, in grief, disappeared to her room; the wedding supper was left untouched; the guests quietly and wonderingly withdrew; the lights in the Edwards mansion were blown out, and darkness settled over all for the night. What the feelings of a lady as sensitive, passionate, and proud as Miss Todd were we can only imagine—no one can ever describe them. By daybreak, after persistent search, Lincoln's friends found him. Restless, gloomy, miserable, desperate, he seemed an object of pity. His friends, Speed among the number, fearing a tragic termination, watched him closely in their rooms day and night. "Knives and razors, and every instrument that could be used for self-destruction were removed from his reach." Mrs. Edwards did not hesitate to regard him as insane, and of course her sister Mary shared in that view. But the case was hardly so desperate. His condition began to improve after a few weeks, and a letter written to his partner Stuart, on the 23d of January, 1841, three weeks after the scene at Edwards' house, reveals more perfectly how he felt. He says: "I am now the most miserable man living. If what I feel were equally distributed to the whole human family, there would not be one cheerful face on earth. Whether I shall ever be better, I cannot tell; I awfully forebode I shall not. To remain as I am is impossible. I must die or be better, as it appears to me. . . . I fear I shall be unable to attend to any business here, and a change of scene might help me. If I could be myself I would rather remain at home with Judge Logan. I can write no more."

During all this time the Legislature to which Lincoln belonged was in special session, but for a time he was unable to attend. Towards the close of the session, however, he resumed his seat. He took little if any part in the proceedings, made no speeches, and contented himself with answers to the monotonous roll call, and votes on a few of the principal measures. After the adjournment of the Legislature, his warm friend Speed, who had disposed of his interests in Springfield, induced Lincoln to accompany him to Kentucky. Speed's parents lived in a magnificent place a few miles from Louisville. Their farm was well stocked, and they, in the current phrase, "lived well." Thither he was taken, and there amid the quiet surroundings he found the "change of scene" which he told Stuart might help him. He was living under the cloud of melancholia, and sent to the *Sangamon Journal* a few lines under the gloomy title of "Suicide." They were published in the paper, and a few years since I hunted over the files, and coming across the number containing them, was astonished to find that some one had cut them out. I have always supposed it was done by Lincoln or by some one at his instigation.

Speed's mother was much impressed with the tall and swarthy stranger her son had brought with him. She was a God-fearing mother, and besides aiding to lighten his spirits, gave him a Bible, advising him to read it and by adopting its precepts obtain a release from his troubles which no other agency, in her judgment, could bring him. "He was much depressed. At first he almost contemplated suicide. In the deepest of his depression he said one day he had done nothing to make any human being remember that he had lived; and that to connect his name with the events transpiring in his day and generation, and so impress himself upon them as to link his name with something that would redound to the interest of his fellowmen, was what he desired to live for." The congenial associations at the Speed farm,[1] the freedom from unpleasant reminders, the company of his staunch friend, and above all the motherly care and delicate attention of Mrs. Speed exerted a marked influence over Lincoln. He improved gradually, day by day gaining strength and confidence in himself, until at last the great cloud lifted and passed away. In the fall he and Speed returned to Springfield. At this point, as affording us the most reliable account of Mr. Lincoln's condition and views, it is proper to insert a portion of his correspondence with Mr. Speed. For some time Mr. Speed was reluctant to give these letters to the world. After some argument, however, he at last shared my view that they were properly a matter of history, and sent them to me, accompanied by a letter, in which he says:

I enclose you copies of all the letters of any interest from Mr. Lincoln to me. Some explanation may be needed that you may rightly understand their import. In the winter of 1840 and 1841, he was unhappy about his engagement to his wife—not being entirely satisfied that his heart was going with his hand. How much he suffered then on that account none knew so well as myself; he disclosed his whole heart to me.

In the summer of 1841 I became engaged to my wife. He was here on a visit when I courted her; and, strange to say, something of the same feeling which I regarded as so foolish in him took possession of me and kept me very unhappy from the time of my engagement until I was married. This will explain the deep interest he manifested in his letters on my account.

One thing is plainly discernible; if I had not been married and happy—far more happy than I ever expected to be—he would not have married.

The first of these letters is one which he gave Speed when the

[1]At the time of Lincoln's visit at the Speed mansion, James Speed, a brother of Joshua, and afterwards Attorney General in Lincoln's Cabinet, was practicing law in Louisville. Lincoln came into his office daily. "He read my books," related Mr. Speed in after years; "talked with me about his life, his reading, his studies, his aspirations." Mr. Speed discredits the thought that Lincoln was insane at the time, although he understood he was saddened and melancholy over an unfortunate love affair.

latter started on his journey from Illinois to Kentucky. It bears no date, but was handed him January 1, 1842, as Speed has testified, in another letter to me, that he left Springfield on that day. It is full of consolation and advice how best to conduct himself when the periods of gloom which he feels sure will follow come upon his friend.

I know [he says,] *what the painful point with you is at all times when you are unhappy; it is an apprehension that you do not love her as you should. What nonsense! How came you to court her? . . . Did you court her for her wealth? Why, you say she had none. But you say you reasoned yourself into it. What do you mean by that? Was it not that you found yourself unable to reason yourself out of it? Did you not think, and partly form the purpose, of courting her the first time you ever saw her or heard of her? What had reason to do with it at that early stage? There was nothing at that time for reason to work upon. Whether she was moral, amiable, sensible, or even of good character, you did not nor could then know, except perhaps you might infer the last from the company you found her in. . . . Say candidly, were not those heavenly black eyes the whole basis of all of your reasoning on the subject? After you and I had once been at the residence, did you not go and take me all the way to Lexington and back for no other purpose but to get to see her again on our return on that evening to take a trip for that express object?*

The next paragraph is significant as affording us an idea of how the writer perhaps viewed Miss Todd's flirtation with Douglas: "What earthly consideration," he asks, "would you take to find her scouting and despising you and giving herself up to another? But of this you need have no apprehension, and therefore you cannot bring it home to your feelings."

February 3, he writes again, acknowledging receipt of a letter dated January 25. The object of Speed's affection had been ill, and her condition had greatly intensified his gloomy spirits. Lincoln proffers his sympathy.

I hope and believe [he continues] *that your present anxiety about her health and her life must and will forever banish those horrid doubts which I know you sometimes felt as to the truth of your affection for her. If they can once and forever be removed (and I almost feel a presentiment that the Almighty has sent your present affliction expressly for that object), surely nothing can come in their stead to fill their immeasurable measure of misery. . . .*

It really appears to me that you yourself ought to rejoice and not sorrow at this indubitable evidence of your undying affection for her. Why, Speed, if you did not love her, although you might not wish her death, you would most certainly be resigned to it. Perhaps this point is no longer a question with you, and my pertinacious dwelling upon it is a rude intrusion upon your feelings. If so you must pardon me. You know the hell I have suffered on that point, and how tender I am upon it. You know I do not mean wrong. I have been quite clear of hypo since you left, even better than I was along in the fall.

The next letter, February 13, was written on the eve of Speed's marriage. After assurances of his desire to befriend him in everything, he suggests:

But you will always hereafter be on ground that I have never occupied, and consequently, if advice were needed, I might advise wrong. I do fondly hope, however, that you will never again need any comfort from abroad . . . I incline to think it probable that your nerves will fail you occasionally for awhile; but once you get them firmly guarded now, that trouble is over forever. If you went through the ceremony calmly or even with sufficient composure not to excite alarm in any present, you are safe beyond question, and in two or three months, to say the most, will be the happiest of men.

Meanwhile Lincoln had been duly informed of Speed's marriage, and on the 25th he responds:

Yours of the 16th, announcing that Miss Fanny and you are 'no more twain, but one flesh,' reached me this morning. I have no way of telling how much happiness I wish you both, though I believe you both can conceive it. I feel somewhat jealous of both of you now. You will be so exclusively concerned for one another that I shall be forgotten entirely . . . I shall be very lonesome without you. How miserably things seem to be arranged in this world! If we have no friends we have no pleasure, and if we have them we are sure to lose them, and be doubly pained by the loss.

In another letter, written the same day, he says,

I have no doubt it is the peculiar misfortune of both you and me to dream dreams of Elysium far exceeding all that anything earthly can realize. Far short of your dreams as you may be, no woman could do more to realize them than that same black-eyed Fanny. If you could but contemplate her through my imagination, it would appear ridiculous to you that any one should for a moment think of being unhappy with her. My old father used to have a saying, that, 'If you make a bad bargain hug it all the tighter,' and it occurs to me that if the bargain just closed can possibly be called a bad one it is certainly the most pleasant one for applying that maxim to which my fancy can by any effort picture.

Speed having now safely married, Lincoln's mind began to turn on things nearer home. His relations with Mary Todd were still strained, but reminders of his period of gloom the year before began now to bring her again into view. In a letter to Speed, March 27, he says:

It cannot be told how it thrills me with joy to hear you say you are 'far happier than you ever expected to be.' That much, I know, is enough. I know you too well to suppose your expectations were not at least sometimes extravagant, and if the reality exceeds them all, I say, 'Enough, dear Lord.' I am not going beyond the truth when I tell you that the short space it took me to read your last letter gave me more pleasure than the total sum of all I have enjoyed since that fatal first of January, 1841. Since then it seems to me I should have been entirely happy but for the never-absent idea that there is one still unhappy whom I have contributed to make so. That kills my soul. I cannot but reproach myself for ever wishing to be happy while she is otherwise. She accompanied a large party on the railroad cars to Jacksonville last Monday, and on her return spoke, so that I heard of it, of having enjoyed the trip exceedingly. God be praised for that!

The last paragraph of this letter contains a bit of sentiment by

Lincoln in acknowledgment of a violet. In the margin of the letter which he gave me, Speed made this note in pencil: "The violet was sent by my wife, who dropped it in the letter as I was in the act of sealing it. How beautiful the acknowledgment!" This is the paragraph:

The sweet violet you enclosed came safely to hand, but it was so dry, and mashed so flat, that it crumbled to dust at the first attempt to handle it. The juice that mashed out of it stained a place in the letter, which I mean to preserve and cherish for the sake of her who procured it to be sent. My renewed good wishes to her.

Meanwhile the coldness that existed between Lincoln and his "Mary" was gradually passing away, and with it went all of Lincoln's resolution never to renew the engagement. In a letter, July 4, he says:

I must gain confidence in my own ability to keep my resolves when they are made. In that ability I once prided myself as the only chief gem of my character; that gem I lost, how and where you know too well. I have not regained it; and until I do I cannot trust myself in any matter of much importance. I believe now that had you understood my case at the time as well as I understood yours afterwards, by the aid you would have given me I should have sailed through clear; but that does not now afford me sufficient confidence to begin that or the like of that again . . . I always was superstitious; I believe God made me one of the instruments of bringing Fanny and you together, which union I have no doubt he had foreordained. Whatever he designs he will do for me yet. 'Stand still and see the salvation of the Lord,' is my text just now. If, as you say, you have told Fanny all, I should have no objection to her seeing this letter, but for its reference to our friend here; let her seeing it depend upon whether she has ever known anything of my affairs; and if she has not, do not let her. I do not think I can come to Kentucky this season. I am so poor and make so little headway in the world that I drop back in a month of idleness as much as I gain in a year's sowing.

The last letter, and the one which closes this series, was written October 5, 1842. In it he simply announced his "duel with Shields," and then goes on to "narrate the particulars of the duelling business, which still rages in this city." This referred to a challenge from the belligerent Shields to William Butler, and another from General Whitesides to Dr. Merryman. In the latter, Lincoln acted as the "friend of Merryman," but in neither case was there any encounter, and both ended in smoke. The concluding paragraph of this letter is the most singular in the entire correspondence. I give it entire without further comment:

But I began this letter not for what I have been writing, but to say something on that subject which you know to be of such infinite solicitude to me. The immense sufferings you endured from the first days of September till the middle of February you never tried to conceal from me, and I well understood. You have now been the husband of a lovely woman nearly eight months. That you are happier now than the day you married her, I well know, for without, you could not be living. But I have your word for it, too, and the returning elasticity of spirits which is manifested in your letters. But I want to ask you a close question: 'Are you in feeling as well as judgment glad you are married as you are?' From anybody but me this would be an impudent question not to be tolerated, but I know you will pardon it in me. Please answer it quickly, as I am impatient to know.

Lincoln again applied himself to the law. He re-entered the practice, after the long hiatus of rest, with renewed vigor. He permitted the memory of his engagement with Mary Todd to trouble him no longer. Their paths had diverged, the pain of the separation was over, and the whole thing was a history of the past. And so it might ever have remained but for the intervention of a very shrewd and sagacious lady—one who was capable of achieving success anywhere in the ranks of diplomacy. This lady was the wife of Simeon Francis, the editor of the *Sangamon Journal*. She was a warm friend of Mary Todd and a leader in society. Her husband was warmly attached to Lincoln. He ran the Whig organ, and entertained great admiration for Lincoln's brains and noble qualities. The esteem was mutual, and it is no stretch of the truth to say that for years Lincoln exercised undisputed control of the columns of the *Journal* himself. Whatever he wrote or had written, went into the editorial page without question. Mrs. Francis, sharing her husband's views of Lincoln's glorious possibilities, and desiring to do Mary Todd a kindly act, determined to bring about a reconciliation. She knew that Miss Todd had by letter a few days after "that fatal first of January, 1841," as Lincoln styled it, released him from the engagement, and that since then their relations had been strained, if not entirely broken off. As she viewed it, a marriage between a man as promising in the political world as Lincoln, and a woman as accomplished and brilliant in society as Mary Todd, would certainly add to the attractions of Springfield and reflect great credit on those who brought the union about. She was a great social entertainer, and one day arranged a gathering at her house for the express purpose of bringing these two people together. Both were invited and both attended; but neither suspected the other's presence. Having arranged things so ingeniously and with so much discretion, it was no difficult task for the hostess to bring the couple together by a warm introduction and the encouraging admonition, "Be friends again." Much to the surprise of both they found the web woven around them. They entered into the spirit of the reconciliation, and found Mrs. Francis' roof an inviting place for many succeeding meetings. A wall reared itself between them and the past, and they started again under the auspicious omens of another engagement. The tact of a woman and the diplomacy of society had accomplished what love had long since despaired of ever doing or seeing done.

The meetings in the parlor of Mrs. Francis' house were conducted with no little privacy. At first even Mrs. Edwards knew nothing of it, but presently it came to her ears. "I asked Mary," said this lady, "why she was so secretive about it. She said evasively that after all that had occurred, it was best to keep the courtship from all eyes and ears. Men and women and the whole world were uncertain and slippery, and if misfortune befell the engagement all knowledge of it would be hidden from the world."

It is unnecessary to prolong the account of this strange and checkered courtship. The intervention of the affair with Shields, which will be detailed in a subsequent chapter, in no way impeded, if it did not hasten the marriage. One morning in

November, Lincoln hastening to the room of his friend James H. Matheny before the latter had arisen from bed, informed that he was to be married that night, and requested him to attend as best man. That same morning Miss Todd called on her friend Julia M. Jayne, who afterward married Lyman Trumbull, and made a similar request. The Edwardses were notified, and made such meagre preparations as were possible on so short notice. License was obtained during the day, the minister, Charles N. Dresser, was sent for, and in the evening of November 4, 1842, "as pale and trembling as if being driven to slaughter," Abraham Lincoln was at last married to Mary Todd.[2]

Marriages in Springfield up to that time had been rather commonplace affairs. Lincoln's was perhaps the first one ever performed with all the requirements of the Episcopal ceremony. A goodly number of friends had gathered, and while witnessing the ceremony one of the most amusing incidents imaginable occurred. No description on paper can do it justice. Among those present was Thomas C. Brown, one of the judges of the Supreme Court. He was in truth an 'old-timer,' and had the virtue of saying just what he thought, without regard to place or surroundings. He had been on the bench for many years and was not less rough than quaint and curious. There was, of course, a perfect hush in the room as the ceremony progressed. Brown was standing just behind Lincoln. Old Parson Dresser, in canonical robes, with much and impressive ceremony recited the Episcopal service. He handed Lincoln the ring, who, placing it on the bride's finger, repeated the church formula, 'With this ring, I thee endow with all my goods and chattels, lands and tenements.' Brown, who had never witnessed such a proceeding, was struck with its utter absurdity. 'God Almighty! Lincoln,' he ejaculated, loud enough to be heard by all, 'the statute fixes all that!' This unlooked-for interruption almost upset the old parson; he had a keen sense of the ridiculous, and for the moment it seemed as if he would break down; but presently recovering his gravity, he hastily pronounced them husband and wife.[3]

[2]While dressing for the wedding in his room at Butler's house, the latter's little boy, Speed, seeing Lincoln so handsomely attired, in boyish innocence asked him where he was going? "To hell, I suppose," was Lincoln's reply.

[3]James H. Matheny to Herndon, August 21, 1888, used as footnote in original edition.

One great trial of his life was now over, and another still greater one was yet to come. To me it has always seemed plain that Mr. Lincoln married Mary Todd to save his honor, and in doing that he sacrificed his domestic peace. He had searched himself subjectively, introspectively, thoroughly; he knew he did not love her, but he had promised to marry her! The hideous thought came up like a nightmare. As the "fatal first of January, 1841," neared, the clouds around him blackened the heavens and his life almost went out with the storm. But soon the skies cleared. Friends interposed their aid to avert a calamity, and at last he stood face to face with the great conflict between honor and domestic peace. He chose the former, and with it years of self-torture, sacrificial pangs, and the loss forever of a happy home.

With Miss Todd a different motive, but one equally as unfortunate, prompted her adherence to the union. To marry Lincoln meant not a life of luxury and ease, for Lincoln was not a man to accumulate wealth; but in him she saw position in society, prominence in the world, and the grandest social distinction. By that means her ambition would be satisfied. Until that fatal New Year's day in 1841 she may have loved him, but his action on that occasion forfeited her affection. He had crushed her proud, womanly spirit. She felt degraded in the eyes of the world. Love fled at the approach of revenge. Some writer—it is Junius, I believe—has said that, "Injuries may be forgiven and forgotten, but insults admit of no compensation; they degrade the mind in its own self-esteem and force it to recover its level by revenge." Whether Mrs. Lincoln really was moved by the spirit of revenge or not she acted along the lines of human conduct. She led her husband a wild and merry dance. If, in time, she became soured at the world it was not without provocation, and if in later years she unchained the bitterness of a disappointed and outraged nature, it followed as logically as an effect does the cause.

I have told this sad story as I know and have learned it. In rehearsing the varied scenes of the drama, I have unearthed a few facts that seem half-buried, perhaps, but they were not destined to lay buried deep or long. The world will have the truth as long as the name of Lincoln is remembered by mankind.

5

Congressman

The marriage of Lincoln in no way diminished his love for politics; in fact, as we shall see later along, it served to stimulate his zeal in that direction. He embraced every opportunity that offered for a speech in public. Early in 1842 he entered into the Washington movement organized to suppress the evils of intemperance. At the request of the society he delivered an admirable address, on Washington's birthday, in the Presbyterian Church, which, in keeping with former efforts, has been so often published that I need not quote it in full. I was then an ardent temperance reformer myself, and remember well how one paragraph of Lincoln's speech offended the church members who were present. Speaking of certain Christians who objected to the association of drunkards, even with the chance of reforming them, he said:

If they (the Christians) believe, as they profess, that Omnipotence condescended to take on himself the form of sinful man, and as such die an ignominious death, surely they will not refuse submission to the infinitely lesser condescension, for the temporal and perhaps eternal salvation of a large, erring, and unfortunate class of their fellow creatures. Nor is the condescension very great. In my judgment such of us as have never fallen victims have been spared more from the absence of appetite than from any mental or moral superiority over those who have. Indeed, I believe, if we take habitual drunkards as a class, their heads and their hearts will bear an advantageous comparison with those of any other class.

The avowal of these sentiments proved to be an unfortunate thing for Lincoln. The professing Christians regarded the suspicion suggested in the first sentence as a reflection on the sincerity of their belief, and the last one had no better effect in reconciling them to his views. I was at the door of the church as the people passed out, and heard them discussing the speech. Many

85

of them were open in the expression of their displeasure. "It's a shame," I heard one man say, "that he should be permitted to abuse us so in the house of the Lord." The truth was the society was composed mainly of the roughs and drunkards of the town, who had evinced a desire to reform. Many of them were too fresh from the gutter to be taken at once into the society of such people as worshipped at the church where the speech was delivered. Neither was there that concert of effort so universal today between the churches and temperance societies to rescue the fallen. The whole thing, I repeat, was damaging to Lincoln, and gave rise to the opposition on the part of the churches which confronted him several years afterwards when he became a candidate against the noted Peter Cartwright for Congress. The charge, therefore, that in matters of religion he was a skeptic was not without its supporters, especially where his opponent was himself a preacher. But, nothing daunted, Lincoln kept on and labored zealously in the interest of the temperance movement. He spoke often again in Springfield, and also in other places over the country, displaying the same courage and adherence to principle that characterized his every undertaking.

Meanwhile, he had one eye open for politics as he moved along. He was growing more self-reliant in the practice of law every day, and felt amply able to take charge of and maintain himself in any case that happened to come into his hands. His propensity for the narration of an apt story was of immeasurable aid to him before a jury, and in cases where the law seemed to lean towards the other side won him many a case. In 1842, Martin Van Buren, who had just left the Presidential chair, made a journey through the West. He was accompanied by his former Secretary of the Navy, Mr. Paulding, and in June they reached the village of Rochester, distant from Springfield six miles. It was evening when they arrived, and on account of the muddy roads they decided to go no farther, but to rest there for the night. Word was sent into Springfield, and of course the leading Democrats of the capital hurried out to meet the distinguished visitor. Knowing the accommodations at Rochester were not intended for or suited to the entertainment of an ex-President, they took with them refreshments in quantity and variety, to make up for all deficiencies. Among others, they prevailed on

Lincoln, although an ardent and pronounced Whig, to accompany them. They introduced him to the venerable statesman of Kinderhook as a representative lawyer, and a man whose wit was as ready as his store of anecdotes was exhaustless. How he succeeded in entertaining the visitor and the company, those who were present have often since testified. Van Buren himself entertained the crowd with reminiscences of politics in New York, going back to the days of Hamilton and Burr, and many of the crowd in turn interested him with graphic descriptions of early life on the western frontier. But they all yielded at last to the piquancy and force of Lincoln's queer stories. "Of these," relates one of the company, "there was a constant supply, one following another in rapid succession, each more irresistible than its predeccessor. The fun continued until after midnight, and until the distinguished traveller insisted that his sides were sore from laughing." The yarns which Lincoln gravely spun out, Van Buren assured the crowd, he never would forget.

After April 14, 1841, when Lincoln retired from the partnership with Stuart, who had gone to Congress, he had been associated with Stephen T. Logan, a man who had, as he deserved, the reputation of being the best *nisi prius* lawyer in the State. Judge Logan was a very orderly but somewhat technical lawyer. He had some fondness for politics, and made one race for Congress, but he lacked the elements of a successful politician. He was defeated, and returned to the law. He was assiduous in study and tireless in search of legal principles. He was industrious and very thrifty, delighted to make and save money, and died a rich man. Lincoln had none of Logan's qualities. He was anything but studious and had no money sense. He was five years younger, and yet his mind and makeup so impressed Logan that he was invited into the partnership with him. Logan's example had a good effect on Lincoln, and it stimulated him to unusual endeavors. For the first time he realized the effectiveness of order and method in work, but his old habits eventually overcame him. He permitted his partner to do all the studying in the preparation of cases, while he himself trusted to his general knowledge of the law and the inspiration of the surroundings to overcome the judge or the jury. Logan was scrupulously exact, and used extraordinary care in the prepara-

tion of papers. His words were well chosen, and his style of
composition was stately and formal. This extended even to his
letters. This Lincoln lacked in every particular. I have before me
a letter written by Lincoln at this time to the proprietors of a
wholesale store in Louisville, for whom suit had been brought,
in which, after notifying the latter of the sale of certain real estate in satisfaction of their judgment, he adds: "As to the real estate we cannot attend to it. We are not real estate agents, we are
lawyers. We recommend that you give the charge of it to Mr.
Isaac S. Britton, a trustworthy man, and one whom the Lord
made on purpose for such business." He gravely signs the firm
name, Logan and Lincoln, to this unlawyerlike letter and sends
it on its way. Logan never would have written such a letter. He
had too much gravity and austere dignity to permit any such
looseness of expression in letters to his clients or to anyone else.

In 1843, Logan and Lincoln both had their eyes set on the
race for Congress. Logan's claim to the honor lay in his age and
the services he had rendered the Whig party, while Lincoln,
overflowing with ambition, lay great stress on his legislative
achievements, and demanded it because he had been defeated in
the nominating conventions by both Hardin and Baker in the
order named. That two such aspiring politicians, each striving to
obtain the same prize, should not dwell harmoniously together
in the same office is not strange. Indeed, we may reasonably
credit the story that they considered themselves rivals, and that
numerous acrimonious passages took place between them. I was
not surprised, therefore, one morning, to see Mr. Lincoln come
rushing up into my quarters and with more or less agitation tell
me he had determined to sever the partnership with Logan. I
confess I was surprised when he invited me to become his
partner. I was young in the practice and was painfully aware of
my want of ability and experience; but when he remarked in his
earnest, honest way, "Billy, I can trust you, if you can trust me,"
I felt relieved, and accepted the generous proposal. It has always
been a matter of pride with me that during our long partnership,
continuing on until it was dissolved by the bullet of the assassin
Booth, we never had any personal controversy or disagreement.
I never stood in his way for political honors or office, and I
believe we understood each other perfectly. In after years, when

he became more prominent, and our practice grew to respectable proportions, other ambitious practitioners undertook to supplant me in the partnership. One of the latter, more zealous than wise, charged that I was in a certain way weakening the influence of the firm. I am flattered to know that Lincoln turned on this last named individual with the retort, "I know my own business, I reckon. I know Billy Herndon better than anybody, and even if what you say of him is true I intend to stick by him."

Lincoln's effort to obtain the Congressional nomination in 1843 brought out several unique and amusing incidents. He and Edward D. Baker were the two aspirants from Sangamon County, but Baker's long residence, extensive acquaintance, and general popularity were obstacles Lincoln could not overcome; accordingly, at the last moment, Lincoln reluctantly withdrew from the field. In a letter to his friend Speed, dated March 24, 1843, he describes the situation as follows: "We had a meeting of the Whigs of the county here on last Monday, to appoint delegates to a district convention; and Baker beat me, and got the delegation instructed to go for him. The meeting, in spite of my attempt to decline it, appointed me one of the delegates; so that in getting Baker the nomination I shall be fixed a good deal like a fellow who is made groomsman to a man that has cut him out, and is marrying his own dear gal." Only a few days before this he had written a friend anent the Congressional matter, "Now if you should hear any one say that Lincoln don't want to go to Congress, I wish you, as a personal friend of mine, would tell him you have reason to believe he is mistaken. The truth is I would like to go very much. Still, circumstances may happen which may prevent my being a candidate. If there are any who be my friends in such an enterprise, what I now want is that they shall not throw me away just yet." To another friend in the adjoining county of Menard a few days after the meeting of the Whigs in Sangamon, he explains how Baker defeated him.

The entire absence of any feeling of bitterness, or what the politicians call revenge, is the most striking feature of the letter. "It is truly gratifying," he says, "to me to learn that while the people of Sangamon have cast me off, my old friends of Menard, who have known me longest and best, stick to me. It would astonish if not amuse the older citizens to learn that I (a strange,

friendless, uneducated, penniless boy, working on a flatboat at
ten dollars per month) have been put down here as the candidate
of pride, wealth, and aristocratic family distinction. Yet so,
chiefly, it was. There was, too, the strangest combination of
church influence against me. Baker is a Campbellite, and
therefore as I suppose, with few exceptions, got all that church.
My wife has some relations in the Presbyterian churches and
some with the Episcopalian churches, and therefore, wherever it
would tell, I was set down as either the one or the other, while it
was everywhere contended that no Christian ought to go for me,
because I belonged to no church, was suspected of being a deist,
and had talked about fighting a duel. With all these things
Baker, of course, had nothing to do; nor do I complain of them.
As to his own church going for him I think that was right
enough; and as to the influences I have spoken of in the other,
though they were very strong, it would be grossly untrue and
unjust to charge that they acted upon them in a body, or were
very near so. I only mean that those influences levied a tax of
considerable per cent and throughout the religious controversy."
To a proposition offering to instruct the Menard delegation for
him he replies: "You say you shall instruct your delegates for me
unless I object. I certainly shall not object. That would be too
pleasant a compliment for me to tread in the dust. And besides,
if anthing should happen (which, however, is not probable) by
which Baker should be thrown out of the fight, I would be at liberty to accept the nomination if I could get it. I do, however, feel
myself bound not to hinder him in any way from getting the
nomination. I should despise myself were I to attempt it."

Baker's friends had used as an argument against Lincoln that
he belonged to a proud and aristocratic family, referring doubtless to some of the distinguished relatives who were connected
with him by marriage. The story reaching Lincoln's ears, he
laughed heartily over it one day in a Springfield store and
remarked:

"That sounds strange to me, for I do not remember of but one
who ever came to see me, and while he was in town he was accused of stealing a jew's harp." In the convention which was
held shortly after at the town of Pekin neither Baker nor Lincoln
obtained the coveted honor; but John J. Hardin, of Morgan des-

tined to lose his life at the head of an Illinois regiment in the Mexican war, was nominated, and in the following August, elected by a good majority. Lincoln bore his defeat manfully. He was no doubt greatly disappointed, but by no means soured. He conceived the strange notion that the publicity given his so-called "aristocratic family distinction" would cost him the friendship of his humbler constituents—his Clary's Grove friends. He took his friend James Matheny out into the woods with him one day and, calling up the bitter features of the canvass, protested "vehemently and with great emphasis" that he was anything but aristocratic and proud. "Why, Jim," he said, "I am now and always shall be the same Abe Lincoln I was when you first saw me."

In the campaign of 1844 Lincoln filled the honorable post of Presidential elector, and he extended the limits of his acquaintance by stumping the State. This was the year the gallant and magnetic Clay went down in defeat. Lincoln, in the latter end of the canvass, crossed over into Indiana and made several speeches. He spoke at Rockport and also at Gentryville, where he met the Grigsbys, the Gentrys, and other friends of his boyhood. The result of the election was a severe disappointment to Mr. Lincoln as well as to all other Whigs. No election since the foundation of the Government created more widespread regret than the defeat of Clay by Polk. Men were never before so enlisted in any man's cause, and when the great Whig chieftain went down his followers fled from the field in utter demoralization. Some doubted the success of popular government, while others, more hopeful still in the face of the general disaster, vowed they would never shave their faces or cut their hair till Henry Clay became President. As late as 1880 I saw one man who had lived up to his insane resolution. One political society organized to aid Clay's election sent the defeated candidate an address, in which they assured him that, after the smoke of battle had cleared away, he would ever be remembered as one "whose name honored defeat and gave it a glory which victory could not have brought." In Lincoln's case his disappointment was no greater than that of any other Whig. Many persons have yielded to the impression that Mr. Lincoln visited Clay at his home in Lexington and felt a personal loss in his defeat, but such is not the case. He took no more gloomy view of the situation than the rest of his party. He had been a leading figure himself in other campaigns, and was fully inured to the chilling blasts of defeat. They may have driven him in, but only for a short time, for he soon evinced a willingness to test the temper of the winds again.

No sooner had Baker been elected to Congress in August 1844, than Lincoln began to manifest a longing for the tempting prize to be contended for in 1846. Hardin and Baker both having been required to content themselves with a single term each, the struggle among Whig aspirants narrowed down to Logan and Lincoln. The latter's claim seemed to find such favorable lodgment with the party workers, and his popularity seemed so apparent, that Logan soon realized his own want of strength and abandoned the field to his late law partner. The convention which nominated Lincoln met at Petersburg May 1, 1846. Hardin, who, in violation of what was then regarded as precedent, had been seeking the nomination, had courteously withdrawn. Logan, ambitious to secure the honor next time for himself, with apparent generosity presented Lincoln's name to the convention, and there being no other candidate he was chosen unanimously. The reader need not be told whom the Democrats placed in the field against him. It was Peter Cartwright, the famous Methodist divine and circuit rider. An energetic canvass of three months followed, during which Lincoln kept his forces well in hand. He was active and alert, speaking everywhere, and abandoning his share of business in the law office entirely. He had a formidable competitor in Cartwright, who not only had an extensive following by reason of his church influence, but rallied many more supporters around his standard by his pronounced Jacksonian attitude. He had come into Illinois with the early immigrants from Kentucky and Tennessee, and had at one time or another preached to almost every Methodist congregation between Springfield and Cairo. He had extensive family connections all over the district, was almost twenty-five years older than Lincoln, and in every respect a dangerous antagonist. Another thing which operated much to Lincoln's disadvantage was the report circulated by Cartwright's friends with respect to Lincoln's religious views. He was charged with the grave offence of infidelity, and sentiments which he was reported to have expressed with reference to the inspiration of the Bible were given the campaign varnish and passed from hand to hand. His slighting allusion expressed in the address at the Presbyterian Church before the Washington Temperance Society, February 22d four years before, to the insincerity of the Christian people, was not forgotten. It, too, played its part, but all these opposing circumstances were of no avail. Cartwright was personally very popular, but it was plain the people of the Springfield district wanted no preacher to represent them in Congress. They believed in an absolute separation of Church and State. The election, therefore, of such a man as Cartwright would not, to their way of thinking, tend to promote such a result. I was enthusiastic and active in Lincoln's interest myself. The very thought of my associate's becoming a member of Congress was a great stimulus to my self-importance. Many other friends in and around Springfield were equally as vigilant, and, in the language of another, "long before the contest closed we snuffed approaching victory in the air." Our laborious efforts met with a suitable reward. Lincoln was elected by a majority of 1511 in the district, a larger vote than Clay's two years before, which was only 914. In Sangamon County his majority was 690, and exceeded that of any of his predecessors on the Whig ticket, commencing with Stuart in 1834 and continuing on down to the days of Yates in 1852.

Before Lincoln's departure for Washington to enter on his duties as a member of Congress, the Mexican war had begun. The volunteers had gone forward, and at the head of the regiments from Illinois some of the bravest men and the best legal talent in Springfield had marched. Hardin, Baker, Bissell, and even the dramatic Shields had enlisted. The issues of the war and the manner of its prosecution were in every man's mouth. Naturally, therefore, a Congressman-elect would be expected to publish his views and define his position early in the day. Although, in common with the Whig party, opposing the declaration of war, Lincoln, now that hostilities had commenced, urged a vigorous prosecution. He admonished us all to permit our Government to suffer no dishonor, and to stand by the flag till peace came and came honorably to us. He declared these sentiments in a speech at a public meeting in Springfield, May 29,

1847. In the following December he took his seat in Congress. He was the only Whig from Illinois. In the Senate Douglas had made his appearance for the first time. The Little Giant is always in sight! Robert C. Winthrop, of Massachusetts, was chosen Speaker. John Quincy Adams, Horace Mann, Caleb Smith, Alexander H. Stephens, Robert Toombs, Howell Cobb, and Andrew Johnson were important members of the House. With many of these the newly elected member from Illinois was destined to sustain another and far different relation.

On the 5th of December, the day before the House organized. Lincoln wrote me a letter about our fee in a lawsuit and reported the result of the Whig caucus the night before. On the 13th he wrote again: "Dear William:—Your letter, advising me of the receipt of our fee in the bank case, is just received, and I don't expect to hear another as good a piece of news from Springfield while I am away." He then directed me from the proceeds of this fee to pay a debt at the bank, and out of the balance left to settle sundry dry-goods and grocery bills. The modest tone of the last paragraph is its most striking feature. "As you are all so anxious for me to distinguish myself," he said, "I have concluded to do so before long." January 8 he writes: "As to speech-making, by way of getting the hang of the House, I made a little speech two or three days ago on a post office question of no general interest. I find speaking here and elsewhere about the same thing. I was about as badly scared, and no worse, as I am when I speak in court. I expect to make one within a week or two in which I hope to succeed well enough to wish you to see it." Meanwhile, in recognition of the assurances I had sent him from friends who desired to approve his course by a reelection, he says: "It is very pleasant to me to learn from you that there are some who desire that I should be reelected. I most heartily thank them for the kind partiality, and I can say, as Mr. Clay said of the annexation of Texas that, 'personally, I would not object' to a reelection, although I thought at the time, and still think, it would be quite as well for me to return to the law at the end of a single term. I made the declaration that I would not be a candidate again, more from a wish to deal fairly with others, to keep peace among our friends, and to keep the district from going to the enemy, than for any cause personal to myself, so that if it should happen that nobody else wishes to be elected I could not refuse the people the right of sending me again. But to enter myself as a competitor of others, or to authorize any one so to enter me, is what my word and honor forbid."

His announcement of a willingness to accept a reelection if tendered him by the people was altogether unnecessary, for within a few days after this letter was written his constituents began to manifest symptoms of grave disapproval of his course on the Mexican war question. His position on this subject was evidenced by certain resolutions offered by him in the House three weeks before. These latter were called the "Spot Resolutions," and they and the speech which followed on the 12th of January in support of them not only sealed Lincoln's doom as a Congressman, but in my opinion, lost the district to the Whigs in 1848, when Judge Logan had succeeded at last in obtaining the nomination.

Although differing with the President as to the justice or even propriety of a war with Mexico, Lincoln was not unwilling to vote, and with the majority of his party did vote, the supplies necessary to carry it on. He did this, however, with great reluctance, protesting all the while that "the war was necessarily and unconstitutionally begun by the President." The "Spot Resolutions," which served as a text for his speech on the 12th of January, and which caused such unwonted annoyance in the ranks of his constituents, were a series following a preamble loaded with quotations from the President's messages. These resolutions requested the President to inform the House:

First. *Whether the* spot *on which the blood of our citizens was shed as in his messages declared was or was not within the territory of Spain, at least after the treaty of 1819, until the Mexican revolution.* Second. *Whether that spot is or is not within the territory which was wrested from Spain by the revolutionary government by Mexico.* Third. *Whether that spot is or is not within a settlement of people, which settlement has existed ever since long before the Texas revolution, and until its inhabitants fled before the approach of the United States army.*

There were eight of these interrogatories, but it is only necessary to reproduce the three which foreshadow the position Lincoln was then intending to assume. On the 12th of January, as before stated, he followed them up with a carefully prepared and well arranged speech, in which he made a severe arraignment of President Polk and justified the pertinence and propriety of the inquiries he had a few days before addressed to him. The speech is too long for insertion here. It was constructed much after the manner of a legal argument. Reviewing the evidence furnished by the President in his various messages, he undertook to "smoke him out" with this:

Let the President answer the interrogatories I proposed, as before mentioned, or other similar ones. Let him answer fully, fairly, candidly. Let him answer with facts, not with arguments. Let him remember, he sits where Washington sat; and so remembering, let him answer as Washington would answer. As a nation should not, and the Almighty will not, be evaded, so let him attempt no evasion, no equivocation. And if, so answering, he can show the soil was ours where the first blood of the war was shed; that it was not within an inhabited country, or if within such; that the inhabitants had submitted themselves to the civil authority of Texas or of the United States; and that the same is true of the site of Fort Brown, then I am with him for his justification . . . But if he cannot or will not do this—if, on any pretence, or no pretence, he shall refuse or omit it—then I shall be fully convinced of what I more than suspect already—that he is deeply conscious of being in the wrong; that he feels the blood of this war, like the blood of Abel, is crying to Heaven against him; that he ordered General Taylor into the midst of a peaceful Mexican settlement purposely to bring on a war; that, originally having some strong motive—which I will not now stop to give my opinion concerning—to involve the countries in a war, and trusting to escape scrutiny by fixing the public gaze upon the exceeding brightness of military glory—that attractive rainbow that rises in showers of blood, that serpent's eye that charms to destroy—he plunged into it, and has swept on and on, till disappointed in his calculation of the ease with which Mexico might be subdued, he now finds himself he knows not where. He is a bewildered, confounded, and miserably perplexed man. God grant that he may be able to show that there is not something about his conscience more painful than all his mental perplexity.

This speech, however clear may have been its reasoning, however rich in illustration, in restrained and burning earnestness, yet was unsuccessful in "smoking out" the President. He remained within the official seclusion his position gave him, and declined to answer. In fact it is doubtless true that Lincoln anticipated no response, but simply took that means of defining clearly his own position.

On the 19th inst., having occasion to write me with reference to a note with which one of our clients, one Louis Candler, had been "annoying" him, "not the least of which annoyance," he complains, "is his cursed unreadable and ungodly handwriting," he adds a line, in which with noticeable modesty he informs me: "I have made a speech, a copy of which I send you by mail." He doubtless felt he was taking rather advanced and perhaps questionable ground. And so he was, for very soon after, murmurs of dissatisfaction began to run through the Whig ranks. I did not, as some of Lincoln's biographers would have their readers believe, inaugurate this feeling of dissatisfaction. On the contrary, as the law partner of the Congressman, and as his ardent admirer, I discouraged the defection all I could. Still, when I listened to the comments of his friends everywhere after the delivery of his speech, I felt that he had made a mistake. I therefore wrote him to that effect, at the same time giving him my own views, which I knew were in full accord with the views of his Whig constituents. My argument in substance was: That the President of the United States is Commander in Chief of the Army and Navy; that as such commander it was his duty, in the absence of Congress, if the country was about to be invaded and armies were organized in Mexico for that purpose, to go—if necessary—into the very heart of Mexico and prevent the invasion. I argued further that it would be a crime in the Executive to let the country be invaded in the least degree. The action of the President was a necessity, and under a similar necessity years afterward Mr. Lincoln himself emancipated the slaves, although he had no special power under the Constitution to do so. In later days, in what is called the Hodges letter, concerning the freedom of the slaves, he used this language:

"I felt that measures otherwise unconstitutional might become lawful by becoming indispensable."

Briefly stated, that was the strain of my argument. My judgment was formed on the law of nations and of war. If the facts were as I believed them, and my premises correct, then I assumed that the President's acts became lawful by becoming indispensable.

February 1 he wrote me: "Dear William: You fear that you and I disagree about the war. I regret this, not because of any fear we shall remain disagreed after you have read this letter, but because if you misunderstand I fear other good friends may also."

Speaking of his vote in favor of the amendment to the supply bill proposed by George Ashmun, of Massachusetts, he continues:

That vote affirms that the war was unnecessarily and unconstitutionally commenced by the President; and I will stake my life that if you had been in my place you would have voted just as I did. Would you have voted what you felt and knew to be a lie? I know you would not. Would you have gone out of the House,—skulked the vote? I expect not. If you had skulked one vote you would have had to skulk many more before the close of the session. Richardson's resolutions, introduced before I made any move or gave any vote upon the subject, make the direct question of the justice of the war; so that no man can be silent if he would. You are compelled to speak; and your only alternative is to tell the truth or tell a lie. I cannot doubt which you would do...I do not mean this letter for the public, but for you. Before it reaches you you will have seen and read my pamphlet speech and perhaps have been scared anew by it. After you get over your scare read it over again, sentence by sentence, and tell me honestly what you think of it. I condensed all I could for fear of being cut off by the hour rule; and when I got through I had spoken but forty-five minutes.

Yours forever,
A. Lincoln.

I digress from the Mexican war subject long enough to insert, because in the order of time it belongs here, a characteristic letter which he wrote me regarding a man who was destined at a later date to play a far different role in the national drama. Here it is:

> Washington, Feb. 2, 1848.

Dear William:

I just take up my pen to say that Mr. Stephens, of Georgia, a little, slim, pale-faced, consumptive man, with a voice like Logan's, has just concluded the very best speech of an hour's length I ever heard. My old, withered, dry eyes are full of tears yet. If he writes it out anything like he delivered it our people shall see a good many copies of it.

> Yours truly,
> A. Lincoln.

To Wm. H. Herndon, Esq.

February 15 he wrote me again in criticism of the President's invasion of foreign soil. He still believed the Executive had exceeded the limit of his authority. "The provision of the Constitution giving the war-making power to Congress," he insists, "was dictated, as I understand it, by the following reasons; kings had always been involving and impoverishing their people in wars, pretending generally, if not always, that the good of the people was the object. This, our convention understood to be the most oppressive of all kingly oppressions; and they resolved to so frame the Constitution that no one man should hold the power of bringing this oppression upon us. But your view destroys the whole matter, and places our President where kings have always stood."

In June the Whigs met in national convention at Philadelphia to nominate a candidate for President. Lincoln attended as a delegate. He advocated the nomination of Taylor because of his belief that he could be elected, and was correspondingly averse to Clay because of the latter's signal defeat in 1844. In a letter from Washington a few days after the convention he predicts the election of "Old Rough." He says: "In my opinion we shall have a most overwhelming glorious triumph. One unmistakable sign is that all the odds and ends are with us—Barnburners, Native Americans, Tyler-men, disappointed office-seeking Locofocos, and the Lord knows what not . . . Taylor's nomination takes the

Locos on the blind side. It turns the war thunder against them. The war is now to them the gallows of Haman, which they built for us and on which they are doomed to be hanged themselves."

Meanwhile, in spite of the hopeful view Lincoln seemed to take of the prospect, things in his own district were in exceedingly bad repair. I could not refrain from apprising him of the extensive defections from the party ranks, and the injury his course was doing him. My object in thus writing to him was not to threaten him. Lincoln was not a man who could be successfully threatened; one had to approach him from a different direction. I warned him of public disappointment over his course, and I earnestly desired to prevent him from committing what I believed to be political suicide. June 22d he answered a letter I had written him on the 15th. He had just returned from a Whig caucus held in relation to the coming Presidential election. "The whole field of the nation was scanned; all is high hope and confidence," he said exultingly. "Illinois is expected to better her condition in this race. Under these circumstances judge how heart-rending it was to come to my room and find and read your discouraging letter of the 15th." But still he does not despair. "Now, as to the young man," he says, "you must not wait to be brought forward by the older men. For instance, do you suppose that I should ever have got into notice if I had waited to be hunted up and pushed forward by older men? You young men get together and form a Rough and Ready club, and have regular meetings and speeches. Take in everybody that you can get . . . As you go along gather up all the shrewd, wild boys about town, whether just of age or a little under age. Let everyone play the part he can play best—some speak, some sing, and all halloo. Your meetings will be of evenings; the older men and the women will go to hear you, so that it will not only contribute to the election of 'Old Zack,' but will be an interesting pastime and improving to the faculties of all engaged." He was evidently endeavoring through me to rouse up all the enthusiasm among the youth of Springfield possible under the circumstances. But I was disposed to take a dispirited view of the situation, and therefore was not easily warmed up. I felt at this time, somewhat in advance of its occurrence, the death throes of the Whig party. I did not conceal my suspicions, and one of the

Springfield papers gave my sentiments liberal quotation in its columns. I felt gloomy over the prospect, and cut out these newspaper slips and sent them to Lincoln. Accompanying these I wrote him a letter equally melancholy in tone, in which among other things I reflected severely on the stubbornness and bad judgment of the old fossils in the party, who were constantly holding the young men back. This brought from him a letter, July 10, 1848, which is so clearly Lincolnian and so full of plain philosophy, that I copy it in full. Not the least singular of all is his allusion to himself as an old man, although he had scarcely passed his thirty-ninth year.

Washington, July 10, 1848.

Dear William:

    Your letter covering the newspaper slips was received last night. The subject of that letter is exceedingly painful to me, and I cannot but think there is some mistake in your impression of the motives of the old men. I suppose I am now one of the old men; and I declare on my veracity, which I think is good with you, that nothing could afford me more satisfaction than to learn that you and others of my young friends at home were doing battle in the contest and endearing themselves to the people and taking a stand far above any I have ever been able to reach in their admiration. I cannot conceive that other men feel differently. Of course, I cannot demonstrate what I say; but I was young once, and I am sure I was never ungenerously thrust back. I hardly know what to say. The way for a young man to rise is to improve himself every way he can, never suspecting that anybody wishes to hinder him. Allow me to assure you that suspicion and jealousy never did help any man in any situation. There may sometimes be ungenerous attempts to keep a young man down; and they will succeed, too, if he allows his mind to be diverted from its true channel to brood over the attempted injury. Cast about and see if this feeling has not injured every person you have ever known to fall into it.

    Now, in what I have said I am sure you will suspect nothing but sincere friendship. I would save you from a fatal error. You have been a laborious, studious young man. You are far better informed on almost all subjects than I ever have been. You can-

*not fail in any laudable object unless you allow your mind to be
improperly directed. I have some the advantage of you in the
world's experience merely by being older; and it is this that in-
duces me to advise.*

> *Your friend, as ever,*
> *A. Lincoln.*

Before the close of the Congressional session he made two
more speeches. One of these, which he hastened to send home in
pamphlet form, and which he supposes "nobody will read," was
devoted to the familiar subject of internal improvements, and
deserves only passing mention. The other, delivered on the 27th
of July, was in its way a masterpiece; and it is no stretch of the
truth to say that while intended simply as a campaign document
and devoid of any effort at classic oratory, it was, perhaps, one
of the best speeches of the session. It is too extended for insertion here without abridgment; but one who reads it will lay it
down convinced that Lincoln's ascendency for a quarter of a
centry among the political spirits in Illinois was by no means an
accident; neither will the reader wonder that Douglas, with all
his forensic ability, averted, as long as he could, a contest with a
man whose plain, analytical reasoning was not less potent than
his mingled drollery and caricature were effective. The speech in
the main is an arraignment of General Cass, the Democratic
candidate for President, who had already achieved great renown
in the political world, principally on account of his career as a
soldier in the war of 1812, and is a triumphant vindication of his
Whig opponent, General Taylor, who seemed to have had a less
extensive knowledge of civil than of military affairs, and was
discreetly silent about both. Lincoln caricatured the military pretensions of the Democratic candidate in picturesque style. This
latter section of the speech has heretofore been omitted by most
of Mr. Lincoln's biographers because of its glaring inappro-
priateness as a Congressional effort. I have always failed to see
wherein its comparison with scores of others delivered in the
halls of Congress since that time could in any way detract from
the fame of Mr. Lincoln, and I therefore reproduce it here:

> *But the gentleman from Georgia* [Mr. Iverson] *further says,
> we have deserted all our principles, and taken shelter under*

General Taylor's military coattail; and he seems to think this is exceedingly degrading. Well, as his faith is, so be it unto him. But can he remember no other military coattail, under which a certain other party have been sheltering for near a quarter of a century? Has he no acquaintance with the ample military coat-tail of General Jackson? Does he not know that his own party have run the last five Presidential races under that coattail? and that they are now running the sixth under the same cover? Yes, sir, that coattail was used not only for General Jackson himself, but has been clung to with the grip of death by every Democrat-ic candidate since. You have never ventured, and dare not now venture from under it. Your campaign papers have constantly been 'Old Hickory's,' with rude likeness of the old general upon them; hickory poles and hickory brooms your never-ending em-blems. Mr. Polk himself was 'Young Hickory,' 'Little Hickory,' or something so; and even now your campaign paper here is proclaiming that Cass and Butler are of the 'Hickory stripe.' No, sir, you dare not give it up. Like a horde of hungry ticks, you have stuck to the tail of the Hermitage lion to the end of his life; and you are still sticking to it, and drawing a loathsome suste-nance from it, after he is dead. A fellow once advertised that he had made a discovery by which he could make a new man out of an old man and have enough of the stuff left to make a little yellow dog. Just such a discovery has General Jackson's popular-ity been to you. You not only twice made Presidents of him out of it, but you have enough of the stuff left to make Presidents of several comparatively small men since; and it is your chief reli-ance now to make still another.

Mr. Speaker, old horses and military coattails, or tails of any sort, are not figures of speech such as I would be the first to in-troduce into discussion here; but as the gentleman from Georgia has thought fit to introduce them, he and you are welcome to all you have made or can make by them. If you have any more old horses, trot them out; any more tails, just cock them and come at us. I repeat, I would not introduce this mode of discussion here; but I wish gentlemen on the other side to understand that the use of degrading figures is a game at which they may find themselves unable to take all the winnings. [A voice 'No, we give it up'] *Aye! you give it up, and well you may; but for a very different reason from that which you would have us understand. The point—the power to hurt—of all figures consists in the truthfulness of their application; and, understanding this, you may well give it up. They are weapons which hit you, but miss us.*

But in my hurry I was very near closing on this subject of the military tails before I was done with it. There is one entire article of the sort I have not discussed yet; I mean the military tail you Democrats are now engaged in dovetailing on to the great Michigander. Yes, sir, all his biographers (and they are legion) have him in hand, tying him to a military tail, like so many mischievous boys tying a dog to a bladder of beans. True, the material is very limited, but they are at it might and main. He invaded Canada without resistance, and he outvaded it without pursuit. As he did both under orders, I suppose there was to him neither credit nor discredit; but they are made to constitute a large part of the tail. He was not at Hull's surrender, but he was close by, he was volunteer aid to General Harrison on the day of the battle of the Thames; and as you said in 1840 Harrison was picking whortleberries two miles off while the battle was fought I suppose it is a just conclusion with you to say Cass was aiding Harrison to pick whortleberries. This is about all, except the mooted question of the broken sword. Some authors say he broke it; some say he threw it away; and some others, who ought to know, say nothing about it. Perhaps it would be a fair historical compromise to say if he did not break it, he did not do anything else with it.

By the way, Mr. Speaker, did you know I am a military hero? Yes, sir, in the days of the Black Hawk war, I fought, bled, and came away. Speaking of General Cass's career, reminds me of my own. I was not at Stillman's defeat, but I was about as near it as Cass was to Hull's surrender; and, like him, I saw the place very soon afterward. It is quite certain I did not break my sword, for I had none to break, but I bent my musket pretty badly on one occasion. If Cass broke his sword, the idea is, he broke it in desperation; I bent the musket by accident. If General Cass went in advance of me picking whortleberries, I guess I surpassed him in charges upon the wild onions. If he saw any live fighting Indians, it was more than I did, but I had a good many bloody strug-

*gles with the mosquitos; and, although I never fainted from loss
of blood, I can truly say I was often very hungry. Mr. Speaker, if
ever I should conclude to doff whatever our Democratic friends
may suppose there is of black-cockade Federalism about me,
and, thereupon they shall take me up as their candidate for the
Presidency, I protest that they shall not make fun of me as they
have of General Cass by attempting to write me into a military
hero.*

After the adjournment of Congress on the 14th of August,
Lincoln went through New York and some of the New England
States making a number of speeches for Taylor, none of which,
owing to the limited facilities attending newspaper reporting in
that day, have been preserved. He returned to Illinois before the
close of the canvass and continued his efforts on the stump till
after the election. At the second session of Congress, which
began in December, he was less conspicuous than before. The
few weeks spent with his constituents had perhaps taught him
that in order to succeed as a Congressman it is not always the
most politic thing to tell the truth because it is the truth, or to do
right because it is right. With the opening of Congress, by virtue
of the election of Taylor, the Whigs obtained the ascendency in
the control of governmental machinery. He attended to the
duties of the Congressional office diligently and with becoming
modesty. He answered the letters of his constituents, sent them
their public documents, and looked after their pension claims.
His only public act of any moment was a bill looking to the
emancipation of the slaves in the District of Columbia. He interested Joshua R. Giddings and others of equally as pronounced
antislavery views in the subject, but his bill eventually found a
lodgment on "the table," where it was carefully but promptly
laid by a vote of the House.

Meanwhile, being chargeable with the distribution of official
patronage, he began to flounder about in explanation of his action in a sea of seemingly endless perplexities. His recommendation of the appointment of T. R. King to be Register or
Receiver of the Land Office had produced no little discord
among the other aspirants for the place. He wrote to a friend
who endorsed and urged the appointment, "either to admit it is

wrong, or come forward and sustain him." He then transmits to this same friend a scrap of paper—probably a few lines approving the selection of King—which is to be copied in the friend's own handwriting. "Get everybody," he insists, "(not three or four, but three or four hundred) to sign it, and then send it to me. Also have six, eight, or ten of our best known Whig friends to write me additional letters, stating the truth in this matter as they understood it. Don't neglect or delay in the matter. I understand," he continues, "information of an indictment having been found against him three years ago for gaming or keeping a gaming house has been sent to the Department." He then closes with the comforting assurance: "I shall try to take care of it at the Department till your action can be had and forwarded on." And still people insist that Mr. Lincoln was such a guileless man and so free from the politician's sagacity!

In June I wrote him regarding the case of one Walter Davis, who was soured and disappointed because Lincoln had overlooked him in his recommendation for the Springfield post office. "There must be some mistake," he responds on the 5th, "about Walter Davis saying I promised him the post office. I did not so promise him. I did tell him that if the distribution of the offices should fall into my hands he should have something; and if I shall be convinced he has said any more than this I shall be disappointed. I said this much to him because, as I understand, he is of good character, is one of the young men, is of the mechanics, is always faithful and never troublesome, a Whig, and is poor, with the support of a widow-mother thrown almost exclusively on him by the death of his brother. If these are wrong reasons then I have been wrong; but I have certainly not been selfish in it, because in my greatest need of friends he was against me and for Baker."

Judge Logan's defeat in 1848 left Lincoln still in a measure in charge of the patronage in his district. After his term in Congress expired the "wriggle and struggle" for office continued; and he was often appealed to for his influence in obtaining, as he termed it, "a way to live without work." Occasionally, when hard pressed, he retorted with bitter sarcasm. I append a letter written in this vein to a gentleman still living in central Illinois, who I suppose, would prefer that his name should be withheld:

Springfield, Dec. 15, 1849.

_____*Esq.*
Dear Sir:

On my return from Kentucky I found your letter of the 7th of November, and have delayed answering it till now for the reason I now briefly state. From the beginning of our acquaintance I had felt the greatest kindness for you and had supposed it was reciprocated on your part. Last summer, under circumstances which I mentioned to you, I was painfully constrained to withhold a recommendation which you desired, and shortly afterwards I learned, in such a way as to believe it, that you were indulging in open abuse of me. Of course my feelings were wounded. On receiving your last letter the question occurred whether you were attempting to use me at the same time you would injure me, or whether you might not have been misrepresented to me. If the former, I ought not to answer you; if the latter, I ought, and so I have remained in suspense. I now enclose you the letter, which you may use if you see fit.

Yours, etc.
A. Lincoln.

No doubt the man, when Lincoln declined at first to recommend him, did resort to more or less abuse. That would have been natural, especially with an unsuccessful and disappointed officeseeker. I am inclined to the opinion, and a careful reading of the letter will warrant it, that Lincoln believed him guilty. If the recommendation which Lincoln, after so much reluctance, gave was ever used to further the applicant's cause I do not know it.

With the close of Lincoln's Congressional career he drops out of sight as a political factor, and for the next few years we take him up in another capacity. He did not solicit or contend for a renomination to Congress, and such was the unfortunate result of his position on public questions that it is doubtful if he could have succeeded had he done so.

6

Lawyer (I)

After the wedding of Lincoln and Miss Todd at the Edwards mansion we hear but little of them as a married couple till the spring of 1843, when the husband writes to his friend Speed, who had been joined to his "black-eyed Fanny" a little over a year, with regard to his life as a married man. "Are you possessing houses and lands," he writes, "and oxen and asses and menservants and maidservants, and begetting sons and daughters? We are not keeping house, but boarding at the Globe Tavern, which is very well kept now by a widow lady of the name of Beck. Our room (the same Dr. Wallace occupied there) and boarding only costs us four dollars a week." Gaining a livelihood was slow and discouraging business with him, for we find him in another letter apologizing for his failure to visit Kentucky, "because," he says, "I am so poor and make so little headway in the world that I drop back in a month of idleness as much as I gain in a year's sowing." But by dint of untiring efforts and the recognition of influential friends he managed through rare frugality to move along. In his struggles, both in the law and for political advancement, his wife shared in his sacrifices. She was a plucky little woman, and in fact endowed with a more restless ambition than he. She was gifted with a rare insight into the motives that actuate mankind, and there is no doubt that much of Lincoln's success was in a measure attributable to her acuteness and the stimulus of her influence. His election to Congress within four years after their marriage afforded her extreme gratification. She loved power and prominence, and when occasionally she came down to our office, it seemed to me then that she was inordinately proud of her tall and ungainly husband. She saw in him bright prospects ahead, and his every move was watched by her with the closest interest. If to other persons he seemed homely, to her he was the embodiment of noble manhood, and each succeeding day impressed upon her the wisdom of her choice of Lincoln over Douglas—if in reality she ever seriously accepted the latter's attentions. "Mr. Lincoln may not be as handsome a figure," she said one day in the office during her husband's absence, when the conversation turned on Douglas, "but the people are perhaps not aware that his heart is as large as his arms are long."

Mrs. Lincoln accompanied her husband to Washington and remained during one session of Congress. While there they boarded at the same house with Joshua R. Giddings, and when in 1856 the Valiant Old Abolitionist came to take part in the canvass in Illinois, he early sought out Lincoln, with whom he had been so favorably impressed several years before. On his way home from Congress Lincoln came by way of Niagara Falls and down Lake Erie to Toledo or Detroit. It happened that, some time after, I went to New York and also returned by way of Niagara Falls. In the office, a few days after my return, I was endeavoring to entertain my partner with an account of my trip, and among other things described the Falls. In the attempt I indulged in a good deal of imagery. As I warmed up with the subject my descriptive powers expanded accordingly. The mad rush of water, the roar, the rapids, and the rainbow furnished me with an abundance of material for a stirring and impressive picture. The recollection of the gigantic and awe-inspiring scene stimulated my exuberant powers to the highest pitch. After wellnigh exhausting myself in the effort I turned to Lincoln for his opinion. "What," I inquired, "made the deepest impression on you when you stood in the presence of the great natural wonder?" I shall never forget his answer, because it in a very characteristic way illustrates how he looked at everything. "The thing that struck me most forcibly when I saw the Falls," he responded, "was where in the world did all that water come from?" He had no eye for the magnificence and grandeur of the scene, for the rapids, the mist, the angry waters, and the roar of the whirlpool, but his mind, working in its accustomed channel, heedless of beauty or awe, followed irresistibly back to the first cause. It was in this light he viewed every question. However great the verbal foliage that concealed the nakedness of a good idea Lincoln stripped it all down till he could see clear the way between cause and effect. If there was any secret in his power this surely was it.

After seeing Niagara Falls he continued his journey homeward. At some point on the way, the vessel on which he had taken passage stranded on a sand bar. The captain ordered the hands to collect all the loose planks, empty barrels and boxes and force them under the sides of the boat. These empty casks were used to buoy it up. After forcing enough of them under the vessel she lifted gradually and at last swung clear of the opposing sand bar. Lincoln had watched this operation very intently. It no doubt carried him back to the days of his navigation on the turbulent Sangamon, when he and John Hanks had rendered similar service at New Salem dam to their employer the volatile Offut. Continual thinking on the subject of lifting vessels over sand bars and other obstructions in the water suggested to him the idea of inventing an apparatus for the purpose. Using the principle involved in the operation he had just witnessed, his plan was to attach a kind of bellows on each side of the hull of the craft just below the water line, and by an odd system of ropes and pulleys, whenever the keel grated on the sand these bellows were to be filled with air, and thus buoyed up, the vessel was expected to float clear of the shoal. On reaching home he at once set to work to demonstrate the feasibility of his plan. Walter Davis, a mechanic having a shop near our office, granted him the use of his tools, and likewise assisted him in making the model of a miniature vessel with the arrangement as above described. Lincoln manifested ardent interest in it. Occasionally he would bring the model in the office, and while whittling on it would descant on its merits and the revolution it was destined to work in steamboat navigation. Although I regarded the thing as impracticable I said nothing, probably out of respect for Lincoln's well-known reputation as a boatman. The model was sent or taken by him to Washington, where a patent was issued, but the invention was never applied to any vessel, so far as I ever learned, and the threatened revolution in steamboat architecture and navigation never came to pass. The model still reposes in undisturbed slumber on the shelves in the Patent Office, and is the only evidence now existing of Lincoln's success as an inventor.

While a member of Congress and otherwise immersed in politics Lincoln seemed to lose all interest in law. Of course, what practice he himself controlled passed into other hands. I retained

all the business I could, and worked steadily on until, when he
returned, our practice was as extensive as that of any other firm
at the bar. Lincoln realized that much of this was due to my efforts, and on his return he therefore suggested that he had no
right to share in the business and profits which I had made. I
responded that, as he had aided me and given me prominence
when I was young and needed it, I could afford now to be grateful if not generous. I therefore recommended a continuation of
the partnership, and we went on as before. I could notice a difference in Lincoln's movement as a lawyer from this time forward. He had begun to realize a certain lack of discipline—a
want of mental training and method. Ten years had wrought
some change in the law, and more in the lawyers, of Illinois. The
conviction had settled in the minds of the people that the pyrotechnics of court room and stump oratory did not necessarily
imply extensive or profound ability in the lawyer who resorted
to it. The courts were becoming graver and more learned, and
the lawyer was learning as a preliminary and indispensable condition to success that he must be a close reasoner, besides having
at command a broad knowledge of the principles on which the
statutory law is constructed. There was of course the same riding on circuit as before, but the courts had improved in tone and
morals, and there was less laxity—at least it appeared so to Lincoln. Political defeat had wrought a marked effect on him. It
went below the skin and made a changed man of him. He was
not soured at his seeming political decline, but still he determined to eschew politics from that time forward and devote
himself entirely to the law. And now he began to make up for
time lost in politics by studying the law in earnest. No man had
greater power of application than he. Once fixing his mind on
any subject, nothing could interfere with or disturb him.
Frequently I would go out on the circuit with him. We, usually,
at the little country inns occupied the same bed. In most cases
the beds were too short for him, and his feet would hang over
the floorboard, thus exposing a limited expanse of shin bone.
Placing a candle on a chair at the head of the bed, he would read
and study for hours. I have known him to study in this position
till two o'clock in the morning. Meanwhile, I and others who
chanced to occupy the same room would be safely and soundly

asleep. On the circuit in this way he studied Euclid until he could with ease demonstrate all the propositions in the six books. How he could maintain his mental equilibrium or concentrate his thoughts on an abstract mathematical proposition, while Davis, Logan, Swett, Edwards, and I so industriously and volubly filled the air with our interminable snoring was a problem none of us could ever solve. I was on the circuit with Lincoln probably one-fourth of the time. The remainder of my time was spent in Springfield looking after the business there, but I know that life on the circuit was a gay one. It was rich with incidents, and afforded the nomadic lawyers ample relaxation from all the irksome toil that fell to their lot. Lincoln loved it. I suppose it would be a fair estimate to state that he spent over half the year following Judges Treat and Davis around on the circuit. On Saturdays the court and attorneys, if within a reasonable distance, would usually start for their homes. Some went for a fresh supply of clothing, but the greater number went simply to spend a day of rest with their families. The only exception was Lincoln, who usually spent his Sundays with the loungers at the country tavern, and only went home at the end of the circuit or term of court. "At first," relates one of his colleagues on the circuit, "we wondered at it, but soon learned to account for his strange disinclination to go home. Lincoln himself never had much to say about home, and we never felt free to comment on it. Most of us had pleasant, inviting homes, and as we struck out for them I'm sure each one of us down in our hearts had a mingled feeling of pity and sympathy for him." If the day was long and he was oppressed, the feeling was soon relieved by the narration of a story. The tavern loungers enjoyed it, and his melancholy, taking to itself wings, seemed to fly away. In the rôle of a storyteller I am prone to regard Mr. Lincoln as without an equal. I have seen him surrounded by a crowd numbering as many as two and in some cases three hundred persons, all deeply interested in the outcome of a story which, when he had finished it, speedily found repetition in every grocery and lounging place within reach. His power of mimicry, as I have before noted, and his manner of recital, were in many respects unique, if not remarkable. His countenance and all his features seemed to take part in the performance. As he neared the pith or point of the joke or story every vestige of seriousness disappeared from his face. His little gray eyes sparkled; a smile seemed to gather up, curtain like, the corners of his mouth; his frame quivered with suppressed excitement; and when the point—or "nub" of the story, as he called it— came, no one's laugh was heartier than his. These backwoods allegories are out of date now, and any lawyer, ambitious to gain prominence, would hardly dare thus to entertain a crowd, except at the risk of his reputation; but with Lincoln it gave him, in some mysterious way, a singularly firm hold on the people.

Lincoln was particularly strong in Menard County, and while on the circuit there he met with William Engle and James Murray, two men who were noted also for their storytelling proclivities. When Lincoln, Murry, and Engle met, there was sure to be a crowd. All were more or less masters in their art. I have seen the little country tavern where these three were wont to meet after an adjournment of court, crowded almost to suffocation with an audience of men who had gathered to witness the contest among the members of the strange triumvirate. The physicians of the town, all the lawyers, and not unfrequently a preacher could be found in the crowd that filled the doors and windows. The yarns they spun and the stories they told would not bear repetition here, but many of them had morals which, while exposing the weaknesses of mankind, stung like a whip-lash. Some were no doubt a thousand years old, with just enough "verbal varnish" and alterations of names and dates to make them new and crisp. By virtue of the last-named application, Lincoln was enabled to draw from Balzac a "droll story," and locating it in "Egypt" [southern Illinois] or in Indiana, pass it off for a purely original conception. Every recital was followed by its "storm of laughter and chorus of cheers." After this had all died down, some unfortunate creature, through whose thickened skull the point had just penetrated, would break out in a guffaw, starting another wave of laughter which, growing to the proportions of a billow, would come rolling in like a veritable breaker. I have known these storytelling jousts to continue long after midnight—in some cases till the very small hours of the morning. I have seen Judge Treat, who was the very impersonation of gravity itself, sit up till the last and laugh until, as he often expressed it, "he almost shook his ribs loose." The next day he would ascend the bench and listen to Lincoln in a murder trial, with all the seeming severity of an English judge in wig and gown. Amid such surroundings, a leading figure in such society, alternately reciting the latest effusion of the barroom or mimicking the clownish antics of the Negro minstrel, he who was destined to be an immortal emancipator, was steadily and unconsciously nearing the great trial of his life. We shall see further on how this rude civilization crystallized both his logic and his wit for use in another day.

Reverting again to Mr. Lincoln as a lawyer, it is proper to add that he detested the mechanical work of the office. He wrote few papers — less perhaps than any other man at the bar. Such work was usually left to me for the first few years we were together. Afterwards we made good use of students who came to learn the law in our office. A Chicago lawyer, in a letter to me about Mr. Lincoln, in 1866, says: "Lincoln once told me that he had taken you in as a partner, supposing you had system and would keep things in order, but that he found out you had no more system than he had, but that you were in reality a good lawyer, so that he was doubly disappointed." Lincoln knew no such thing as order or method in his law practice. He made no preparation in advance, but trusted to the hour for its inspiration and to Providence for his supplies. In the matter of letter-writing he made no distinction between one of a business nature or any other kind. If a happy thought of expression struck him he was by no means reluctant to use it. As early as 1839 he wrote to a gentleman about a matter of business, observing crustily that "a d——d hawk-billed Yankee is here besetting me at every turn I take, saying that Robert Kenzie never received the $80 to which he was entitled." In July, 1851, he wrote a facetious message to one of his clients, saying: "I have news from Ottawa that we win our case. As the Dutch justice said when he married folks, 'Now where is my hundred tollars.' " He was proverbially careless as to habits. In a letter to a fellow lawyer in another town, apologizing for failure to answer sooner, he explains: "First, I have been very busy in the United States Court; second, when I received the letter I put it in my old hat and buying a new one the next day the old one was set aside, and so the letter was lost sight of for a time." This hat of Lincoln's—a silk plug—was an extraordinary receptacle. It was his desk and his memorandum book. In it he carried his bank book and the bulk of his letters. Whenever in his reading or researches he wished to preserve an idea, he jotted it down on an envelope or stray piece of paper and placed it inside the lining. Afterwards when the memorandum was needed there was only one place to look for it.[1]

How Lincoln appeared and acted in the law office has been graphically and, I must confess, truthfully told by a gentleman now in New York, who was for several years a student in our office. I beg to quote a few lines from him: "My brother met Mr. Lincoln in Ottawa, Ill., one day, and said to him: 'I have a brother who I would very much like to have enter your office as a student.' 'All right!' was his reply; 'send him down and we will take a look at him.' I was then studying law at Grand Rapids, Mich., and on hearing from my brother I immediately packed up and started for Springfield. I arrived there on Saturday night. On Sunday Mr. Lincoln was pointed out to me. I well remember this first sight of him. He was striding along, holding little Tad, then about six years old, by the hand, who could with the greatest difficulty keep up with his father. In the morning I applied at the office of Lincoln and Herndon for admission as a student. The office was on the second floor of a brick building on the public square, opposite the courthouse. You went up one flight of stairs and then passed along a hallway to the rear office, which was a medium-sized room. There was one long table in the center of the room, and a shorter one running in the opposite direction, forming a T, and both were covered with green baize. There were two windows which looked into the back yard. In one corner was an old-fashioned secretary with pigeonholes and a drawer, and here Mr. Lincoln and his partner kept their law papers. There was also a bookcase containing about 200 volumes

---

[1]Lincoln had always on the top of our desk a bundle of papers into which he slipped anything he wished to keep and afterwards refer to. It was a receptacle of general information. Some years ago, on removing the furniture from the office, I took down the bundle and blew from the top the liberal coat of dust that had accumulated thereon. Immediately underneath the string was a slip bearing this endorsement, in his hand: "When you can't find it anywhere else, look in this."

of law as well as miscellaneous books. The morning I entered the office Mr. Lincoln and his partner, Mr. Herndon, were both present. Mr. Lincoln addressed his partner thus: 'Billy, this is the young man of whom I spoke to you. Whatever arrangement you make with him will be satisfactory to me.' Then, turning to me, he said, 'I hope you will not become so enthusiastic in your studies of Blackstone and Kent as did two young men whom we had here. Do you see that spot over there?' pointing to a large ink stain on the wall. 'Well, one of these young men got so enthusiastic in his pursuit of legal lore that he fired an inkstand at the other one's head, and that is the mark he made.' I immediately began to clean up about the office a little. Mr. Lincoln had been in Congress and had the usual amount of seeds to distribute to the farmers. These were sent out with Free Soil and Republican documents. In my efforts to clean up, I found that some of the seeds had sprouted in the dirt that had collected in the office. Judge Logan and Milton Hay occupied the front offices on the same floor with Lincoln and Herndon, and one day Mr. Hay came in and said with apparent astonishment: 'What's happened here?' 'Oh, nothing,' replied Lincoln, pointing to me, 'only this young man has been cleaning up a little.' One of Lincoln's striking characteristics was his simplicity, and nowhere was this trait more strikingly exhibited than in his willingness to receive instruction from anybody and everybody. One day he came into the office and addressing his partner, said: 'Billy, what's the meaning of antithesis?' Mr. Herndon gave him the definition of the word, and I said: 'Mr. Lincoln, if you will allow me, I will give you an example.' 'All right, John, go ahead,' said Mr. Lincoln in his hearty manner. Phillips says, in his essay on Napoleon, "A pretended patriot, he impoverished the country; a professed Catholic, he imprisoned the Pope, " etc. Mr. Lincoln thanked me and seemed very much pleased. Returning from off the circuit once he said to Mr. Herndon: 'Billy, I heard a good story while I was up in the country. Judge D — — was complimenting the landlord on the excellence of his beef "I am surprised," he said, "that you have such good beef.You must have to kill a whole critter when you want any." "Yes," said the landlord, "we never kill less than a whole critter." '

"Lincoln's favorite position when unraveling some knotty law point was to stretch both of his legs at full length upon a chair in front of him. In this position, with books on the table near by and in his lap, he worked up his case. No matter how deeply interested in his work, if any one came in he had something humorous and pleasant to say, and usually wound up by telling a joke or an anecdote. I have heard him relate the same story three times within as many hours to persons who came in at different periods, and every time he laughed as heartily and enjoyed it as if it were a new story. His humor was infectious. I had to laugh because I thought it funny that Mr. Lincoln enjoyed a story so repeatedly told.

"There was no order in the office at all. The firm of Lincoln and Herndon kept no books. They divided their fees without taking any receipts or making any entries on books. One day Mr. Lincoln received $5,000 as a fee in a railroad case. He came in and said; 'Well, Billy,' addressing his partner, Mr. Herndon, 'here is our fee; sit down and let me divide.' He counted out $2,500 to his partner, and gave it to him with as much nonchalance as he would have given a few cents for a paper. Cupidity had no abiding place in his nature.

"I took a good deal of pains in getting up a speech which I wanted to deliver during a political campaign. I told Mr. Lincoln that I would like to read it to him. He sat down in one chair, put his feet into another one, and said: 'John, you can fire away with that speech; I guess I can stand it.' I unrolled the manuscript, and proceeded with some trepidation. 'That's a good point, John,' he would say, at certain places, and at others: 'That's good—very good indeed,' until I felt very much elated over my effort. I delivered the speech over fifty times during the campaign. Elmer E. Ellsworth, afterwards colonel of the famous Zouaves, who was killed in Alexandria, early in the war, was nominally a student in Lincoln's office. His head was so full of military matters, however, that he thought little of law. Of Ellsworth, Lincoln said: 'That young man has a real genius for war!' "

During the six years following his retirement from Congress, Lincoln, realizing in a marked degree his want of literary knowledge, extended somewhat his research in that direction. He was naturally indisposed to undertake anything that savored of exertion, but his brief public career had exposed the limited area of his literary attainments. Along with his Euclid therefore he carried a well-worn copy of Shakespeare, in which he read no little in his leisure moments. "In travelling on the circuit," relates one of his associates at the bar, "he was in the habit of rising earlier than his brothers of the bar. On such occasions he was wont to sit by the fire, having uncovered the coals, and muse, and ponder, and soliloquize, inspired, no doubt, by that strange psychological influence which is so poetically described by Poe in 'The Raven.' On one of these occasions, at the town of Lincoln, sitting in the position described, he quoted aloud and at length the poem called 'Immortality.' When he had finished he was questioned as to the authorship and where it could be found. He had forgotten the author, but said that to him it sounded as much like true poetry as anything he had ever heard. He was particularly pleased with the last two stanzas."

Beyond a limited acquaintance with Shakespeare, Byron, and Burns, Mr. Lincoln, comparatively speaking, had no knowledge of literature. He was familiar with the Bible, and now and then evinced a fancy for some poem or short sketch to which his attention was called by some one else, or which he happened to run across in his cursory reading of books or newspapers. He never in his life sat down and read a book through, and yet he could readily quote any number of passages from the few volumes whose pages he had hastily scanned. In addition to his well-known love for the poem "Immortality" or "Why should the Spirit of Mortal be Proud," he always had a great fondness for Oliver Wendell Holmes' "Last Leaf," the fourth stanza of which beginning with the verse, "The mossy marbles rest," I have often heard him repeat. He once told me of a song a young lady had sung in his hearing at a time when he was laboring under some dejection of spirits. The lines struck his fancy, and although he did not know the singer—having heard her from the sidewalk as he passed her house—he sent her a request to write the lines out for him. Within a day or two he came into the office, carrying in his hand a delicately perfumed envelope which bore the address, "Mr. Lincoln—Present," in an unmistakable female hand. In it, written on gilt-edged paper, were the lines of the song. The plaintive strain of the piece and its melancholy sentiment struck a responsive chord in a heart already filled with gloom and sorrow. Though ill-adapted to dissipate one's depression, something about it charmed Lincoln, and he read and reread it with increasing relish. I had forgotten the circumstance until recently, when, in going over some old papers and letters turned over to me by Mr. Lincoln, I ran across the manuscript, and the incident was brought vividly to my mind. The envelope, still retaining a faint reminder of the perfumed scent given it thirty years before, bore the laconic endorsement, "Poem—I like this," in the handwriting of Mr. Lincoln. Unfortunately no name accompanied the manuscript, and unless the lady on seeing this chooses to make herself known, we shall probably not learn who the singer was. The composition is headed, "The Inquiry." I leave it to my musical friends to render it into song. Following are the lines:

Tell me, ye winged winds
That round my pathway roar,
Do ye not know some spot
Where mortals weep no more?
Some lone and pleasant vale
Some valley in the West,
Where, free from toil and pain,
The weary soul may rest?
The loud wind dwindled to a whisper low,
And sighed for pity as it answered, No.

Tell me, thou mighty deep,
Whose billows round me play,
Knows't thou some favored spot,
Some island far away,
Where weary man may find
The bliss for which he sighs;
Where sorrow never lives
And friendship never dies?
The loud waves rolling in perpetual flow
Stopped for awhile and sighed to answer, No.

And thou, serenest moon,
That with such holy face

Dost look upon the earth
Asleep in Night's embrace—
Tell me, in all thy round
Hast thou not seen some spot
Where miserable man
Might find a happier lot?
Behind a cloud the moon withdrew in woe,
And a voice sweet but sad responded, No.

Tell me, my secret soul.
Oh, tell me, Hope and Faith,
Is there no resting place
From sorrow, sin, and death?
Is there no happy spot
Where mortals may be blessed,
Where grief may find a balm
And weariness a rest?
Faith, Hope, and Love, best boon to mortals given,
Waved their bright wings and whispered, Yes, in Heaven.[2]

A lawyer in Beardstown relates this: "Lincoln came into my office one day with the remark: 'I see you've been suing some of my clients, and I've come down to see about it.' He had reference to a suit I had brought to enforce the specific performance of a contract. I explained the case to him and showed my proofs. He seemed surprised that I should deal so frankly with him, and said he would be as frank with me; that my client was justly entitled to a decree, and he should so represent it to the court; and that it was against his principles to contest a clear matter of right. So my client got a deed for a farm which, had another lawyer been in Mr. Lincoln's place, would have been consumed by the costs of litigation for years, with the result probably the same in the end." A young man once wrote to Lincoln, inquiring for the best mode of obtaining a thorough knowledge of the law. "The mode is very simple," he responded, "though laborious and tedious. It is only to get books and read and study them

[2]Persons familiar with literature will recognize this as a poem written by Charles Mackay, an English writer who represented a London newspaper in the United States during the Rebellion as its war correspondent. It was set to music as a chant, and as such was frequently rendered in public by the famous Hutchinson family of singers. I doubt if Mr. Lincoln ever knew who wrote it.

carefully. Begin with Blackstone's *Commentaries,* and after reading carefully through, say twice, take up Chitty's *Pleadings,* Greenleaf's *Evidence,* and Story's *Equity* in succession. Work, work, work, is the main thing."

Lincoln never believed in suing for a fee. If a client would not pay on request he never sought to enforce collection. I remember once a man who had been indicted for forgery or fraud employed us to defend him. The illness of the prosecuting attorney caused some delay in the case, and our client, becoming dissatisfied at our conduct of the case, hired someone else, who superseded us most effectually. The defendant declining to pay us the fee demanded, on the ground that we had not represented him at the trial of the cause, I brought suit against him in Lincoln's absence and obtained judgment for our fee. After Lincoln's return from the circuit the fellow hunted him up and by means of a carefully constructed tale prevailed on him to release the judgment without receiving a cent of pay. The man's unkind treatment of us deserved no such mark of generosity from Lincoln, and yet he could not resist the appeal of any one in poverty and want. He could never turn from a woman in tears. It was no surprise to me or any of his intimate friends that so many designing women with the conventional widow's weeds and easy flowing tears overcame him in Washington. It was difficult for him to detect an impostor, and hence it is not to be marveled at that he cautioned his secretaries: "Keep them away—I cannot stand it."

On many questions I used to grow somewhat enthusiastic, adopting sometimes a lofty metaphor by way of embellishment. Lincoln once warned me: "Billy, don't shoot too high—aim lower and the common people will understand you. They are the ones you want to reach—at least they are the ones you ought to reach. The educated and refined people will understand you anyway. If you aim too high your ideas will go over the heads of the masses, and only hit those who need no hitting." While it is true that from his peculiar construction Lincoln dwelt entirely in the head and in the land of thought, and while he was physically a lazy man, yet he was intellectually energetic; he was not only energetic, but industrious; not only industrious, but tireless; not only tireless, but indefatigable. Therefore if in debate with him a man stood on a questionable foundation he might well watch whereon he stood. Lincoln could look a long distance ahead and calculate the triumph of right. With him justice and truth were paramount. If to him a thing seemed untrue he could not in his nature simulate truth. His retention by a man to defend a lawsuit did not prevent him from throwing it up in its most critical stage if he believed he was espousing an unjust cause. This extreme conscientiousness and disregard of the alleged sacredness of the professional cloak robbed him of much so-called success at the bar. He once wrote to one of our clients: "I do not think there is the least use of doing anything more with your lawsuit. I not only do not think you are sure to gain it, but I do think you are sure to lose it. Therefore the sooner it ends the better." Messrs. Stuart and Edwards once brought a suit against a client of ours which involved the title to considerable property. At that time we had only two or three terms of court, and the docket was somewhat crowded. The plaintiff's attorneys were pressing us for a trial, and we were equally as anxious to ward it off. What we wanted were time and a continuance to the next term. We dared not make an affidavit for continuance, founded on facts, because no such pertinent and material facts as the law contemplated existed. Our case for the time seemed hopeless. One morning, however, I accidentally overheard a remark from Stuart indicating his fear lest a certain fact should happen to come into our possession. I felt some relief, and at once drew up a fictitious plea, averring as best I could the substance of the doubts I knew existed in Stuart's mind. The plea was as skillfully drawn as I knew how, and was framed as if we had the evidence to sustain it. The whole thing was a sham, but so constructed as to work the desired continuance, because I knew that Stuart and Edwards believed the facts were as I pleaded them. This was done in the absence and without the knowledge of Lincoln. The plea could not be demurred to, and the opposing counsel dared not take issue on it. It perplexed them sorely. At length, before further steps were taken, Lincoln came into court. He looked carefully over all the papers in the case, as was his custom, and seeing my ingenious subterfuge, asked, "Is this seventh plea a good one?" Proud of the exhibition of my skill, I answered that it was. "But," he inquired, incredulously, "is it founded on fact?"

I was obliged to respond in the negative, at the same time following up my answer with an explanation of what I had overheard Stuart intimate, and of how these alleged facts could be called facts if a certain construction were put upon them. I insisted that our position was justifiable, and that our client must have time or be ruined. I could see at once it failed to strike Lincoln as just right. He scratched his head thoughtfully and asked, "Hadn't we better withdraw that plea? You know it's a sham, and a sham is very often but another name for a lie. Don't let it go on record. The cursed thing may come staring us in the face long after this suit has been forgotten." The plea was withdrawn. By some agency—not our own—the case was continued and our client's interests were saved. I only relate this incident to illustrate Lincoln's far-seeing capacity; it serves to show how overcautious he seemed to be with regard to how his record might look in the future. I venture the assertion that he was the only member of the bar in Springfield who would have taken such a conscientious view of the matter.

One phase of Lincoln's character, almost lost sight of in the commonly accepted belief in his humility and kindly feeling under all circumstances, was his righteous indignation when aroused. In such cases he was the most fearless man I ever knew. I remember a murder case in which we appeared for the defense, and during the trial of which the judge—a man of ability far inferior to Lincoln's—kept ruling against us. Finally, a very material question, in fact one around which the entire case seemed to revolve, came up, and again the Court ruled adversely. The prosecution was jubilant, and Lincoln, seeing defeat certain unless he recovered his ground, grew very despondent. The notion crept into his head that the Court's rulings, which were absurd and almost spiteful, were aimed at him, and this angered him beyond reason. He told me of his feelings at dinner, and said: "I have determined to crowd the Court to the wall and regain my position before night." From that time forward it was interesting to watch him. At the reassembling of court he arose to read a few authorities in support of his position. In his comments he kept within the bounds of propriety just far enough to avoid a reprimand for contempt of court. He characterized the continued rulings against him as not only unjust but foolish; and, figuratively speaking, he peeled the Court from head to foot. I shall never forget the scene. Lincoln had the crowd, a portion of the bar, and the jury with him. He knew that fact, and it, together with the belief that injustice had been done him, nerved him to a feeling of desperation. He was wrought up to the point of madness. When a man of large heart and head is wrought up and mad, as the old adage runs, "he's mad all over." Lincoln had studied up the points involved, but knowing full well the calibre of the judge, relied mostly on the moral effect of his personal bearing and influence. He was alternately furious and eloquent, pursuing the Court with broad facts and pointed inquiries in marked and rapid succession. I remember he made use of this homely incident in illustration of some point: "In early days a party of men went out hunting for a wild boar. But the game came upon them unawares, and scampering away they all climbed the trees save one, who, seizing the animal by the ears, undertook to hold him, but despairing of success cried out to his companions in the trees, 'For God's sake, boys, come down and help me let go.' " The prosecution endeavored to break him down or even "head him off," but all to no purpose. His masterly arraignment of law and facts had so effectually badgered the judge that, strange as it may seem, he pretended to see the error in his former position, and finally reversed his decision in Lincoln's favor. The latter saw his triumph, and surveyed a situation of which he was the master. His client was acquitted, and he had swept the field.

In the case of Parker vs. Hoyt, tried in the United States Court in Chicago, Lincoln was one of the counsel for the defendant. The suit was on the merits of an infringement of a patent water wheel. The trial lasted several days and Lincoln manifested great interest in the case. In his earlier days he had run, or aided in running, a sawmill, and explained in his argument the action of the water on the wheel in a manner so clear and intelligible that the jury were enabled to comprehend the points and line of defense without the least difficulty. It was evident he had carried the jury with him in a most masterly argument, the force of which could not be broken by the reply of the opposing counsel. After the jury retired he became very anxious and uneasy. The jury were in another building, the windows of which opened on the street, and had been out for some two hours. "In passing along the street, one of the jurors on whom we very much relied," relates Lincoln's associate in the case, "he being a very intelligent man and firm in his convictions, held up to him one finger. Mr. Lincoln became very much excited, fearing it indicated that eleven of the jury were against him. He knew if this man was for him he would never yield his opinion. He added, if he was like a juryman he had in Tazewell County, the defendant was safe. He was there employed, he said, to prosecute a suit for divorce. His client was a pretty, refined, and interesting little woman in court. The defendant, her husband, was a gross, morose, querulous, fault-finding, and uncomfortable man, and entirely unfitted for the husband of such a woman; but although he was able to prove the use of very offensive and vulgar epithets applied by the husband to his wife and all sorts of annoyances, yet there were no such acts of personal violence as were required by the statute to justify a divorce. Lincoln did the best he could and appealed to the jury to have compassion on the woman, and not to bind her to such a man and such a life as awaited her if required to live longer with him. The jury took about the same view of it in their deliberations. They desired to find for his fair client, but could discover no evidence which would really justify a verdict for her. At last they drew up a verdict for the defendant, and all signed but one fellow, who on being approached with the verdict, said, coolly: 'Gentlemen, I am going to lie down to sleep, and when you get ready to give a verdict for that little woman, then wake me and not until then; for before I will give a verdict against her I will lie here till I rot and the pismires carry me out through the keyhole.' 'Now,' observed Lincoln, 'if that juryman will stick like the man in Tazewell County we are safe.' Strange to relate, the jury did come in, and with a verdict for the defendant. Lincoln always regarded this as one of the gratifying triumphs of his professional life."

7

Lawyer (II)

A law office is a dull, dry place so far as pleasurable or interesting incidents are concerned. If one is in search of stories of fraud, deceit, cruelty, broken promises, blasted homes, there is no better place to learn them than a law office. But to the majority these painful recitals are anything but attractive, and it is well perhaps that it should be so. In the office, as in the court room, Lincoln, when discussing any point, was never arbitrary or insinuating. He was deferential, cool, patient, and respectful. When he reached the office, about nine o'clock in the morning, the first thing he did was to pick up a newspaper, spread himself out on an old sofa, one leg on a chair, and read aloud, much to my discomfort. Singularly enough Lincoln never read any other way but aloud. This habit used to annoy me almost beyond the point of endurance. I once asked him why he did so. This was his explanation: "When I read aloud two senses catch the idea: first, I see what I read; second, I hear it, and therefore I can remember it better." He never studied law books unless a case was on hand for consideration—never followed up the decisions of the supreme courts, as other lawyers did. It seemed as if he depended for his effectiveness in managing a law suit entirely on the stimulus and inspiration of the final hour. He paid but little attention to the fees and money matters of the firm—usually leaving all such to me. He never entered an item in the account book. If any one paid money to him which belonged to the firm, on arriving at the office he divided it with me. If I was not there, he would wrap up my share in a piece of paper and place it in my drawer—marking it with a pencil, "Case of Roe vs. Doe.— Herndon's half."

On many topics he was not a good conversationalist, because he felt that he was not learned enough. Neither was he a good listener. Putting it a little strongly, he was often not even polite. If present with others, or participating in a conversation he was rather abrupt, and in his anxiety to say something apt or to illustrate the subject under discussion, would burst in with a story. In our office I have known him to consume the whole forenoon relating stories. If a man came to see him for the purpose of finding out something, which he did not care to let him know and at the same time did not want to refuse him, he was very adroit. In such cases Lincoln would do most of the talking, swinging around what he suspected was the vital point, but never nearing it, interlarding his answers with a seemingly endless supply of stories and jokes. The interview being both interesting and pleasant, the man would depart in good humor, believing he had accomplished his mission. After he had walked away a few squares and had cooled off, the question would come up, "Well, what did I find out?" Blowing away the froth of Lincoln's humorous narratives he would find nothing substantial left.

"As he entered the trial," relates one of his colleagues at the bar, "where most lawyers would object, he would say he 'reckoned' it would be fair to let this in, or that; and sometimes when his adversary could not quite prove what Lincoln knew to be the truth, he 'reckoned' it would be fair to admit the truth to be so-and-so. When he did object to the Court, and when he heard his objections answered, he would often say, 'Well, I reckon I must be wrong.' Now, about the time he had practiced this three-fourths through the case, if his adversary didn't understand him, he would wake up in a few minutes learning that he had feared the Greeks too late and find himself beaten. He was wise as a serpent in the trial of a cause, but I have had too many scars from his blows to certify that he was harmless as a dove. When the whole thing was unraveled, the adversary would begin to see that what he was so blandly giving away was simply what he couldn't get and keep. By giving away six points and carrying the seventh he carried his case, and the whole case hanging on the seventh, he traded away everything which would give him the least aid in carrying that. Any man who took Lincoln for a simple-minded man would very soon wake up with his back in a ditch."

Lincoln's restless ambition found its gratification only in the field of politics. He used the law merely as a stepping-stone to what he considered a more attractive condition in the political world. In the allurements held out by the latter he seemed to be happy. Nothing in Lincoln's life has provoked more discussion than the question of his ability as a lawyer. I feel warranted in saying that he was at the same time a very great and a very insignificant lawyer. Judge David Davis, in his eulogy on Lincoln at Indianapolis, delivered at the meeting of the bar there in May, 1865, said this: "In all the elements that constituted a lawyer he had few equals. He was great at *nisi prius* and before an appellate tribunal. He seized the strong points of a cause and presented them with clearness and great compactness. His mind was logical and direct, and he did not indulge in extraneous discussion. Generalities and platitudes had no charm for him. An unfailing vein of humor never deserted him, and he was able to claim the attention of court and jury when the cause was most uninteresting by the appropriateness of his anecdotes. His power of comparison was large, and he rarely failed in a legal discussion to use that mode of reasoning. The framework of his mental and moral being was honesty, and a wrong case was poorly defended by him. The ability which some eminent lawyers possess of explaining away the bad points of a cause by ingenious sophistry was denied him. In order to bring into full activity his great powers it was necessary that the should be convinced of the right and justice of the matter which he advocated. When so convinced, whether the cause was great or small he was usually successful."

This statement of Judge Davis in general is correct, but in some particulars is faulty. It was intended as a eulogy on Lincoln, and as such would not admit of as many limitations and modifications as if spoken under other circumstances. In 1866 Judge Davis said in a statement made to me in his home at Bloomington, which I still have, "Mr. Lincoln had no managing faculty nor organizing power; hence a child could conform to the simple and technical rules, the means and the modes of getting at justice better than he. The law has its own rules, and a student could get at them or keep within them better than Lincoln. Sometimes he was forced to study these if he could not get the rubbish of a case removed. But all the way through his lack of method and organizing ability was clearly apparent."

The idea that Mr. Lincoln was a great lawyer in the higher courts and a good *nisi prius* lawyer, and yet that a child or student could manage a case in court better than he, seems strangely inconsistent, but the facts of his life as a lawyer will reconcile this and other apparent contradictions.

I was not only associated with Mr. Lincoln in Springfield, but was frequently on the circuit with him, but of course not so much as Judge Davis, who held the court, and whom Lincoln followed around on the circuit for at least six months out of the year. I easily realized that Lincoln was strikingly deficient in the technical rules of the law. Although he was constantly reminding young legal aspirants to study and "work, work," yet I doubt if he ever read a single elementary law book through in his life. In fact, I may truthfully say, I never knew him to read through a law book of any kind. Practically, he knew nothing of the rules of evidence, of pleading, or practice, as laid down in the textbooks, and seemed to care nothing about them. He had a keen sense of justice, and struggled for it, throwing aside forms, methods, and rules, until it appeared pure as a ray of light flashing through a fog bank. He was not a general reader in any field of knowledge, but when he had occasion to learn or investigate any subject he was thorough and indefatigable in his search. He not only went to the root of the question, but dug up the root, and separated and analyzed every fibre of it. He was in every respect a case lawyer, never cramming himself on any question till he had a case in which the question was involved. He thought slowly and acted slowly; he must needs have time to analyze all the facts in a case and wind them into a connected story. I have seen him lose cases of the plainest justice, which the most inexperienced member of the bar would have gained without effort. Two things were essential to his success in managing a case. One was time; the other a feeling of confidence in the justice of the cause he represented. He used to say, "If I can free this case from technicalities and get it properly swung to the jury, I'll win it." But if either of these essentials were lacking, he was the weakest man at the bar. He was greatest in my opinion as a lawyer in the Supreme Court of Illinois. There the cases were never hurried. The attorneys generally prepared their cases in the form of briefs, and the movements of the court and counsel were so slow that no one need be caught by surprise. I was with Lincoln once and listened to an oral argument by him in which he rehearsed an extended history of the law. It was a carefully prepared and masterly discourse, but, as I thought, entirely useless. After he was through and we were walking home I asked him why he went so far back in the history of the law. I presumed the court knew enough history. "That's where you're mistaken," was his instant rejoinder. "I dared not trust the case on the presumption that the court knows everything—in fact I argued it on the presumption that the court didn't know anything," a statement which, when one reviews the decisions of our appellate courts, is not so extravagant as one would at first suppose.

I used to grow restless at Lincoln's slow movements and speeches in court. "Speak with more vim," I would frequently say, "and arouse the jury—talk faster and keep them awake." In answer to such a suggestion he one day made use of this illustration: "Give me your little penknife, with its short blade, and hand me that old jackknife, lying on the table." Opening the blade of the penknife he said: "You see, this blade at the point travels rapidly, but only through a small portion of space till it stops; while the long blade of the jackknife moves no faster but through a much greater space than the small one. Just so with the long, labored movements of my mind. I may not emit ideas as rapidly as others, because I am compelled by nature to speak slowly, but when I do throw off a thought it seems to me, though it comes with some effort, it has force enough to cut its own way and travel a greater distance." This was said to me when we were alone in our office simply for illustration. It was not said boastingly.

As a specimen of Lincoln's method of reasoning I insert here the brief or notes of an argument used by him in a lawsuit as late as 1850. I copy from the original.

Legislature and adjudication must follow and conform to the progress of society.
The progress of society now begins to produce cases of the

transfer for debts of the entire property of railroad corporations; and to enable transferees to use and enjoy the transferred property legislation *and* adjudication *begin to be necessary.*

Shall this class of legislation just now beginning with us be general *or* special?

Section Ten of our Constitution requires that it should be general, if possible. (Read the Section.)

Special legislation always trenches upon the judical department; and in so far violates Section Two of the Constitution. (Read it.)

Just reasoning—policy—is in favor of general legislation—else the legislature will be loaded *down with the investigation of smaller cases—a work which the courts ought to perform, and can perform much more perfectly. How can the Legislature rightly decide the facts between P. & B. and S. C. & Co.*

It is said that under a general law, whenever a R. R. Co. gets tired of its debts, it may transfer fraudulently *to get rid of them. So they may—so may individuals; and which—the* Legislature *or the courts—is best suited to try the question of fraud in either case?*

It is said, if a purchaser have acquired legal rights, let him not be robbed of them, but if he needs legislation *let him submit to just terms to obtain it.*

Let him, say we, have general law in advance (guarded in every possible way against fraud), so that, when he acquires a legal right, he will have no occasion to wait for additional legislation; and if he has practiced fraud let the courts so decide.

David Davis said this of Lincoln: "When in a lawsuit he believed his client was oppressed—as in the Wright case—he was hurtful in denunciation. When he attacked meanness, fraud, or vice, he was powerful, merciless in his castigation." The Wright case referred to was a suit brought by Lincoln and myself to compel a pension agent to refund a portion of a fee which he had withheld from the widow of a revolutionary soldier. The entire pension was $400, of which sum the agent had retained one-half. The pensioner, an old woman crippled and bent with age, came hobbling into the office and told her story.

It stirred Lincoln up, and he walked over to the agent's office and made a demand for a return of the money, but without success. Then suit was brought. The day before the trial I hunted up for Lincoln, at his request, a history of the Revolutionary War, of which he read a good portion. He told me to remain during the trial until I had heard his address to the jury. "For," said he, "I am going to skin Wright, and get that money back." The only witness we introduced was the old lady, who through her tears told her story. In his speech to the jury, Lincoln recounted the causes leading to the outbreak of the Revolutionary struggle, and then drew a vivid picture of the hardships of Valley Forge, describing with minuteness the men, barefooted and with bleeding feet, creeping over the ice. As he reached that point in his speech wherein he narrated the hardened action of the defendant in fleecing the old woman of her pension his eyes flashed, and throwing aside his handkerchief, which he held in his right hand, he fairly launched into him. His speech for the next five to ten minutes justified the declaration of Davis, that he was "hurtful in denunciation and merciless in castigation." There was no rule of court to restrain him in his argument, and I never, either on the stump or on other occasions in court, saw him so wrought up. Before he closed, he drew an ideal picture of the plaintiff's husband, the deceased soldier, parting with his wife at the threshold of their home, and kissing their little babe in the cradle, as he started for the war. "Time rolls by," he said in conclusion; "the heroes of '76 have passed away and are encamped on the other shore. The soldier has gone to rest, and now, crippled, blind, and broken, his widow comes to you and to me, gentlemen of the jury, to right her wrongs. She was not always thus. She was once a beautiful young woman. Her step was elastic, her face fair, and her voice as sweet as any that rang in the mountains of old Virginia. But now she is poor and defenseless. Out here on the prairies of Illinois, many hundreds of miles away from the scenes of her childhood, she appeals to us, who enjoy the privileges achieved for us by the patriots of the Revolution, for our sympathetic aid and manly protection. All I ask is, shall we befriend her?" The speech made the desired impression on the jury. Half of them were in tears, while the defendant sat in the court room, drawn up and writhing

under the fire of Lincoln's fierce invective. The jury returned a
verdict in our favor for every cent we demanded. Lincoln was
so much interested in the old lady that he became her surety
for costs, paid her way home, and her hotel bill while she was
in Springfield. When the judgment was paid we remitted the
proceeds to her and made no charge for our services. Lincoln's
notes for the argument were unique: "No contract.—Not professional services.—Unreasonable charge.—Money retained by
Def't not given by Pl'ff.—Revolutionary War.—Describe Valley
Forge privations.—Ice—Soldier's bleeding feet.—Pl'ffs husband.—Soldier leaving home for army.—*Skin Def't*. Close."

It must not be inferred from this that Lincoln was in the habit
of slopping over. He never hunted up acts of injustice, but if they
came to him he was easily enlisted. In 1855 he was attending
court at the town of Clinton, Illinois. Fifteen ladies from a
neighboring village in the county had been indicted for trespass.
Their offense consisted in sweeping down on one Tanner, the
keeper of a saloon in the village, and knocking in the heads of
his barrels. Lincoln was not employed in the case, but sat
watching the trial as it proceeded. In defending the ladies their
attorney seemed to evince a little want of tact, and this prompted one of the former to invite Mr. Lincoln to add a few words to
the jury, if he thought he could aid their cause. He was too
gallant to refuse and, their attorney having consented, he made
use of the following argument: "In this case I would change the
order of indictment and have it read The State vs. Mr. Whisky,
instead of The State vs. The Ladies; and touching these there are
three laws: The law of self-protection; the law of the land, or
statute law; and the moral law, or law of God. First, the law of
self-protection is a law of necessity, as evinced by our forefathers
in casting the tea overboard and asserting their right to the
pursuit of life, liberty, and happiness. In this case it is the
only defense the ladies have, for Tanner neither feared God
nor regarded man. Second, the law of the land, or statute law,
and Tanner is recreant to both. Third, the moral law, or law
of God, and this is probably a law for the violation of which
the jury can fix no punishment. Lincoln gave some of his own
observations on the ruinous effects of whisky in society, and
demanded its early suppression. After he had concluded, the

Court, without awaiting the return of the jury, dismissed the ladies, saying: "Ladies, go home. I will require no bond of you, and if any fine is ever wanted of you, we will let you know."

A widow who owned a piece of valuable land employed Lincoln and myself to examine the title to the property, with the view of ascertaining whether certain alleged tax liens were just or not. In tracing back the title we were not satisfied with the description of the ground in one of the deeds of conveyance. Lincoln, to settle the matter, took his surveying instruments and surveyed the ground himself. The result proved that Charles Matheny, a former grantor, had sold the land at so much per acre, but that in describing it he had made an error and conveyed more land than he received pay for. This land descended to our client, and Lincoln after a careful survey and calculation, decided that she ought to pay to Matheny's heirs the sum which he had shown was due them by reason of the erroneous conveyance. To this she entered strenuous objections, but when assured that unless she consented to this act of plain justice we would drop the case, she finally, though with great reluctance, consented. She paid the required amount, and this we divided up into smaller sums proportioned to the number of heirs. Lincoln himself distributed these to the heirs, obtaining a receipt from each one.

While Mr. Lincoln was no financier and had no propensity to acquire property—no avarice of the get—yet he had the capacity of retention, or the avarice of the keep. He never speculated in lands or anything else. In the days of land offices and "choice lots in a growing town" he had many opportunities to make safe ventures promising good returns, but he never availed himself of them. His brother lawyers were making good investments and lucky turns, some of them, Davis, for example, were rapidly becoming wealthy; but Lincoln cared nothing for speculation; in fact there was no venturesome spirit in him. His habits were very simple. He was not fastidious as to food or dress. His hat was brown, faded, and the nap usually worn or rubbed off. He wore a short cloak and sometimes a shawl. His coat and vest hung loosely on his gaunt frame, and his trousers were invariably too short. On the circuit he carried in one hand a faded green umbrella, with "A. Lincoln" in large white cotton or

muslin letters sewed on the inside. The knob was gone from the
handle, and when closed a piece of cord was usually tied around
it in the middle to keep it from flying open. In the other hand he
carried a literal carpetbag, in which were stored the few papers
to be used in court, and underclothing enough to last till his return to Springfield. He slept in a long, coarse, yellow flannel
shirt, which reached halfway between his knees and ankles. It
probably was not made to fit his bony figure as completely as
Beau Brummel's shirt, and hence we can somewhat appreciate
the sensation of a young lawyer who, on seeing him thus ar-
rayed for the first time observed afterwards that, "He was the
ungodliest figure I ever saw."

"He never complained of the food, bed, or lodgings. If every
other fellow grumbled at the bill of fare which greeted us at
many of the dingy taverns," says David Davis, "Lincoln said
nothing." He was once presiding as judge in the absence of
Davis, and the case before him was an action brought by a
merchant against the father of a minor son for a suit of clothes
sold to the son without paternal authority. The real question
was whether the clothes were necessary, and suited to the condition of the son's life. The father was a wealthy farmer; the bill
for the clothing was twenty-eight dollars. I happened in court
just as Lincoln was rendering his decision. He ruled against the
plea of necessity. "I have rarely in my life," said he, "worn a suit
of clothes costing twenty-eight dollars."

"Several of us lawyers," remarked one of his colleagues, "in
the eastern end of the circuit annoyed Lincoln once while he was
holding court for Davis by attempting to defend against a note
to which there were many makers. We had no legal, but a good
moral defense, but what we wanted most of all was to stave it off
till the next term of court by one expedient or another. We
bothered 'the court' about it till late on Saturday, the day of adjournment. He adjourned for supper with nothing left but this
case to dispose of. After supper he heard our twaddle for nearly
an hour, and then made this odd entry: 'L. D. Chaddon vs. J. D.
Beasley *et al.* April term, 1856. Champaign County Court. Plea
in abatement by B. Z. Green, a defendant not served, filed Saturday at 11 o'clock A.M. April 24, 1856, stricken from the files by
order of court. Demurrer to declaration, if there ever was one,

overruled. Defendants who are served now, at 8 o'clock, P.M., of the last day of the term, ask to plead to the merits, which is denied by the court on the ground that the offer comes too late and therefore, as by *nil dicet*, judgment is rendered for Pl'ff. Clerk assess damages. A. Lincoln, Judge *pro tem.*' " The lawyer who reads this singular entry will appreciate its oddity if no else does. After making it one of the lawyers, on recovering from his astonishment, ventured to inquire, "Well, Lincoln, how can we get this case up again?" Lincoln eyed him quizzically a moment, and then answered, "You have all been so 'mighty smart about this case you can find out how to take it up again yourselves."

The same gentleman who furnishes the incident concerning Lincoln on the bench, and who was afterwards a trusted friend of Mr. Lincoln, Henry C. Whitney, has described most happily the delights of a life on the circuit. A bit of it, referring to Lincoln, I apprehend, cannot be deemed out of place here. "In October, 1854, Abraham Lincoln," he relates, "drove into our town (Urbana) to attend court. He had the appearance of a rough, intelligent farmer, and his rude, homemade buggy and raw-boned horse enforced this belief. I had met him for the first time in June of the same year. David Davis and Leonard Swett had just preceded him. The next morning he started North, on the Illinois Central Railroad, and as he went in an old omnibus he played on a boy's harp all the way to the depot. I used to attend the Danville court, and while there, usually roomed with Lincoln and Davis. We stopped at McCormick's hotel, an old-fashioned frame country tavern. Jurors, counsel, prisoners, everybody ate at a long table. The judge, Lincoln, and I had the ladies' parlor fitted up with two beds. Lincoln, Swett, McWilliams, of Bloomington, Voorhees, of Covington, Ind., O. L. Davis, Drake, Ward Lamon, Lawrence, Beckwith, and O. F. Harmon, of Danville, Whiteman, of Iroquois County, and Chandler, of Williamsport, Ind., constituted the bar. Lincoln, Davis, Swett, I, and others who came from the western part of the state would drive from Urbana. The distance was thirty-six miles. We sang and exchanged stories all the way. We had no hesitation in stopping at a farmhouse and ordering them to kill and cook a chicken for dinner. By dark we reached Danville. Lamon would have whiskey in his office for the drinking ones, and those who indulged in petty gambling would get by themselves and play till late in the night. Lincoln, Davis, and a few local wits would spend the evening in Davis's room, talking politics, wisdom, and fun. Lincoln and Swett were the great lawyers, and Lincoln always wanted Swett in jury cases. We who stopped at the hotel would all breakfast together and frequently go out into the woods and hold court. We were of more consequence than a court and bar is now. The feelings were those of great fraternity in the bar, and if we desired to restrict our circle it was no trouble for Davis to freeze out any disagreeable persons. Lincoln was fond of going all by himself to any little show or concert. I have known him to slip away and spend the entire evening at a little magic lantern show intended for children. A traveling concert company, calling themselves the 'Newhall Family,' were sure of drawing Lincoln. One of their number, Mrs. Hillis, a good singer, he used to tell us was the only woman who ever seemed to exhibit any liking for him. I attended a Negro minstrel show in Chicago, where we heard Dixie sung. It was entirely new, and pleased him greatly. In court he was irrepressible and apparently inexhaustible in his fund of stories. Where in the world a man who had traveled so little and struggled amid the restrictions of such limited surroundings could gather up such apt and unique yarns we never could guess. Davis appreciated Lincoln's talent in this direction, and was always ready to stop business to hear one of his stories. Lincoln was very bashful when in the presence of ladies. I remember once we were invited to take tea at a friend's house, and while in the parlor I was called to the front gate to see a client. When I returned, Lincoln, who had undertaken to entertain the ladies, was twisting and squirming in his chair, and as bashful as a schoolboy. Everywhere, though we met a hard crowd at every court, and though things were free and easy, we were treated with great respect."

Probably the most important lawsuit Linclon and I conducted was one in which we defended the Illinois Central Railroad in an action brought by McLean County, Illinois, in August, 1853, to recover taxes alleged to be due the county from the road. The Legislature had granted the road immunity from taxation, and this was a case intended to test the constitutionality of the law. The road sent a retainer fee of $250. In the lower court the case was decided in favor of the railroad. An appeal to the Supreme Court followed, and there it was argued twice, and finally decided in our favor. This last decision was rendered some time in 1856. Mr. Lincoln soon went to Chicago and presented our bill for legal services. We only asked for $2,000 more. The official to whom he was referred—supposed to have been the superintendent George B. McClellan who afterwards became the eminent general—looking at the bill expressed great surprise. "Why, sir," he exclaimed, "this is as much as Daniel Webster himself would have charged. We cannot allow such a claim." Stung by the rebuff, Lincoln withdrew the bill, and started for home. On the way he stopped at Bloomington. There he met Grant Goodrich, Archibald Williams, Norman B. Judd, O. H. Browning, and other attorneys, who, on learning of his modest charge for such valuable services rendered the railroad, induced him to increase the demand to $5,000, and to bring suit for that sum. This was done at once. On the trial six lawyers certified that the bill was reasonable, and judgment for that sum went by default. The judgment was promptly paid. Lincoln gave me my half, and much as we deprecated the avarice of great corporations, we both thanked the Lord for letting the Illinois Central Railroad fall into our hands.

In the summer of 1857 Lincoln was employed by one Manny, of Chicago, to defend him in an action brought by McCormick, who was the inventor of the reaping machine, for infringement of patent. Lincoln had been recommended to Manny by E. B. Washburne, then a member of Congress from northern Illinois. The case was to be tried before Judge McLean at Cincinnati, in the Circuit Court of the United States. The counsel for McCormick was Reverdy Johnson. Edwin M. Stanton and George Harding, of Philadelphia, were associated on the other side with Lincoln. The latter came to Cincinnati a few days before the argument took place, and stopped at the house of a friend. "The case was one of great importance pecuniarily," relates a lawyer in Cincinnati who was a member of the bar at the time, "and in the law questions involved. Reverdy Johnson represented the plaintiff. Mr. Lincoln had prepared himself with the greatest care; his ambition was up to speak in the case and to measure swords with the renowned lawyer from Baltimore. It was understood between his client and himself before his coming that Mr. Harding, of Philadelphia, was to be associated with him in the case, and was to make the 'mechanical argument.' After reaching Cincinnati, Mr. Lincoln was a little surprised and annoyed to learn that his client had also associated with him Mr. Edwin M. Stanton, of Pittsburgh, and a lawyer of our own bar, the reason assigned being that the importance of the case required a man of the experience and power of Mr. Stanton to meet Mr. Johnson. The Cincinnati lawyer was appointed for his 'local influence.' These reasons did not remove the slight conveyed in the employment without consultation with him of this additional counsel. He keenly felt it, but acquiesced. The trial of the case came on; the counsel for defense met each morning for consultation. On one of these occasions one of the counsel moved that only two of them should speak in the case. This matter was also acquiesced in. It had always been understood that Mr. Harding was to speak to explain the mechanism of the reapers. So this motion excluded either Mr. Lincoln or Mr. Stanton—which? By the custom of the bar, as between counsel of equal standing and in the absence of any action of the client, the original counsel speaks. By this rule Mr. Lincoln had precedence. Mr. Stanton suggested to Mr. Lincoln to make the speech. Mr. Lincoln answered. 'No, you speak.' Mr. Stanton replied, 'I will,' and taking up his hat, said he would go and make preparation. Mr. Lincoln acquiesced in this, but was greatly grieved and mortified; he took but little more interest in the case, though remaining until the conclusion of the trial. He seemed to be greatly depressed, and gave evidence of that tendency to melancholy which so marked his character. His parting on leaving the city cannot be forgotten. Cordially shaking the hand of his hostess he said: 'You have made my stay here most agreeable, and I am a thousand times obliged to you; but in reply to your request for me to come again, I must say to you I never expect to be in Cincinnati again. I have nothing against the city, but things have so happened here as to make it undesirable for me ever to return.' Lincoln felt that Stanton had not only been very discourteous to him, but had purposely ignored him in the case, and that he had received rather rude, if not unkind, treatment from all hands. Stanton, in his brusque and abrupt way, it is said, described him as a 'long, lank creature from Illinois, wearing a dirty linen duster for a coat, on the back of which the perspiration had splotched wide stains that resembled a map of the continent.' Mr. Lincoln," adds Mr. Dickson, "remained in Cincinnati about a week, moving freely around, yet not twenty men knew him personally or knew he was here; not a hundred would have known who he was had his name been given to them. He came with the fond hope of making fame in a forensic contest with Reverdy Johnson. He was pushed aside, humiliated and mortified. He attached to the innocent city the displeasure that filled his bosom, and shook its dust from his feet." On his return to Springfield he was somewhat reticent regarding the trial, and, contrary to his custom, communicated to his associates at the bar but few of its incidents. He told me that he had been "roughly handled by that man Stanton"; that he overheard the latter from an adjoining room, while the door was slightly ajar, referring to Lincoln, inquire of another, "Where did that long-armed creature come from, and what can he expect to do in this case?" During the trial Lincoln formed a poor opinion of Judge McLean. He characterized him as an "old granny," with considerable vigor of mind, but no perception at all. "If you were to point your finger at him," he put it, "and a darning needle at the same time he never would know which was the sharpest."

As Lincoln grew into public favor and achieved such marked success in the profession, half the bar of Springfield began to be envious of his growing popularity. I believe there is less jealousy and bitter feeling among lawyers than professional men of any other class; but it should be borne in mind that in that day a portion of the bar in every county seat, if not a majority of the lawyers everywhere, were politicians. Stuart frequently differed from Lincoln on political questions, and was full of envy. Likewise those who coincided with Lincoln in his political views were disturbed in the same way. Even Logan was not wholly free from the degrading passion. But in this respect Lincoln suffered no more than other great characters who preceded him in the world's history.

That which Lincoln's adversaries in a lawsuit feared most of all was his apparent disregard of custom or professional propriety in managing a case before a jury. He brushed aside all rules,

and very often resorted to some strange and strategic performance which invariably broke his opponent down or exercised
some peculiar influence over the jury. Hence the other side in a
case were in constant fear of one of his dramatic strokes, or
trembled lest he should "ring in" some ingeniously planned interruption not on the programme. In a case where Judge
Logan—always earnest and grave—opposed him, Lincoln created no little merriment by his reference to Logan's style of dress.
He carried the surprise in store for the latter, till he reached his
turn before the jury. Addressing them, he said: "Gentlemen, you
must be careful and not permit yourselves to be overcome by the
eloquence of counsel for the defense. Judge Logan, I know, is an
effective lawyer. I have met him too often to doubt that; but
shrewd and careful though he be, still he is sometimes wrong.
Since this trial has begun I have discovered that, with all his
caution and fastidiousness, he hasn't knowledge enough to put
his shirt on right." Logan turned red as crimson, but sure
enough, Lincoln was correct, for the former had donned a new
shirt, and by mistake had drawn it over his head with the pleat-
ed bosom behind. The general laugh which followed destroyed
the effect of Logan's eloquence over the jury—the very point at
which Lincoln aimed.

The trial of William Armstrong for the murder of James P.
Metzger, in May, 1858, at Beardstown, Illinois, in which Lincoln secured the acquittal of the defendant, was one of the gratifying triumphs in his career as a lawyer. Lincoln's defense,
wherein he floored the principal prosecuting witness, who had
testified positively to seeing the fatal blow struck in the
moonlight, by showing from an almanac that the moon had set,
was not more convincing than his eloquent and irresistible appeal in his client's favor. The latter's mother, old Hannah
Armstrong, the friend of his youth, had solicited him to defend
her son. "He told the jury," relates the prosecuting attorney, "of
his once being a poor, friendless boy; that Armstrong's parents
took him into their house, fed and clothed him, and gave him a
home. There were tears in his eyes as he spoke. The sight of his
tall, quivering frame, and the particulars of the story he so
pathetically told, moved the jury to tears also, and they forgot
the guilt of the defendant in their admiration of his advocate. It

was the most touching scene I ever witnessed." Before passing it may be well to listen to the humble tribute of old Hannah Armstrong, the defendant's mother: "Lincoln had said to me, 'Hannah, your son will be cleared before sundown.' I left the courtroom, and they came and told me that my son was cleared and a free man. I went up to the courthouse. The jury shook hands with me; so did the judge and Lincoln; tears streamed down Lincoln's eyes. . . . After the trial I asked him what his fee would be; told him I was poor. 'Why, Hannah,' he said, 'I sha'n't charge you a cent, and anything else I can do for you, will do it willingly and without charge.' He afterwards wrote to me about a piece of land which certain men were trying to get from me, and said: 'Hannah, they can't get your land. Let them try it in the Circuit Court, and then you appeal it; bring it to the Supreme Court and I and Herndon will attend to it for nothing.'"

The last suit of any importance in which Lincoln was personally engaged, was known as the Johnson sandbar case. It involved the title to certain lands, the accretion on the shores of Lake Michigan, in or near Chicago. It was tried in the United States Circuit Court at Chicago in April and May, 1860. During the trial, the Court—Judge Drummond—and all the counsel on both sides dined at the residence of Isaac N. Arnold, afterwards a member of Congress. "Douglas and Lincoln," relates Mr. Arnold, "were at the time both candidates for the nomination for President. There were active and ardent political friends of each at the table, and when the sentiment was proposed, 'May Illinois furnish the next President,' it was drank with enthusiasm by the friends of both Lincoln and Douglas."

8

The Slavery Question

While Lincoln in a certain sense was buried in the law from the time his career in Congress closed till, to use his own words, "the repeal of the Missouri Compromise aroused him again," yet he was a careful student of his times and kept abreast of the many and varied movements in politics. He was generally on the Whig electoral tickets, and made himself heard during each successive canvass, but he seemed to have lost that zealous interest in politics which characterized his earlier days. He plodded on unaware of, and seemingly without ambition for, the great distinction that lay in store for him. John T. Stuart relates that, as he and Lincoln were returning from the court in Tazewell County in 1850, and were nearing the little town of Dillon, they engaged in a discussion of the political situation. "As we were coming down the hill," are Stuart's words, "I said, 'Lincoln, the time is coming when we shall have to be all either Abolitionists or Democrats.' He thought a moment and then answered, ruefully and emphatically. 'When that time comes my mind is made up, for I believe the slavery question can never be successfully compromised.' I responded with equal emphasis. 'My mind is made up too'." Thus it was with Lincoln. But he was too slow to suit the impetuous demand of the few pronounced Abolitionists whom he met in his daily walks. The sentiment of the majority in Springfield tended in the other direction, and thus environed, Lincoln lay down like the sleeping lion. The future would yet arouse him. At that time I was an ardent Abolitionist in sentiment. I used to warn Lincoln against his apparent conservatism when the needs of the hour were so great; but his only answer would be, "Billy, you're too rampant and spontaneous." I was in correspondence with Sumner, Greeley, Phillips, and Garrison, and was thus thoroughly imbued with all the rancor drawn from such strong antislavery sources. I adhered to Lincoln, relying on the final outcome of his sense of justice and right. Every time a good speech on the great issue was made I sent for it. Hence you could find on my table the latest utterances of Giddings,

Phillips, Sumner, Seward, and one whom I considered grander than all the others—Theodore Parker. Lincoln and I took such papers as the *Chicago Tribune, New York Tribune, Anti-Slavery Standard, Emancipator,* and *National Era.* On the other side of the question we took the *Charleston Mercury* and the *Richmond Enquirer.* I also bought a book called *Sociology,* written by one Fitzhugh, which defended and justified slavery in every conceivable way. In addition I purchased all the leading histories of the slavery movement, and other works which treated on that subject. Lincoln himself never bought many books, but he and I both read those I have named. After reading them we would discuss the questions they touched upon and the ideas they suggested, from our different points of view. I was never conscious of having made much of an impression on Mr. Lincoln, nor do I believe I ever changed his views. I will go further and say, that, from the profound nature of his conclusions and the labored method by which he arrived at them, no man is entitled to the credit of having either changed or greatly modified them. I remember once, after having read one of Theodore Parker's sermons on slavery, saying to Mr. Lincoln substantially this: "I have always noticed that ill-gotten wealth does no man any good. This is as true of nations as individuals. I believe that all the ill-gotten gain wrenched by us from the Negro through his enslavement will eventually be taken from us, and we will be set back where we began." Lincoln thought my prophecy rather direful. He doubted seriously if either of us would live to see the righting of so great a wrong; but years after, when writing his second Inaugural address, he endorsed the idea. Clothing it in the most beautiful language, he says: "Yet if God wills that it [the war] continue till all the wealth piled by the bondsman's two hundred and fifty years of unrequited toil shall be sunk, and until every drop of blood drawn by the lash shall be paid by another drawn by the sword, as was said three thousand years ago, so still it must be said, 'The judgments of the Lord are true and righteous altogether.'"

The passage in May, 1854, of the Kansas-Nebraska bill swept out of sight the Missouri Compromise and the Compromise measures of 1850. This bill, designed and carried through by Douglas, was regarded by him as the masterpiece of all his

varied achievements in legislation. It served to prove more clearly than anything he had ever before done his flexibility and want
of political conscience. Although in years gone before he had invoked the vengeance of Heaven on the ruthless hand that should
dare to disturb the sanctity of the compact of 1821, yet now he
was the arrogant and audacious leader in the very work he had
so heartily condemned. When we consider the bill and the unfortunate results which followed it in the border States we are irresistibly led to conclude that it was, all things considered, a
great public wrong and a most lamentable piece of political
jugglery. The stump speech which Thomas H. Benton charged
that Douglas had "injected into the belly of the bill" contains all
there was of Popular Sovereignty—"It being the true intent and
meaning of this act not to legislate slavery into any Territory or
State nor to exclude it therefrom, but to leave the people thereof
perfectly free to form and regulate their domestic institutions in
their own way, subject only to the Constitution of the United
States," an argument which, using Lincoln's words, "amounts to
this: That if any one man chooses to enslave another no third
man shall be allowed to object." The widespread feeling the passage of this law aroused everywhere over the Union is a matter
of general history. It stirred up in New England the latent hostil-
ity to the aggression of slavery; it stimulated to extraordinary
endeavors the derided Abolitionists, arming them with new
weapons; it sounded the deathknell of the gallant old Whig
party; it drove together strange, discordant elements in readiness to fight a common enemy; it brought to the forefront a
leader in the person of Lincoln.

Lincoln had made a few speeches in aid of Scott during the
campaign of 1852, but they were efforts entirely unworthy of
the man. Now, however, a live issue was presented to him. No
one realized this sooner than he. In the office discussions he
grew bolder in his utterances. He insisted that the social and political difference between slavery and freedom was becoming
more marked; that one must overcome the other; and that post-
poning the struggle between them would only make it the more
deadly in the end. "The day of compromise," he still contended,
"has passed. These two great ideas have been kept apart only by
the most artful means. They are like two wild beasts in sight of

each other, but chained and held apart. Some day these deadly antagonists will one or the other break their bonds, and then the question will be settled." In a conversation with a fellow lawyer (Joseph Gillespie) he said of slavery: "It is the most glittering, ostentatious, and displaying property in the world, and now, if a young man goes courting, the only inquiry is how many Negroes he or his ladylove owns. The love for slave property is swallowing up every other mercenary possession. Slavery is a great and crying injustice—an enormous national crime." At another time he made the observation that it was "singular that the courts would hold that a man never lost his right to his property that had been stolen from him, but that he instantly lost his right to himself if he was stolen." It is useless to add more evidence—for it could be piled mountain high—showing that at the very outset Mr. Lincoln was sound to the core on the injustice and crime of human slavery.

After a brief rest at his home in Chicago Mr. Douglas betook himself to the country, and in October, during the week of the State Fair we find him in Springfield. On Tuesday he made a speech in the State House which, in view of the hostile attitude of some of his own party friends, was a labored defense of his position. It was full of ingenious sophistry and skilful argument. An unprecedented concourse of people had gathered from all parts of the State, and Douglas, fresh from the halls of Congress, was the lion of the hour. On the following day Mr. Lincoln, as the champion of the opponents of Popular Sovereignty, was selected to represent those who disagreed with the new legislation, and to answer Douglas. His speech encouraged his friends no less than it startled his enemies. At this time I was zealously interested in the new movement, and not less so in Lincoln. I frequently wrote the editorials in the *Springfield Journal*, the editor, Simeon Francis, giving to Lincoln and to me the utmost liberty in that direction. Occasionally Lincoln would write out matter for publication, but I believe I availed myself of the privilege oftener than he. The editorial in the issue containing the speeches of Lincoln and Douglas on this occasion was my own, and while in description it may seem rather strongly imbued with youthful enthusiasm, yet on reading it in maturer years I am still inclined to believe it reasonably faithful to the facts and the situation. "The anti-Nebraska speech of Mr. Lincoln," says the article, "was the profoundest in our opinion that he has made in his whole life. He felt upon his soul the truths burn which he uttered, and all present felt that he was true to his own soul. His feelings once or twice swelled within, and came near stifling utterance. He quivered with emotion. The whole house was as still as death. He attacked the Nebraska bill with unusual warmth and energy; and all felt that a man of strength was its enemy, and that he intended to blast it if he could by strong and manly efforts. He was most successful, and the house approved the glorious triumph of truth by loud and continued huzzas. Women waved their white handkerchiefs in token of woman's silent but heartfelt assent. Douglas felt the sting; the animal within him was roused because he frequently interrupted Mr. Lincoln. His friends felt that he was crushed by Lincoln's powerful argument, manly logic, and illustrations from nature around us. The Nebraska bill was shivered, and like a tree of the forest was torn and rent asunder by the hot bolts of truth. Mr. Lincoln exhibited Douglas in all the attitudes he could be placed, in a friendly debate. He exhibited the bill in all its aspects to show its humbuggery and falsehood, and, when thus torn to rags, cut into slips, held up to the gaze of the vast crowd, a kind of scorn and mockery was visible upon the face of the crowd and upon the lips of their most eloquent speaker. At the conclusion of this speech every man and child felt that it was unanswerable. He took the heart captive and broke like a sun over the understanding."

Anent the subject of editorial writing it may not be inappropriate to relate that Lincoln and I both kept on furnishing political matter of many varieties for the *Springfield Journal* until 1860. Many of the editorials that I wrote were intended directly or indirectly to promote the interest of Lincoln. I wrote one on the advisability of annexing Cuba to the United States, taking the rather advanced ground that slavery would be abolished in Cuba before it would in this country—a position which aroused no little controversy with other papers. One little incident occurs to me in this connection which may not be without inter-

est to newspaper men. A newspaper had been started in Springfield called the *Conservative*, which, it was believed, was being
run in the interest of the Democratic party. While pretending to
support Fillmore it was kept alive by Buchanan men and other
kindred spirits, who were somewhat proslavery in their views.
The thing was damaging Lincoln and the friends of freedom
more than an avowed Democratic paper could. The editor, an
easy, good-natured fellow, simply placed in charge to execute
the will of those who gave the paper its financial backing, was a
good friend of mine, and by means of this friendship I was
always well informed of matters in the *Conservative* editorial
room. One day I read in the *Richmond Enquirer* an article en-
dorsing slavery, and arguing that from principle the enslavement of either whites or blacks was justifiable and right. I
showed it to Lincoln who remarked that it was "rather rank doctrine for Northern Democrats to endorse. I should like to see,"
he said, with emphasis, "some of these Illinois newspapers
champion that." I told him if he would only wait and keep his
own counsel I would have a proslavery organ in Springfield
publish that very article. He doubted it, but when I told him
how it was to be done he laughed and said, "Go in." I cut the
slip out and succeeded in getting it in the paper named. Of
course it was a trick, but it acted admirably. Its appearance in
the new organ, although without comment, almost ruined that
valuable journal, and my good-natured friend the editor was
nearly overcome by the denunciation of those who were responsible for the organ's existence. My connection, and Lincoln's
too—for he endorsed the tricks—with the publication of the
condemned article was eventually discovered, and we were
thereafter effectually prevented from getting another line in the
paper. The antislavery people quoted the article as having
been endorsed by a Democratic newspaper in Springfield, and
Lincoln himself used it with telling effect. He joined in the
popular denunciation, expressing great astonishment that such
a sentiment could find lodgment in any paper in Illinois,
although he knew full well how the whole thing had been
carried through.

During the remainder of the State-Fair week, speeches were

made by Lyman Trumbull, Sidney Breese, E. D. Taylor, and John Calhoun, none of which unfortunately have been preserved. Among those who mingled in the crowd and listened to them was Owen Lovejoy, a radical, fiery, brave, fanatical man, it may be, but one full of the virus of Abolitionism. I had been thoroughly inoculated with the latter myself and so had many others, who helped to swell the throng. The Nebraska movement had kindled anew the old zeal, and inspired us with renewed confidence to begin the crusade. As many of us as could, assembled together to organize for the campaign before us. As soon therefore as Lincoln finished his speech in the hall of the House of Representatives, Lovejoy, moving forward from the crowd, announced a meeting in the same place that evening of all the friends of Freedom. That of course meant the Abolitionists with whom I had been in conference all the day. Their plan had been to induce Mr. Lincoln to speak for them at their meeting. Strong as I was in the faith, yet I doubted the propriety of Lincoln's taking any stand yet. As I viewed it, he was ambitious to climb to the United States Senate, and on grounds of policy it would not do for him to occupy at that time such advanced ground as we were taking. On the other hand, it was equally as dangerous to refuse a speech for the Abolitionists. I did not know how he felt on the subject, but on learning that Lovejoy intended to approach him with an invitation, I hunted up Lincoln and urged him to avoid meeting the enthusiastic champion of Abolitionism. "Go home at once," I said. "Take Bob with you and drive somewhere into the country and stay till this thing is over." Whether my admonition and reasoning moved him or not I do not know, but it only remains to state that under pretence of having business in Tazewell County he drove out of town in his buggy, and did not return till the apostles of Abolitionism had separated and gone to their homes. I have always believed this little arrangement—it would dignify it too much to call it a plan—saved Lincoln. If he had endorsed the resolutions passed at the meeting, or spoken simply in favor of freedom that night, he would have been identified with all the rancor and extremes of Abolitionism. If, on the contrary, he had been invited to join them, and then had refused to take a position as advanced as theirs, he would have lost their support. In either event he was in great danger; and so he who was aspiring to succeed his old rival, James Shields, in the United States Senate was forced to avoid the issue by driving hastily in his one horse buggy to the court in Tazewell County. A singular coincidence suggests itself in the fact that, twelve years before, James Shields and a friend drove hastily in the same direction, and destined for the same point, to force Lincoln to take issue in another and entirely different matter.

By request of party friends Lincoln was induced to follow after Douglas and, at the various places where the latter had appointments to speak, reply to him. On the 16th of October they met at Peoria, where Douglas enjoyed the advantages of an "open and close." Lincoln made an effective speech, which he wrote out and furnished to the *Sangamon Journal* for publication, and which can be found among his public utterances. His party friends in Springfield and elsewhere, who had urged him to push after Douglas till he cried "enough," were surprised a few days after the Peoria debate to find him at home, with the information that by an agreement with the latter they were both to return home and speak no more during the campaign. Judge of his astonishment a few days later to find that his rival, instead of going direct to his home in Chicago, had stopped at Princeton and violated his express agreement by making a speech there! Lincoln was much displeased at this action of Douglas, which tended to convince him that the latter was really a man devoid of fixed political morals. I remember his explanation in our office made to me, William Butler, William Jayne, Ben F. Irwin, and other friends, to account for his early withdrawal from the stump. After the Peoria debate Douglas approached him and flattered him by saying that he was giving him more trouble on the territorial and slavery questions than all the United States Senate, and he therefore proposed to him that both should abandon the field and return to their homes. Now Lincoln could never refuse a polite request—one in which no principle was involved. I have heard him say, "It's a fortunate thing I wasn't born a woman, for I cannot refuse anything, it seems." He therefore consented to the cessation of debate proposed by Douglas, and the next day both went to the town of

Lacon, where they had been billed for speeches. Their agreement was kept from their friends, and both declined to speak—Douglas, on the ground of hoarseness, and Lincoln gallantly refusing to take advantage of "Judge Douglas's indisposition." Here they separated, Lincoln going directly home, and Douglas, as before related, stopping at Princeton and colliding in debate with Owen Lovejoy. Upon being charged afterwards with his breech of agreement Douglas responded that Lovejoy "bantered and badgered" him so persistently he could not gracefully resist the encounter. The whole thing thoroughly displeased Lincoln.

During this campaign Lincoln was nominated and elected to the Legislature. This was done in the face of his unwillingness and over his protest. On the ticket with him was Judge Logan. Both were elected by a majority of about 600 votes. Lincoln, being ambitious to reach the United States Senate, and warmly encouraged in his aspirations by his wife, resigned his seat in the Legislature in order that he might the more easily be elected to succeed his old rival James Shields, who was then one of the senators from Illinois. His canvass for that exalted office was marked by his characteristic activity and vigilance. During the anxious moments that intervened between the general election and the assembling of the Legislature he slept, like Napoleon, with one eye open. While attending court at Clinton on the 11th of November, a few days after the election, he wrote to a party friend in the town of Paris: "I have a suspicion that a Whig has been elected to the Legislature from Edgar. If this is not so, why then, 'nix cum arous;' but if it is so, then could you not make a mark with him for me for U.S. Senator? I really have some chance. Please write me at Springfield giving me the names, post offices, and political positions of your Representative and Senator, whoever they may be. Let this be confidential."

That man who thinks Lincoln calmly sat down and gathered his robes about him, waiting for the people to call him, has a very erroneous knowledge of Lincoln. He was always calculating, and always planning ahead. His ambition was a little engine that knew no rest. The vicissitudes of a political campaign brought into play all his tact and management and developed to its fullest extent his latent industry. In common with other politicians he never overlooked a newspaper man who had it in his power to say a good or bad thing of him. The press of that day was not so powerful an institution as now, but ambitious politicians courted the favor of a newspaper man with as much zeal as the same class of men have done in later days. I remember a letter Lincoln once wrote to the editor of an obscure little country newspaper in southern Illinois in which he warms up to him in the following style. "Friend Harding: I have been reading your paper for three or four years and have paid you nothing for it." He then encloses ten dollars and admonishes the editor with innocent complacency: "Put it into your pocket, saying nothing further about it." Very soon thereafter, he prepared an article on political matters and sent it to the rural journalist, requesting its publication in the editorial columns of his "valued paper," but the latter having followed Lincoln's directions and stowed the ten dollars away in his pocket, and alive to the importance of his journal's influence, declined, "because," he said, "I long ago made it a rule to publish nothing as editorial matter not written by myself." Lincoln read the editor's answer to me. Although the laugh was on Lincoln he enjoyed the joke heartily. "That editor," he said, "has a rather lofty but proper conception of true journalism."

Meanwhile the Legislature had convened and the Senatorial question came on for solution. The history of this contest is generally understood, and the world has repeatedly been told how Lincoln was led to expect the place and would have won but for the apostasy of the five Anti-Nebraska men of Democratic antecedents who clung to and finally forced the election of Lyman Trumbull. The student of history in after years will be taught to revere the name of Lincoln for his exceeding magnanimity in inducing his friends to abandon him at the crucial period and save Trumbull, while he himself disappeared beneath the waves of defeat.

This frustration of Lincoln's ambition had a marked effect on his political views. It was plain to him now that the "irrepressible conflict" was not far ahead. With the strengthening of his faith in a just cause so long held in abeyance he became more defiant each day. But in the very nature of things he dared not be as bold and outspoken as I. With him every word and sentence had to be weighed and its effects calculated, before being uttered; but with me that operation had to be reversed if done at all. An incident that occurred about this time will show how his views were broadening. Some time after the election of Trumbull a young Negro, the son of a colored woman in Springfield known as Polly, went from his home to St. Louis and there hired as a hand on a lower Mississippi boat—for what special service, I do not recollect—arriving in New Orleans without what were known as free papers. Though born free he was subjected to the tyranny of the "black code," all the more stringent because of the recent utterances of the Abolitionists in the North, and was kept in prison until his boat had left. Then, as no one was especially interested in him, he was forgotten. After a certain length of time established by law, he would inevitably have been sold in slavery to defray prison expenses had not Lincoln and I interposed our aid. The mother came to us with the story of the wrong done her son and induced us to interfere in her behalf. We went first to see the Governor of Illinois, who, after patient and thorough examination of the law, responded that he had no right or power to interfere. Recourse was then had to the Governor of Louisiana, who responded in like manner. We were sorely perplexed. A second interview with the Governor of Illinois resulting in nothing favorable, Lincoln rose from his chair, hat in hand, and exclaimed with some emphasis: "By God, Governor, I'll make the ground in this country too hot for the foot of a slave, whether you have the legal power to secure the release of this boy or not." Having exhausted all legal means to recover the Negro we dropped our relation as lawyers to the case. Lincoln drew up a subscription list, which I circulated, collecting funds enough to purchase the young man's liberty. The money was sent to Col. A. P. Field, a friend of ours in New Orleans, who applied it as directed, and it restored the prisoner to his overjoyed mother.

The political history of the country, commencing in 1854 and continuing until the outbreak of the Rebellion, furnishes the student a constant succession of stirring and sometimes bloody scenes. No sooner had Lincoln emerged from the senatorial contest in February, 1855, and absorbed himself in the law, than the outrages on the borders of Missouri and Kansas began to arrest public attention. The stories of raids, election frauds, murders, and other crimes were moving eastward with marked rapidity. These outbursts of frontier lawlessness, led and sanctioned by the avowed proslavery element, were not only stirring up the Abolitionists to fever heat, but touching the hearts of humanity in general. In Illinois an association was formed to aid the cause of "Free-Soil" men in Kansas. In the meetings of these bands the Abolitionists of course took the most prominent part. At Springfield we were energetic, vigilant, almost revolutionary. We recommended the employment of any means, however desperate, to promote and defend the cause of freedom. At one of these meetings Lincoln was called on for a speech. He responded to the request, counselling moderation and less bitterness in dealing with the situation before us. We were belligerent in tone, and clearly out of patience with the Government. Lincoln opposed the notion of coercive measures with the possibility of resulting bloodshed, advising us to eschew resort to the bullet. "You can better succeed," he declared, "with the ballot. You can peaceably then redeem the Government and preserve the liberties of mankind through your votes and voice and moral influence. . . . Let there be peace. Revolutionize through the ballot box, and restore the Government once more to the affections and hearts of men by making it express, as it was intended to do, the highest spirit of justice and liberty. Your attempt, if there be such, to resist the laws of Kansas by force is criminal and wicked; and all your feeble attempts will be follies and end in bringing sorrow on your heads and ruin the cause you would freely die to preserve!" These judicious words of counsel, while they reduced somewhat our ardor and our desperation, only placed before us in their real colors the grave features of the situation. We raised a neat sum of money, Lincoln showing his sincerity by joining in the subscription, and forwarded it to our friends in Kansas.

The Whig party, having accomplished its mission in the political world, was now on the eve of a great break-up. Lincoln realized this and, though proverbially slow in his movements, prepared to find a firm footing when the great rush of waters should come and the maddening freshet sweep former landmarks out of sight. Of the strongest significance in this connection is a letter written by him at this juncture to an old friend in Kentucky, who called to his attention their differences of views on the wrong of slavery. Speaking of his observation of the treatment of the slaves, he says: "I confess I hate to see the poor creatures hunted down and caught and carried back to their unrequited toils; but I bite my lips and keep quiet. In 1841 you and I had rather a tedious low-water trip on a steamboat from Louisville to St. Louis. You may remember, as I well do, that from Louisville to the mouth of the Ohio, there were on board ten or a dozen slaves shackled together with irons. That sight was a continued torment to me; and I see something like it every time I touch the Ohio or any slave border. It is not fair for you to assume that I have no interest in a thing which has, and continually exercises, the power of making me miserable. You ought rather to appreciate how much the great body of the Northern people do crucify their feelings in order to maintain their loyalty to the Constitution and the Union. I do oppose the extension of slavery because my judgment and feeling so prompt me; and I am under no obligation to the contrary. If for this you and I must differ, differ we must."

Finding himself drifting about with the disorganized elements that floated together after the angry political waters had subsided, it became apparent to Lincoln that if he expected to figure as a leader he must take a stand himself. Mere hatred of slavery and opposition to the injustice of the Kansas-Nebraska legislation were not all that were required of him. He must be a Democrat, Know-Nothing, Abolitionist, or Republican, or forever float about in the great political sea without compass, rudder, or sail. At length he declared himself. Believing the times were ripe for more advanced movements, in the spring of 1856 I drew up a paper for the friends of freedom to sign, calling a county convention in Springfield to select delegates for the forthcoming Republican State convention in Bloomington. The paper was freely circulated and generously signed. Lincoln was absent at the time and, believing I knew what his "feeling and judgment" on the vital questions of the hour were, I took the liberty to sign his name to the call. The whole was then published in the

Springfield *Journal*. No sooner had it appeared than John T. Stuart, who, with others, was endeavoring to retard Lincoln in his advanced movements, rushed into the office and excitedly asked if "Lincoln had signed the Abolition call in the *Journal?*" I answered in the negative, adding that I had signed his name myself. To the question, "Did Lincoln authorize you to sign it?" I returned an emphatic "No." "Then," exclaimed the startled and indignant Stuart, "you have ruined him." But I was by no means alarmed at what others deemed inconsiderate and hasty action. I thought I understood Lincoln thoroughly, but in order to vindicate myself if assailed I immediately sat down, after Stuart had rushed out of the office, and wrote Lincoln, who was then in Tazewell County attending court, a brief account of what I had done and how much stir it was creating in the ranks of his conservative friends. If he approved or disapproved my course I asked him to write or telegraph me at once. In a brief time came his answer: "All right; go ahead. Will meet you—radicals and all." Stuart subsided, and the conservative spirits who hovered around Springfield no longer held control of the political fortunes of Abraham Lincoln.

The Republican party came into existence in Illinois as a party at Bloomington, May 29, 1856. The State convention of all opponents of Anti-Nebraska legislation, referred to in a foregoing paragraph, had been set for that day. Judd, Yates, Trumbull, Swett, and Davis were there; so also was Lovejoy, who, like Otis of colonial fame, was a flame of fire. The firm of Lincoln and Herndon was represented by both members in person. The gallant William H. Bissell, who had ridden at the head of the Second Illinois Regiment at the battle of Buena Vista in the Mexican war, was nominated as governor. The convention adopted a platform ringing with strong Anti-Nebraska sentiments, and then and there gave the Republican party its official christening. The business of the convention being over, Mr. Lincoln, in response to repeated calls, came forward and delivered a speech of such earnestness and power that no one who heard it will ever forget the effect it produced. In referring to this speech some years ago I used the following rather graphic language: "I have heard or read all of Mr. Lincoln's great speeches, and I give it as my opinion that the Bloomington speech was the grand effort of this life. Heretofore he had simply argued the slavery question on grounds of policy—the statesman's grounds—never reaching the question of the radical and the eternal right. Now he was newly baptized and freshly born; he had the fervor of a new convert; the smothered flame broke out; enthusiasm unusual to him blazed up; his eyes were aglow with an inspiration; he felt justice; his heart was alive to the right; his sympathies, remarkably deep for him, burst forth, and he stood before the throne of the eternal Right. His speech was full of fire and energy and force; it was logic; it was pathos; it was enthusiasm; it was justice, equity, truth, and right set ablaze by the divine fires of a soul maddened by the wrong; it was hard, heavy, knotty, gnarly, backed with wrath. I attempted for about fifteen minutes as was usual with me then to take notes, but at the end of that time I threw pen and paper away and lived only in the inspiration of the hour. If Mr. Lincoln was six feet, four inches high usually, at Bloomington that day he was seven feet, and inspired at that. From that day to the day of his death he stood firm in the right. He felt his great cross, had his great idea, nursed it, kept it, taught it to others, in his fidelity bore witness of it to his death, and finally sealed it with his precious blood." The foregoing paragraph, used by me in a lecture in 1866, may to the average reader seem somewhat vivid in description, besides inclining to extravagance in imagery, yet although more than twenty years have passed since it was written I have never seen the need of altering a single sentence. I still adhere to the substantial truthfulness of the scene as described. Unfortunately Lincoln's speech was never written out nor printed, and we are obliged to depend for its reproduction upon personal recollection.

Not only in Springfield but everywhere else the founders of the Republican party—the apostles of freedom—went out to battle for the righteousness of their cause. Lincoln, having as usual been named as one of the Presidential electors, canvassed the State, making in all about fifty speeches. He was in demand everywhere. I have before me a package of letters addressed to him, inviting him to speak at almost every county seat in the

State. Yates wanted him to go to one section of the State, Washburne to another, and Trumbull still another; while every crossroads politician and legislative aspirant wanted him "down in our country, where we need your help." Joshua R. Giddings wrote him words of encouragement. "You may start," said the valiant old Abolitionist in a letter from Peoria, "on the one great issue of restoring Kansas and Nebraska to freedom, or rather of restoring the Missouri Compromise, and in this State no power on earth can withstand you on that issue." The demand for Lincoln was not confined to his own State. Indiana sent for him, Wisconsin also, while Norman B. Judd and Ebenezer Peck, who were stumping Iowa, sent for him to come there. A town committee invited him to come during "our Equestrian Fair on the 9th, 10th, and 11th," evidently anticipating a three days' siege. An enthusiastic officer in a neighboring town urges him: "Come to our place, because in you do our people place more confidence than in any other man. Men who do not read want the story told as you only can tell it. Others may make fine speeches, but it would not be 'Lincoln said so in his speech'." A jubilant friend in Chicago writes: "Push on the column of freedom. Give the Buck Africans plenty to do in Egypt. The hour of our redemption draweth nigh. We are coming to Springfield with 20,000 majority!" A postmaster, acting under the courage of his convictions, implores him to visit his neighborhood. "The Democrats here," he insists, "are dyed in the wool. Thunder and lightning would not change their political complexion. I am postmaster here," he adds, confidentally, "for which reason I must ask you to keep this private, for if old Frank (President Pierce) were to hear of my support of Fremont I would get my walking papers sure enough." A settlement of Germans in southern Indiana asked to hear him; and the president of a college, in an invitation to address the students under his charge, characterizes him as "one providentially raised up for a time like this, and even should defeat come in the contest, it would be some consolation to remember we had Hector for a leader."

And thus it was everywhere. Lincoln's importance in the conduct of the campaign was apparent to all, and his canvass was characterized by his usual vigor and effectiveness. He was

especially noted for his attempt to break down the strength of
Fillmore, who was nominated as a third party candidate and was
expected to divide the Republican vote. He tried to wean away
Fillmore's adherents by an adroit and ingenious letter[1] sent to
those suspected of the latter's support, and marked confidential,
in which he strove to show that in clinging to their candidate
they were really aiding the election of Buchanan. But the effort
proved unavailing, for in spite of all his arguments and appeals a
large number of the Fillmore men clung tenaciously to their
leader, resulting in Buchanan's election. The vote in Illinois

[1] One of these letters which Lincoln wrote to counteract the Fillmore movement
is still in my possession. As it is more or less characteristic I copy it entire:

Springfield, September 8, 1856.

Harrison Maltby, Esq.
Dear Sir:
*I understand you are a Fillmore man. Let me prove to you that every vote
withheld from Fremont and given to Fillmore in this State actually lessens Fillmore's chance of being President.*

*Suppose Buchanan gets all the slave States and Pennsylvania and any other
one State besides; then he is elected, no matter who gets all the rest. But suppose Fillmore gets the two slave States of Maryland and Kentucky, then
Buchanan is not elected; Fillmore goes into the House of Representatives and
may be made President by a compromise. But suppose again Fillmore's friends
throw away a few thousand votes on him in Indiana and Illinois; it will inevitably give these States to Buchanan, which will more than compensate him for
the loss of Maryland and Kentucky; it will elect him, and leave Fillmore no
chance in the House of Representatives or out of it.*

*This is as plain as adding up the weight of three small hogs. As Mr. Fillmore
has no possible chance to carry Illinois for himself it is plainly to his interest to
let Fremont take it and thus keep it out of the hands of Buchanan. Be not
deceived. Buchanan is the hard horse to beat in this race. Let him have Illinois,
and nothing can beat him; and he will get Illinois if men persist in throwing
away votes upon Mr. Fillmore. Does some one persuade you that Mr. Fillmore
can carry Illinois? Nonsense! There are over seventy newspapers in Illinois opposing Buchanan, only three or four of which support Mr. Fillmore, all the rest
going for Fremont. Are not these newspapers a fair index of the proportion of
the votes? If not, tell me why.*

*Again, of these three or four Fillmore newspapers, two at least are sup-
ported in part by the Buchanan men, as I understand. Do not they know
where the shoe pinches? They know the Fillmore movement helps them,
and therefore they help it.*

Do think these things over and then act according to your judgment.

Yours very truly,
A. Lincoln.

(Confidential)

stood, Buchanan 105,344, Fremont 96,180, and Fillmore 37,451. At the same time Bissell was elected governor by a majority of 4,729 over W. A. Richardson, Democrat. After the heat and burden of the day Lincoln returned home, bearing with him more and greater laurels than ever. The signs of the times indicated, and the result of the canvass demonstrated, that he and he alone was powerful enough to meet the redoubtable Little Giant in a greater conflict yet to follow.

9
Debates with Douglas

I shall be forced to omit much that happened during the interval between the election of Buchanan and the campaign of 1858, for the reason that it would not only swell this work to undue proportions, but be a mere repetition of what has been better told by other writers. It is proper to note in passing, however, that Mr. Lincoln's reputation as a political speaker was no longer bounded by the border lines of Illinois. It had passed beyond the Wabash, the Ohio, and the Mississippi rivers, and while his pronounced stand on the slavery question had increased the circle of his admirers in the North it provoked a proportionate amount of execration in the South. He could not help the feeling that he was now the leading Republican in his State, and he was therefore more or less jealous of his prerogative. Formidable in debate, plain in speech, without pretence of literary acquirements, he was none the less self-reliant. He already envied the ascendency and domination Douglas exercised over his followers, and felt keenly the slight given him by others of his own faith whom he conceived were disposed to prevent his attaining the leadership of his party. I remember early in 1858 of his coming into the office one morning and speaking in very dejected terms of the treatment he was receiving at the hands of Horace Greeley. "I think Greeley," he complained, "is not doing me right. His conduct, I believe, savors a little of injustice. I am a true Republican and have been tried already in the hottest part of the anti-slavery fight, and yet I find him taking up Douglas, a veritable dodger—once a tool of the South, now its enemy—and pushing him to the front. He forgets that when he does that he pulls me down at the same time. I fear Greeley's attitude will damage me with Sumner, Seward, Wilson, Phillips, and other friends in the East." This was said with so much of mingled sadness and earnestness that I was deeply impressed. Lincoln was gloomy and restless the entire day. Greeley's letters were driving the enthusiasm out of him. He seemed unwilling to attend to any business, and finally, just

before noon, left the office, going over to the United States
Court room to play a game of chess with Judge Treat, and did
not return again that day. I pondered a good deal over Lincoln's
dejection, and that night, after weighing the matter well in
mind, resolved to go to the eastern States myself and endeavor
to sound some of the great men there. The next day, on apprising Lincoln of my determination, he questioned its propriety.
Our relations, he insisted, were so intimate that a wrong construction might be put upon the movement. I listened carefully
to him, but as I had never been beyond the Alleghenies I packed
my valise and went, notwithstanding his objections. I had been
in correspondence on my own account with Greeley, Seward,
Sumner, Phillips, and others for several years, had kept them informed of the feelings of our people and the political campaigns
in their various stages, but had never met any of them save
Greeley. I enjoyed heartily the journey and the varied sights and
scenes that attended it. Aside from my mission, the trip was a
great success. The magnificent buildings, the display of wealth
in the large cities and prosperous manufacturing towns,
broadened the views of one whose vision had never extended
beyond the limits of the Illinois prairies. In Washington I saw
and dined with Trumbull, who went over the situation with me.
Trumbull had written to Lincoln shortly before that he thought
it "useless to speculate upon the further course of Douglas or the
effect it is to have in Illinois or other States. He himself does not
know where he is going or where he will come out." At my interview with Trumbull, however, he directed me to assure Mr.
Lincoln that Douglas did not mean to join the Republican party,
however great the breach between himself and the administration might be. "We Republicans here," he said exultingly in
another letter to Lincoln, "are in good spirits, and are standing
back to let the fight go on between Douglas and his former associates. Lincoln will lose nothing by this if he can keep the attention of our Illinois people from being diverted from the great
and vital question of the day to the minor and temporary issues
which are now being discussed." In Washington I saw also
Seward, Wilson, and others of equal prominence. Douglas was
confined to his house by illness, but on receiving my card he
directed me to be shown up to his room. We had a pleasant and

interesting interview. Of course the conversation soon turned on Lincoln. In answer to an inquiry regarding the latter I remarked that Lincoln was pursuing the even tenor of his way. "He is not in anybody's way," I contended, "not even in yours, Judge Douglas." He was sitting up in a chair smoking a cigar. Between puffs he responded that neither was he in the way of Lincoln or any one else, and did not intend to invite conflict. He conceived that he had achieved what he had set out to do, and hence did not feel that his course need put him in opposition to Mr. Lincoln or his party. "Give Mr. Lincoln my regards," he said, rather warmly, "when you return, and tell him I have crossed the river and burned my boat." Leaving Washington, my next point was New York, where I met the editor of the *Anti-Slavery Standard*, Horace Greeley, Henry Ward Beecher, and others. I had a long talk with Greeley, whom I noticed leaned toward Douglas. I found, however, he was not at all hostile to Lincoln. I presented the latter's case in the best phase I knew how, but while I drew but little from him, I left feeling that he hadn't been entirely won over. He introduced me to Beecher, who, as everybody else did, inquired after Lincoln and through me sent him words of encouragement and praise. From New York I went to Boston, and from the latter place I wrote Lincoln a letter which happily I found not long since in a bundle of Lincoln's letters, and which I insert here, believing it affords a better reflex of the situation at the time than anything I might see fit to say now. Here it is:

Revere House,
Boston, Mass., March 24, 1858.

Friend Lincoln.

I am in this city of notions, and am well—very well indeed. I wrote you a hasty letter from Washington some days ago, since which time I have been in Philadelphia, Baltimore, New York, and now here. I saw Greeley, and so far as any of our conversation is interesting to you I will relate. And we talked, say twenty minutes. He evidently wants Douglas sustained and sent back to the Senate. He did not say so in so many words, yet his feelings are with Douglas. I know it from the spirit and drift of his conversation. He talked bitterly—somewhat so—against the papers in Illinois, and said they were fools. I asked him this question,

'Greeley, do you want to see a third party organized, or do you want Douglas to ride to power through the North, which he has so much abused and betrayed?' and to which he replied, 'Let the future alone; it will all come right. Douglas is a brave man. Forget the past and sustain the righteous.' Good God, righteous, eh!

Since I have landed in Boston I have seen much that was entertaining and interesting. This morning I was introduced to Governor Banks. He and I had a conversation about Republicanism and especially about Douglas. He asked me this question, 'You will sustain Douglas in Illinois, won't you?' and to which I said 'No, never!' He affected to be much surprised, and so the matter dropped and turned on Republicanism, or in general—Lincoln. Greeley's and other sheets that laud Douglas, Harris, et al., want them sustained, and will try to do it. Several persons have asked me the same question which Banks asked, and evidently they get their cue, ideas, or what not from Greeley, Seward, et al. By-the-bye, Greeley remarked to me this, "The Republican standard is too high; we want something practical.'

This may not be interesting to you, but however it may be, it is my duty to state what is going on, so that you may head it off—counteract it in some way. I hope it can be done. The northern men are cold to me—somewhat repellent.

> Your friend,
> W.H. Herndon.

On my return home I had encouraging news to relate. I told Lincoln of the favorable mention I had heard of him by Phillips, Sumner, Seward, Garrison, Beecher, and Greeley. I brought with me additional sermons and lectures by Theodore Parker, who was warm in his commendation of Lincoln. One of these was a lecture on "The Effect of Slavery on the American People," which was delivered in the Music Hall in Boston, and which I gave to Lincoln, who read and returned it. He liked especially the following expression, which he marked with a pencil, and which he in substance afterwards used in his Gettysburg address: "Democracy is direct self-government, over all the people, for all the people, by all the people."

Meanwhile, passing by other events which have become inter-

woven in the history of the land, we reach April, 1858, at which
time the Democratic State convention met and, besides nominating candidates for State offices, endorsed Mr. Douglas' services
in the Senate, thereby virtually renominating him for that exalted office. In the very nature of things Lincoln was the man
already chosen in the hearts of the Republicans of Illinois for the
same office, and therefore with singular appropriateness they
passed, with great unanimity, at their convention in Springfield
on the 16th of June, the characteristic resolution: "That Hon.
Abraham Lincoln is our first and only choice for United States
Senator to fill the vacancy about to be created by the expiration
of Mr. Douglas' term of office." There was of course no surprise
in this for Mr. Lincoln. He had been all along led to expect it,
and with that in view had been earnestly and quietly at work
preparing a speech in acknowledgment of the honor about to be
conferred on him. This speech he wrote on stray envelopes and
scraps of paper, as ideas suggested themselves, putting them
into that miscellaneous and convenient receptacle, his hat. As
the convention drew near he copied the whole on connected
sheets, carefully revising every line and sentence, and fastened
them together, for reference during the delivery of the speech,
and for publication. The former precaution, however, was unnecessary, for he had studied and read over what he had written
so long and carefully that he was able to deliver it without the
least hesitation or difficulty. A few days before the convention,
when he was at work on the speech, I remember that Jesse K.
Dubois, who was Auditor of State, came into the office and,
seeing Lincoln busily writing, inquired what he was doing or
what he was writing. Lincoln answered gruffly, "It's something
you may see or hear sometime, but I'll not let you see it now."
I myself knew what he was writing, but he having asked neither
my opinion nor that of anyone else, I did not venture to offer
any suggestions. After he had finished the final draft of the
speech, he locked the office door, drew the curtain across the
glass panel in the door, and read it to me. At the end of each
paragraph he would halt and wait for my comments. I remember
what I said after hearing the first paragraph, wherein occurs the
celebrated figure of the house divided against itself: "It is true,
but is it wise or politic to say so?" He responded: "That expres-

sion is a truth of all human experience, 'a house divided against itself cannot stand,' and 'he that runs may read.' The proposition also is true, and has been for six thousand years. I want to use some universally known figure expressed in simple language as universally well-known, that may strike home to the minds of men in order to raise them up to the peril of the times. I do not believe I would be right in changing or omitting it. I would rather be defeated with this expression in the speech, and uphold and discuss it before the people, than be victorious without it." This was not the first time Lincoln had endorsed the dogma that our Government could not long endure part slave and part free. He had incorporated it in a speech at Bloomington in 1856, but in obedience to the emphatic protest of Judge T. Lyle Dickey and others, who conceived the idea that its "delivery would make abolitionists of all the North and slavery propagandists of all the South, and thereby precipitate a struggle which might end in disunion," he consented to suspend its repetition, but only for that campaign. Now, however, the situation had changed somewhat. There had been a shifting of scenes, so to speak. The Republican party had gained some in strength and more in moral effectiveness and force. Nothing could keep back in Lincoln, any longer, sentiments of right and truth, and he prepared to give the fullest expression to both in all future contests.

Before delivering his speech he invited a dozen or so of his friends over to the library of the State House, where he read and submitted it to them. After the reading he asked each man for his opinion. Some condemned and not one endorsed it. One man, more forcible than elegant, characterized it as a "d—d fool utterance;" another said the doctrine was "ahead of its time;" and still another contended that it would drive away a good many voters fresh from the Democrats' ranks. Each man attacked it in his criticism. I was the last to respond. Although the doctrine announced was rather rank, yet it suited my views, and I said, "Lincoln, deliver that speech as read and it will make you President." At the time I hardly realized the force of my prophecy. Having patiently listened to these various criticisms from his friends—all of which with a single exception were adverse—he rose from his chair, and after alluding to the careful study and intense thought he had given the question, he answered all their objections substantially as follows: "Friends, this thing has been retarded long enough. The time has come when these sentiments should be uttered; and if it is decreed that I should go down because of this speech, then let me go down linked to the truth—let me die in the advocacy of what is just and right." The next day, the 17th, the speech was delivered just as we had heard it read. Up to this time Seward had held sway over the North by his "higher-law" sentiments, but the "house-divided-against-itself" speech by Lincoln in my opinion drove the nail into Seward's political coffin.[1]

Lincoln had now created in reality a more profound impression than he or his friends anticipated. Many Republicans deprecated the advanced ground he had taken, the more so as the Democrats rejoiced that it afforded them an issue clear and well-defined. Numbers of his friends distant from Springfield, on reading his speech, wrote him censorious letters; and one well-informed coworker predicted his defeat, charging it to the first ten lines of the speech. These complaints, coming apparently from every quarter, Lincoln bore with great patience. To one complainant who followed him into his office he said proudly, "If I had to draw a pen across my record, and erase my whole life from sight, and I had one poor gift or choice left as to what I should save from the wreck, I should choose that speech and leave it to the world unerased."

Meanwhile Douglas had returned from Washington to his home in Chicago. Here he rested for a few days until his friends and coworkers had arranged the details of a public reception on the 9th of July, when he delivered from the balcony of the Tremont House a speech intended as an answer to the one made by Lincoln in Springfield. Lincoln was present at this reception, but took no part in it. The next day, however, he replied. Both speeches were delivered at the same place. Leaving Chicago, Douglas passed on down to Bloomington and Springfield, where

[1] If any student of oratorical history, after reading Lincoln's speech on this occasion, will refer to Webster's reply to Hayne in the Senate, he will be struck with the similarity in figure and thought in the opening lines of both speeches. In fact, it may not be amiss to note that, in this instance, Webster's effort was carefully read by Lincoln and served in part as his model.

he spoke on the 16th and 17th of July respectively. On the evening of the latter day Lincoln responded again in a most effective and convincing effort. The contest now took on a different
phase. Lincoln's Republican friends urged him to draw Douglas
into a joint debate, and he accordingly sent him a challenge on
the 24th of July. It is not necessary, I suppose, to reproduce here
the correspondence that passed between these great leaders. On
the 30th Douglas finally accepted the proposition to "divide
time, and address the same audiences," naming seven different
places, one in each Congressional district, outside of Chicago
and Springfield, for joint meetings. The places and dates were,
Ottawa, August 21; Freeport, August 27; Jonesboro, September 15;
Charleston, September 18; Galesburg, October 7; Quincy, October 13; and Alton, October 15. "I agree to your suggestion,"
wrote Douglas, "that we shall alternately open and close the discussion. I will speak at Ottawa one hour, you can reply, occupy-
ing an hour and a half, and I will then follow for half an hour.
At Freeport you shall open the discussion and speak one hour, I
will follow for an hour and a half, and you can then reply for
half an hour. We will alternate in like manner in each successive
place." To this arrangement Lincoln on the 31st gave his consent, "although," he wrote, "by the terms as you propose you
take four openings and closes to my three."

History furnishes few characters whose lives and careers were
so nearly parallel as those of Lincoln and Douglas. They met for
the first time at the Legislature in Vandalia in 1834, where Lincoln was a member of the House of Representatives and Douglas
was in the lobby. The next year Douglas was also a member. In
1839 both were admitted to practice in the Supreme Court of Illinois on the same day. In 1841 both courted the same young
lady. In 1846 both represented Illinois in Congress at Washington, the one in the upper and the other in the lower House. In
1858 they were opposing candidates for United States Senator;
and finally, to complete the remarkable counterpart, both were
candidates for the Presidency in 1860. While it is true that their
ambitions ran in parallel lines, yet they were exceedingly unlike
in all other particulars. Douglas was short—something over five
feet high—heavy set, with a large head, broad shoulders, deep
chest, and striking features. He was polite and affable, but fear-

less. He had that unique trait, magnetism, fully developed in his nature, and that attracted a host of friends and readily made him a popular idol. He had had extensive experience in debate, and had been trained by contact for years with the great minds and orators of Congress. He was full of political history, well informed on general topics, eloquent almost to the point of brilliancy, self-confident to the point of arrogance, and a dangerous competitor in every respect. What he lacked in ingenuity he made up in strategy, and if in debate he could not tear down the structure of his opponent's argument by a direct and violent attack, he was by no means reluctant to resort to a strained restatement of the latter's position or to the extravagance of ridicule. Lincoln knew his man thoroughly and well.[2] He had often met Douglas on the stump; was familiar with his tactics, and though fully aware of his "want of fixed political morals," was not averse to measuring swords with the elastic and flexible "Little Giant."

Lincoln himself was constructed on an entirely different foundation. His base was plain common sense, direct statement, and the inflexibility of logic. In physical make-up he was cold—at least not magnetic—and made no effort to dazzle people by his bearing. He cared nothing for a following, and though he had often before struggled for a political prize, yet in his efforts he never had strained his well-known spirit of fairness or open love of the truth. He analyzed everything, laid every statement bare, and by dint of his broad reasoning powers and manliness of admission inspired his hearers with deep conviction of his earnestness and honesty. Douglas may have electrified the crowd with his eloquence or charmed them with his majestic bearing and dexterity in debates, but as each man, after the meetings

---

[2] An erroneous impression has grown up in recent years concerning Douglas's ability and standing as a lawyer. One of the latest biographies of Lincoln credits him with many of the artifices of the "shyster." This is not only unfair, but decidedly untrue. I always found Douglas at the bar to be a broad, fair, and liberal-minded man. Although not a thorough student of the law his large fund of good common sense kept him in the front rank. He was equally generous and courteous, and he never stooped to gain a case. I know that Lincoln entertained the same view of him. It was only in politics that Douglas demonstrated any want of inflexibility and rectitude, and then only did Lincoln manifest a lack of faith in his morals.

were over and the applause had died away, went to his home, his head rang with Lincoln's logic and appeal to manhood.

A brief description of Mr. Lincoln's appearance on the stump and of his manner when speaking may not be without interest. When standing erect he was six feet four inches high. He was lean in flesh and ungainly in figure. Aside from the sad, pained look due to habitual melancholy, his face had no characteristic or fixed expression. He was thin through the chest, and hence slightly stoop-shouldered. When he arose to address courts, juries, or crowds of people, his body inclined forward to a slight degree. At first he was very awkward, and it seemed a real labor to adjust himself to his surroundings. He struggled for a time under a feeling of apparent diffidence and sensitiveness, and these only added to his awkwardness. I have often seen and sympathized with Mr. Lincoln during these moments. When he began speaking, his voice was shrill, piping, and unpleasant. His manner, his attitude, his dark, yellow face, wrinkled and dry, his oddity of pose, his diffident movements—everything seemed to be against him, but only for a short time. After having arisen, he generally placed his hands behind him, the back of his left hand in the palm of his right, the thumb and fingers of his right hand clasped around the left arm at the wrist. For a few moments he displayed the combination of awkwardness, sensitiveness, and diffidence. As he proceeded he became somewhat animated, and to keep in harmony with his growing warmth his hands relaxed their grasp and fell to his side. Presently he clasped them in front of him, interlocking his fingers, one thumb meanwhile chasing another. His speech now requiring more emphatic utter-ance, his fingers unlocked and his hands fell apart. His left arm was thrown behind, the back of his hand resting against his body, his right hand seeking his side. By this time he had gained sufficient composure, and his real speech began. He did not ges-ticulate as much with his hands as with his head. He used the latter frequently, throwing it with vim this way and that. This movement was a significant one when he sought to enforce his statement. It sometimes came with a quick jerk, as if throwing off electric sparks into combustible material. He never sawed the air nor rent space into tatters and rags as some orators do. He never acted for stage effect. He was cool, considerate, reflective—in time self-possessed and self-reliant. His style was clear, terse, and compact. In argument he was logical, demonstrative, and fair. He was careless of his dress, and his clothes, instead of fitting neatly as did the garments of Douglas on the latter's well-rounded form, hung loosely on his giant frame. As he moved along in his speech he became freer and less uneasy in his movements; to that extent he was graceful. He had a perfect naturalness, a strong individuality; and to that extent he was dignified. He despised glitter, show, set forms, and shams. He spoke with effectiveness and to move the judgment as well as the emotions of men. There was a world of meaning and emphasis in the long, bony finger of his right hand as he dotted the ideas on the minds of his hearers. Sometimes, to express joy or pleasure, he would raise both hands at an angle of about fifty degrees, the palms upward, as if desirous of embracing the spirit of that which he loved. If the sentiment was one of detestation—denunciation of slavery, for example—both arms, thrown upward and fists clenched, swept through the air, and he expressed an execration that was truly sublime. This was one of his most effective gestures, and signified most vividly a fixed determination to drag down the object of his hatred and trample it in the dust. He always stood squarely on his feet, toe even with toe; that is, he never put one foot before the other. He neither touched nor leaned on anything for support. He made but few changes in his positions and attitudes. He never ranted, never walked backward and forward on the platform. To ease his arms he frequently caught hold, with his left hand, of the lapel of his coat, keeping his thumb upright and leaving his right hand free to gesticulate. The designer of the monument recently erected in Chicago has happily caught him in just this attitude. As he proceeded with his speech the exercise of his vocal organs altered somewhat the tone of his voice. It lost in a measure its former acute and shrilling pitch, and mellowed into a more harmonious and pleasant sound. His form expanded, and, notwithstanding the sunken breast, he rose up a splendid and imposing figure. His little gray eyes flashed in a face aglow with the fire of his profound thoughts; and his uneasy movements and diffident manner sunk themselves beneath the wave of righteous indignation that came sweeping over him. Such was Lincoln the orator.

We can somewhat appreciate the feeling with which Douglas, aggressive and fearless though he was, welcomed a contest with such a man as Lincoln. Four years before, in a joint debate with him, he had asked for a cessation of forensic hostilities, conceding that his opponent of rail-splitting fame had given him "more trouble than all the United States Senate together." Now he was brought face to face with him again.

It is unnecessary and not in keeping with the purpose of this work to reproduce here the speeches made by either Lincoln or Douglas in their justly renowned debate. Briefly stated, Lincoln's position was announced in his opening speech at Springfield:

'A house divided against itself cannot stand.' I believe this Government cannot endure permanently half slave and half free. I do not expect the Union to be dissolved, I do not expect the house to fall—but I do expect it will cease to be divided. It will become all the one thing or the other. Either the opponents of slavery will arrest the further spread of it and place it where the public mind shall rest in the belief that it is in the course of ultimate extinction; or its advocates will push it forward till it becomes alike lawful in all the states, old as well as new, North as well as South.

The position of Douglas on the question of slavery was one of indifference. He advocated with all his power the doctrine of "Popular Sovereignty," a proposition, as quaintly put by Lincoln, which meant that, "if one man chooses to enslave another, no third man has a right to object." At the last joint discussion in Alton, Lincoln, after reflecting on the patriotism of any man who was so indifferent to the wrong of slavery that he cared not whether it was voted up or down, closed his speech with this stirring summary:

That [slavery] is the real issue. That is the issue that will continue in this country when these poor tongues of Judge Douglas and myself shall be silent. It is the eternal struggle between these two principles—right and wrong—throughout the world. They are the two principles that have stood face to face from the beginning of time, and will ever continue to struggle.

*The one is the common right of humanity, and the other the
divine right of kings. It is the same principle, in whatever shape
it develops itself. It is the same spirit that says: 'You work and
toil and earn bread, and I eat it.' No matter in what shape it
comes, whether from the mouth of a king who seeks to bestride
the people of his own nation and live by the fruit of their labor,
or from one race of men as an apology for enslaving another
race, it is the same tyrannical principle.*

During the canvass Mr. Lincoln, in addition to the seven meetings with Douglas, filled thirty-one appointments made by the
State Central Committee, besides speaking at many other times
and places not previously advertised. In his trips to and fro over
the State, between meetings, he would stop at Springfield sometimes, to consult with his friends or to post himself up on questions that occurred during the canvass. He kept me busy hunting up old speeches and gathering facts and statistics at the
State library. I made liberal clippings bearing in any way on the
questions of the hour from every newspaper I happened to see,
and kept him supplied with them; and on one or two occasions,
in answer to letters and telegrams, I sent books forward to him.
He had a little leather bound book, fastened in front with a
clasp, in which he and I both kept inserting newspaper slips and
newspaper comments until the canvass opened. In arranging for
the joint meetings and managing the crowds Douglas enjoyed
one great advantage. He had been United States Senator for several years, and had influential friends holding comfortable government offices all over the State. These men were on hand at
every meeting, losing no opportunity to applaud lustily all the
points Douglas made and to lionize him in every conceivable
way. The ingeniously contrived display of their enthusiasm had
a marked effect on certain crowds—a fact of which Lincoln
frequently complained to his friends. One who accompanied him
during the canvass relates this: "Lincoln and I were at the
Centralia agricultural fair the day after the debate an Jonesboro.
Night came on and we were tired, having been on the fair
grounds all day. We were to go north on the Illinois Central
railroad. The train was due at midnight, and the depot was full
of people. I managed to get a chair for Lincoln in the office of

the superintendent of the railroad, but small politicians would
intrude so that he could scarcely get a moment's sleep. The train
came and was filled instantly. I got a seat near the door for Lincoln and myself. He was worn out, and had to meet Douglas the
next day at Charleston. An empty car, called a saloon car, was
hitched on to the rear of the train and locked up. I asked the
conductor, who knew Lincoln and myself well—we were both
attorneys of the road—if Lincoln could not ride in that car; that
he was exhausted and needed rest; but the conductor refused. I
afterwards got him in by a stratagem. At the same time George
B. McClellan in person was taking Douglas around in a special
car and special train; and that was the unjust treatment Lincoln
got from the Illinois Central railroad. Every interest of that road
and every employee was against Lincoln and for Douglas."

The heat and dust and bonfires of the campaign at last came
to an end. The election took place on the second of November,
and while Lincoln received of the popular vote a majority of over
four thousand, yet the returns from the legislative districts fore-
shadowed his defeat. In fact, when the Senatorial election took
place in the Legislature, Douglas received fifty-four and Lincoln
forty-six votes—one of the results of the lamentable apportionment law then in operation.

Before passing to later events in Mr. Lincoln's life it is proper
to include in this chapter, as a specimen of his oratory at this
time, his eloquent reference to the Declaration of Independence
found in a speech delivered at Beardstown, August 12, and not
at Lewiston five days later, as many biographers have it. Aside
from its concise reasoning, the sublime thought it suggests entit-
les it to rank beside that great masterpiece, his Gettysburg
address. After alluding to the suppression by the Fathers of the
Republic of the slave trade, he says:

*These by their representatives in old Independence Hall said
to the whole race of men: 'We hold these truths to be self-
evident: that all men are created equal; that they are endowed
by their Creator with certain inalienable rights; that among
these are life, liberty, and the pursuit of happiness.' This was
their majestic interpretation of the economy of the universe.
This was their lofty, and wise, and noble understanding of the*

justice of the Creator to his creatures—yes, gentlemen, to all his creatures, to the whole great family of men. In their enlightened belief, nothing stamped with the divine image and likeness was sent into the world to be trodden on and degraded and imbruted by its fellows. They grasped not only the whole race of man then living, but they reached forward and seized upon the farthest posterity. They erected a beacon to guide their children, and their children's children, and the countless myriads who should inhabit the earth in other ages. Wise statesmen as they were, they knew the tendency of prosperity to breed tyrants, and so they established these great self-evident truths, that when in the distant future some man, some faction, some interest, should set up the doctrine that none but rich men, none but white men, or none but Anglo-Saxon white men were entitled to life, liberty, and the pursuit of happiness, their posterity might look up again to the Declaration of Independence and take courage to renew the battle which their fathers began, so that truth and justice and mercy and all the humane and Christian virtues might not be extinguished from the land; so that no man would hereafter dare to limit and circumscribe the great principles on which the temple of liberty was being built.

Now, my countrymen, if you have been taught doctrines conflicting with the great landmarks of the Declaration of Independence; if you have listened to suggestions which would take away from its grandeur and mutilate the fair symmetry of its proportions; if you have been inclined to believe that all men are not created equal in those inalienable rights enumerated by our chart of liberty: let me entreat you to come back. Return to the fountain whose waters spring close by the blood of the Revolution. Think nothing of me; take no thought for the political fate of any man whomsoever, but come back to the truths that are in the Declaration of Independence. You may do anything with me you choose, if you will but heed these sacred principles. You may not only defeat me for the Senate, but you may take me and put me to death. While pretending no indifference to earthly honors, I do claim to be actuated in this contest by something higher than an anxiety for office. I charge you to drop every paltry and insignificant thought for any man's success. It is nothing; I am nothing; Judge Douglas is nothing. But do not de-

stroy that immortal emblem of humanity—the Declaration of American Independence.

One of the newspaper men who heard this majestic oration wrote me as follows: "The apostrophe to the Declaration of Independence to which you refer was written by myself from a vivid recollection of Mr. Lincoln's speech at Beardstown, August 12, 1858. On the day following the delivery of the speech, as Mr. Lincoln and I were proceeding by steamer from Beardstown to Havana, I said to him that I had been greatly impressed by his concluding remarks of the day previous, and that if he would write them out for me I felt confident their publication would be highly beneficial to our cause as well as honorable to his own fame. He replied that he had but a faint recollection of any portion of the speech; that, like all his campaign speeches, it was necessarily extemporaneous; and that its good or bad effect depended upon the inspiration of the moment. He added that I had probably over-estimated the value of the remarks referred to. In reply to my question whether he had any objection to my writing them out from memory and putting them in the form of a verbatim report, he said, 'None at all.' I accordingly did so. I felt confident then and I feel equally assured now that I transcribed the peroration with absolute fidelity as to ideas and commendable fidelity as to language. I certainly aimed to reproduce his exact words, and my recollection of the passage as spoken was very clear. After I had finished writing I read it to Mr. Lincoln. When I had finished the reading he said, 'Well, those are my views, and if I said anything on the subject I must have said substantially that, but not nearly so well as that is said.' I remember this remark quite distinctly, and if the old steamer *Editor* is still in existence I could show the place where we were sitting. Having secured his assent to the publication I forwarded it to our paper, but inasmuch as my report of the Beardstown meeting had been already mailed I incorporated the remarks on the Declaration of Independence in my letter from Lewiston two or three days subsequently. . . . I do not remember ever having related these facts before, although they have often recurred to me as I have seen the peroration resuscitated again and again, and published (with good effect, I trust) in the newspapers of this country and England."

10

"A Nearer and More Personal View"

Before Mr. Lincoln surrenders himself completely to the public—for it is apparent he is fast approaching the great crisis of his career—it may not be entirely inappropriate to take a nearer and more personal view of him. A knowledge of his personal views and actions, a glimpse through the doorway of his home, and a more thorough acquaintance with his marked and strong points as they developed, will aid us greatly in forming our general estimate of the man. When Mr. Lincoln entered the domain of investigation he was a severe and persistent thinker, and had wonderful endurance; hence he was abstracted, and for that reason at times was somewhat unsocial, reticent, and uncommunicative. After his marriage it cannot be said that he liked the society of ladies; in fact, it was just what he did not like, though one of his biographers says otherwise. Lincoln had none of the tender ways that please a woman, and he could not, it seemed, by any positive act of his own make her happy. If his wife was happy, she was naturally happy, or made herself so in spite of countless drawbacks. He was, however, a good husband in his own peculiar way, and in his own way only.

If exhausted from severe and long-continued thought, he had to touch the earth again to renew his strength. When this weariness set in he would stop thought, and get down and play with a little dog or kitten to recover; and when the recovery came he would push it aside to play with its own tail. He treated men and women in much the same way. For fashionable society he had a marked dislike, although he appreciated its value in promoting the welfare of a man ambitious to succeed in politics. If he was invited out to dine or to mingle in some social gathering, and came in contact with the ladies, he treated them with becoming politeness; but the consciousness of his short-comings as a society man rendered him unusually diffident, and at the very first opportunity he would have the men separated from their ladies and crowded close around him in one corner of the parlor, listening to one of his characteristic stories. That a lady as proud and as ambitious to excercise the rights of supremacy in society as Mary Todd should repent of her marriage to the man I have just described surely need occasion no surprise in the mind of anyone. Both she and the man whose hand she accepted acted along the lines of human conduct and both reaped the bitter harvest of conjugal infelicity. In dealing with Mr. Lincoln's home life perhaps I am revealing an element of his character that has heretofore been kept from the world; but in doing so I feel sure I am treading on no person's toes, for all the actors in this domestic drama are dead, and the world seems ready to hear the facts. As his married life, in the opinion of all his friends, exerted a peculiar influence over Mr. Lincoln's political career there can be no impropriety, I apprehend, in throwing the light on it now. Mrs. Lincoln's disposition and nature have been dwelt upon in another chapter, and enough has been told to show that one of her greatest misfortunes was her inability to control her temper. Admit that, and everything can be explained. However cold and abstracted her husband may have appeared to others, however impressive, when aroused, may have seemed his indignation in public, he never gave vent to his feelings at home. He always meekly accepted as final the authority of his wife in all matters of domestic concern. This may explain somewhat the statement of Judge Davis that, "as a general rule, when all the lawyers of a Saturday evening would go home and see their families and friends, Lincoln would find some excuse and refuse to go. We said nothing, but it seemed to us all he was not domestically happy." He exercised no government of any kind over his household. His children did much as they pleased. Many of their antics he approved, and he restrained them in nothing. He never reproved them or gave them a fatherly frown. He was the most indulgent parent I have ever known. He was in the habit, when at home on Sunday, of bringing his two boys, Willie and Thomas—or "Tad"—down to the office to remain while his wife attended church. He seldom accompanied her there. The boys were absolutely unrestrained in their amusement. If they pulled down all the books from the shelves, bent the points of all the pens, overturned inkstands, scattered lawpapers over the floor, or threw the pencils into the spittoon, it never disturbed the serenity of their father's good-nature. Frequently absorbed in thought, he never observed their mischievous but destructive pranks—as his unfortunate partner did, who thought much, but said nothing—and, even if brought to his attention, he virtually encouraged their repetition by declining to show any substantial evidence of parental disapproval. After church was over the boys and their father, climbing down the office stairs, ruefully turned their steps homeward. They mingled with the throngs of well-dressed people returning from church, the majority of whom might well have wondered if the trio they passed were going to a fireside where love and white-winged peace reigned supreme. A near relative of Mrs. Lincoln, in explanation of the unhappy condition of things in that lady's household, offered this sugges-tion: "Mrs. Lincoln came of the best stock, and was raised like a lady. Her husband was her opposite, in origin, in educa-tion, in breeding, in everything; and it is therefore quite natural that she should complain if he answered the door-bell himself instead of sending the servant to do so; neither is she to be con-demned if, as you say, she raised 'merry war' because he persist-ed in using his own knife in the butter, instead of the silver-handled one intended for that purpose."[1] Such want of social polish on the part of her husband of course gave Mrs. Lincoln great offense, and therefore in commenting on it she cared nei-ther for time nor place. Her frequent outbursts of temper precipi-tated many an embarrassment from which Lincoln with great difficulty extricated himself.

Mrs. Lincoln, on account of her peculiar nature, could not long retain a servant in her employ. The sea was never so placid but that a breeze would ruffle its waters. She loved show and at-tention, and if, when she glorified her family descent or indulged in one of her strange outbreaks, the servant could simulate

---

[1] A lady relative who lived for two years with the Lincolns told me that Mr. Lincoln was in the habit of lying on the floor with the back of a chair for a pillow when he read. One evening, when in this position in the hall, a knock was heard at the front door and although in his shirtsleeves he answered the call. Two ladies were at the door whom he invited into the parlor, notifying them in his open familiar way, that he would "trot the women folks out." Mrs. Lincoln from an adjoining room witnessed the ladies' entrance and overheard her husband's jocose expression. Her indignation was so instantaneous she made the situation exceedingly interesting for him, and he was glad to retreat from the mansion. He did not return till very late at night and then slipped quietly in at a rear door.

absolute obsequiousness or had tact enough to encourage her social pretensions, Mrs. Lincoln was for the time her firmest friend. One servant, who adjusted herself to suit the lady's capricious ways, lived with the family for several years. She told me that at the time of the debate between Douglas and Lincoln she often heard the latter's wife boast that she would yet be mistress of the White House. The secret of her ability to endure the eccentricities of her mistress came out in the admission that Mr. Lincoln gave her an extra dollar each week on condition that she would brave whatever storms might arise, and suffer whatever might befall her, without complaint. It was a rather severe condition, but she lived rigidly up to her part of the contract. The money was paid secretly and without the knowledge of Mrs. Lincoln. Frequently, after tempestuous scenes between the mistress and her servant, Lincoln at the first opportunity would place his hand encouragingly on the latter's shoulder with the admonition, "Mary, keep up your courage." It may not be without interest to add that the servant afterwards married a man who enlisted in the army. In the spring of 1865 his wife managed to reach Washington to secure her husband's release from the service. After some effort she succeeded in obtaining an interview with the President. He was glad to see her, gave her a basket of fruit, and directed her to call the next day and obtain a pass through the lines and money to buy clothes for herself and children. That night he was assassinated.

The following letter to the editor of a newspaper in Springfield will serve as a specimen of the perplexities which frequently beset Mr. Lincoln when his wife came in contact with others. What in this instance she said to the paper carrier we do not know; we can only intelligently infer. I have no personal recollection of the incident, although I knew the man to whom it was addressed quite well. The letter only recently came to light. I insert it without further comment.

[*Private.*]

Springfield, Ill., February 20, 1857.

John E. Rosette, Esq.

Dear Sir:—Your note about the little paragraph in the Republican was received yesterday, since which time I have been too unwell to notice it. I had not supposed you wrote or approved it. The whole originated in mistake. You know by the conversation with me that I thought the establishment of the paper unfortunate, but I always expected to throw no obstacle in its way, and to patronize it to the extent of taking and paying for one copy. When the paper was brought to my house, my wife said to me, 'Now are you going to take another worthless little paper?' I said to her evasively, 'I have not directed the paper to be left.' From this, in my absence, she sent the message to the carrier. This is the whole story.

Yours truly,
A. Lincoln.

A man once called at the Lincoln house to learn why Mrs. Lincoln had so unceremoniously discharged his niece from her employ. Mrs. Lincoln met him at the door, and being somewhat wrought up, gave vent to her feelings, resorting to such violent gestures and emphatic language that the man was glad to beat a hasty retreat. He at once started out to find Lincoln, determined to exact from him proper satisfaction for his wife's action. Lincoln was entertaining a crowd in a store at the time. The man, still laboring under some agitation, called him to the door and made the demand. Lincoln listened for a moment to his story. "My friend," he interrupted, "I regret to hear this, but let me ask you in all candor, can't you endure for a few moments what I have had as my daily portion for the last fifteen years?" These words were spoken so mournfully and with such a look of distress that the man was completely disarmed. It was a case that appealed to his feelings. Grasping the unfortunate husband's hand, he expressed in no uncertain terms his sympathy, and even apologized for having approached him. He said no more about the infuriated wife, and Lincoln afterward had no better friend in Springfield.

Mr. Lincoln never had a confidant, and therefore never unbosomed himself to others. He never spoke of his trials to me or, so far as I knew, to any of his friends. It was a great burden to carry, but he bore it sadly enough and without a murmur. I could always realize when he was in distress, without being told. He was not exactly an early riser, that is, he never usually appeared at the office till about nine o'clock in the morning. I usually preceded him an hour. Sometimes, however, he would come down as early as seven o'clock—in fact, on one occasion I remember he came down before daylight. If, on arriving at the office, I found him in, I knew instantly that a breeze had sprung up over the domestic sea, and that the waters were troubled. He would either be lying on the lounge looking skyward, or doubled up in a chair with his feet resting on the sill of a back window. He would not look up on my entering, and only answered my "Good morning" with a grunt. I at once busied myself with pen and paper, or ran through the leaves of some book; but the evidence of his melancholy and distress was so plain, and his silence so significant, that I would grow restless myself, and finding some excuse to go to the courthouse or elsewhere, would leave the room.

The door of the office opening into a narrow hallway was half glass, with a curtain on it working on brass rings strung on wire. As I passed out on these occasions I would draw the curtain across the glass, and before I reached the bottom of the stairs I could hear the key turn in the lock, and Lincoln was alone in his gloom. An hour in the clerk's office at the courthouse, an hour longer in a neighboring store having passed, I would return. By that time either a client had dropped in and Lincoln was propounding the law, or else the cloud of despondency had passed away, and he was busy in the recital of an Indiana story to whistle off the recollections of the morning's gloom. Noon having arrived I would depart homeward for my dinner. Returning within an hour, I would find him still in the office, although his house stood but a few squares away— lunching on a slice of cheese and a handful of crackers which, in my absence, he had brought up from a store below. Separating for the day at five or six o'clock in the evening, I would still leave him behind, either sitting on a box at the foot of the stairway, entertaining a few loungers, or killing time in the same way on the courthouse steps. A light in the office after dark attested his presence there till late along in the night, when, after all the world had gone to sleep, the tall form of a man destined to be the nation's President could have been seen strolling along in the shadows of trees and buildings, and quietly slipping in through the door of a modest frame house, which it pleased the world, in a conventional way, to call his home.

Some persons may insist that this picture is too highly colored. If so, I can only answer, they do not know the facts. The majority of those who have a personal knowledge of them are persistent in their silence. If their lips could be opened and all could be known, my conclusions and statements, to say the least of them, would be found to be fair, reasonable, and true. A few words more as to Lincoln's domestic history, and I pass to a different phase of his life. One of his warmest and closest friends, who still survives, maintains the theory that, after all, Lincoln's political ascendency and final elevation to the Presidency were due more to the influence of his wife than to any other person or cause. "The fact," insists this friend, "that Mary Todd, by her turbulent nature and unfortunate manner, prevented her husband from becoming a domestic man, operated largely in his favor; for he was thereby kept out in the world of business and politics. Instead of spending his evenings at home, reading the papers and warming his toes at his own fireside, he was constantly out with the common people, was mingling with the politicians, discussing public questions with the farmers who thronged the offices in the courthouse and state house, and exchanging views with the loungers who surrounded the stove of winter evenings in the village store. The result of this continuous contact with the world, was that he was more thoroughly known than any other man in his community. His wife, therefore, was one of the unintentional means of his promotion. If, on the other hand, he had married some less ambitious but more domestic woman, some honest farmer's quiet daughter——one who would have looked up to and worshipped him because he uplifted her—the result might have been different. For, although it doubtless would have been her pride to see that he had clean clothes whenever he needed them; that his slippers were always in their place; that he was warmly clad and had plenty to eat; and, although the privilege of ministering to his every wish and whim might have been to her a pleasure rather than a duty; yet I fear he would have been buried in the pleasures of a loving home, and the country would never have had Abraham Lincoln for its President."

In her domestic troubles I have always sympathized with Mrs. Lincoln. The world does not know what she bore or how ill-adapted she was to bear it. Her fearless, witty, and austere nature shrank instinctively from association with the calm, imperturbable, and simple ways of her thoughtful and absent-minded husband.

By reason of his practical turn of mind Mr. Lincoln never speculated any more in the scientific and philosophical than he did in the financial world. He never undertook to fathom the intricacies of psychology and metaphysics. Investigation into first causes, abstruse mental phenomena, the science of being, he brushed aside as trash—mere scientific absurdities. He discovered through experience that his mind, like the minds of other men, had its limitations, and hence he economized his forces and his time by applying his powers in the field of the practical. Scientifically regarded he was a realist as opposed to an idealist, a sensationist as opposed to an intuitionist, a materialist as opposed to a spiritualist.

There was more or less superstition in his nature, and, although he may not have believed implicitly in the signs of his many dreams, he was constantly endeavoring to unravel them. His mind was readily impressed with some of the most absurd superstitions. His visit to the Voodoo fortune-teller in New Orleans in 1831; his faith in the virtues of the mad-stone, when he took his son Robert to Terre Haute, Indiana, to be cured of the bite of a rabid dog; and the strange double image of himself which he told his secretary, John Hay, he saw reflected in a mirror just after his election in 1860, strongly attest his inclination to superstition. He held most firmly to the doctrine of fatalism all his life. His wife, after his death, told me what I already knew, that "his only philosophy was, what is to be will be, and no prayers of ours can reverse the decree." He always contended that he was doomed to a sad fate, and he repeatedly said to me when we were alone in our office: "I am sure I shall meet with some terrible end." In proof of his strong leaning towards fatalism he once quoted the case of Brutus and Caesar, arguing that the former was forced by laws and conditions over which he had no control to kill the latter, and, vice versa, that the latter was specially created to be disposed of by the former. This superstitious view of life ran through his being like the thin blue vein through the whitest marble, giving the eye rest from the weariness of continued unvarying color.

For many years I subscribed for and kept on our office table the *Westminster* and *Edinburgh Review* and a number of other English periodicals. Besides them I purchased the works of Spencer, Darwin, and the utterances of other English scientists, all of which I devoured with great relish. I endeavored, but had little success in inducing Lincoln to read them. Occasionally he would snatch one up and peruse it for a little while, but he soon threw it down with the suggestion that it was entirely too heavy for an ordinary mind to digest. A gentleman in Springfield gave him a book called, I believe, "Vestiges of Creation," which interested him so much that he read it through. The volume was published in Edinburgh, and undertook to demonstrate the doctrine of development or evolution. The treatise interested him greatly, and he was deeply impressed with the notion of the so-called "universal law"—evolution; he did not extend greatly his researches, but by continued thinking in a single channel seemed to grow into a warm advocate of the new doctrine. Beyond what I have stated he made no further investigation into the realm of philosophy. "There are no accidents," he said one day, "in my philosophy. Every effect must have its cause. The past is the cause of the present, and the present will be the cause of the future. All these are links in the endless chain stretching from the finite to the infinite." From what has been said it would follow logically that he did not believe, except in a very restricted sense, in the freedom of the will. We often argued the question, I taking the opposite view; he changed the expression, calling it the freedom of the mind, and insisted that man always acted from a motive. I once contended that man was free and could act without a motive. He smiled at my philosophy, and answered that it was impossible, because the motive was born before the man.

The foregoing thoughts are prefatory to the much-mooted question of Mr. Lincoln's religious belief. For what I have heretofore said on this subject, both in public lectures and in letters which have frequently found their way into the newspapers, I have been freely and sometimes bitterly assailed, but I do not intend now to reopen the discussion or to answer the many persons who have risen up and asked to measure swords with me. I merely purpose to state the bare facts, expressing no opinion of my own, and allowing each and every one to put his or her construction on them.

Inasmuch as he was so often a candidate for public office Mr. Lincoln said as little about his religious opinions as possible, especially if he failed to coincide with the orthodox world. In illustration of his religious code I once heard him say that it was like that of an old man named Glenn, in Indiana, whom he heard speak at a church meeting, and who said: "When I do good I feel good, when I do bad I feel bad, and that's my religion." In 1834, while still living in New Salem and before he became a lawyer, he was surrounded by a class of people exceedingly liberal in matters of religion. Volney's *Ruins* and Paine's *Age of Reason* passed from hand to hand, and furnished food for the evening's discussion in the tavern and village store. Lincoln read both these books and thus assimilated them into his own being. He prepared an extended essay—called by many, a book—in which he made an argument against Christianity, striving to prove that the Bible was not inspired, and therefore not God's revelation, and that Jesus Christ was not the son of God. The manuscript containing these audacious and comprehensive propositions he intended to have published or given a wide circulation in some other way. He carried it to the store, where it was read and freely discussed. His friend and employer, Samuel Hill, was among the listeners, and, seriously questioning the propriety of a promising young man like Lincoln fathering such unpopular notions, he snatched the manuscript from his hands and thrust it into the stove. The book went up in flames, and Lincoln's political future was secure. But his infidelity and his skeptical views were not diminished. He soon removed to Springfield, where he attracted considerable notice by his rank doctrine. Much of what he then said may properly be credited to the impetuosity and exuberance of youth. One of his closest friends, whose name is withheld, narrating scenes and reviewing discussions that in 1838 took place in the office of the county clerk, says: "Sometimes Lincoln bordered on atheism. He went far that way, and shocked me. I was then a young man, and believed what my good mother told me. . . . He would come into the clerk's office where I and some young men were writing and staying, and would bring the Bible with him; would read a chapter and argue against it. . . .Lincoln was enthusiastic in his infidelity. As he grew older he grew more discreet; didn't talk much before strangers about his religion; but to friends, close and bosom ones, he was always open and avowed, fair and honest; to strangers, he held them off from policy." John T. Stuart, who was Lincoln's first partner, substantially endorses the above. "He was an avowed and open infidel," declares Stuart, "and sometimes bordered on atheism;. . . went further against Christian beliefs and doctrines and principles than any man I ever heard; he shocked me. I don't remember the exact line of his argument; suppose it was against the inherent defects, so-called, of the Bible, and on grounds of reason. Lincoln always denied that Jesus was the Christ of God—denied that Jesus was the son of God as understood and maintained by the Christian Church." David Davis tells us this: "The idea that Lincoln talked to a stranger about his religion or religious views, or made such speeches and remarks about it as are published, is to me absurd. I knew the man so well; he was the most reticent, secretive man I ever saw or expect to see. He had no faith, in the Christian sense of the term—had faith in laws, principles, causes and effects." Another man testifies as follows: "Mr. Lincoln told me that he was a kind of immortalist; that he never could bring himself to believe in eternal punishment; that man lived but a little while here; and that if eternal punishment were man's doom, he should spend that little life in vigilant and ceaseless preparation by never-ending prayer." Another intimate friend furnishes this: "In my intercourse with Mr. Lincoln I learned that he believed in a Creator of all things, who had neither beginning nor end, possessing all power and wisdom, established a principle in obedience to which worlds move and are upheld, and animal and vegetable life come into existence. A reason he gave for his belief was that in view of the order and harmony of all nature which we behold, it would have been more miraculous to have come about by chance than to have been created and arranged by some great thinking power. As to the Christian theory that Christ is God or equal to the Creator, he said that it had better be taken for granted; for by the test of reason we might become infidels on that subject, for evidence of Christ's divinity came to us in a somewhat doubtful shape; but that the system of Christianity was an ingenious one at least, and perhaps was calculated to do good." Jesse W. Fell, to whom Lincoln first confided the details of his biography, furnishes a more elaborate account of the latter's religious views than any-one else. In a statement made September 22, 1870, Fell says: "If there were any traits of character that stood out in bold relief in the person of Mr. Lincoln they were those of truth and candor. He was utterly incapable of insincerity or professing views on this or any other subject he did not entertain. Knowing such to be his true character, that insincerity, much more duplicity, were traits wholly foreign to his nature, many of his old friends were not a little surprised at finding in some of the biographies of this great man statements concerning his religious opinions so utter-ly at variance with his known sentiments. True, he may have changed or modified these sentiments after his removal from among us, though this is hardly reconcilable with the history of the man, and his entire devotion to public matters during his four years' residence at the national capital. It is possible, how-ever, that this may be the proper solution of this conflict of opinions; or it may be that, with no intention on the part of any one to mislead the public mind, those who have represented him as believing in the popular theological views of the times may have misapprehended him, as experience shows to be quite com-mon where no special effort has been made to attain critical ac-curacy on a subject of this nature. This is the more probable from the well-known fact, that Mr. Lincoln seldom communi-cated to any one his views on this subject; but be this as it may, I have no hesitation whatever in saying that whilst he held many opinions in common with the great mass of Christian believers, he did not believe in what are regarded as the ortho-dox or evangelical views of Christianity.

"On the innate depravity of man, the character and office of the great Head of the Church, the atonement, the infallibility of the written revelation, the performance of miracles, the nature and design of present and future rewards and punishments (as they are popularly called), and many other subjects he held opinions utterly at variance with what are usually taught in the Church. I should say that his expressed views on these and kindred topics were such as, in the estimation of most believers, would place him outside the Christian pale. Yet, to my mind, such was not the true position, since his principles and practices and the spirit of his whole life were of the very kind we universally agree to call Christian; and I think this conclusion is in no wise affected by the circumstance that he never attached himself to any religious society whatever.

"His religious views were eminently practical, and are summed up, as I think, in these two propositions: the Fatherhood of God, and the brotherhood of man. He fully believed in a superintending and overruling Providence that guides and controls the operations of the world, but maintained that law and order, and not their violation or suspension, are the appointed means by which this Providence is exercised.

"I will not attempt any specification of either his belief or disbelief on various religious topics, as derived from the conversations with him at different times during a considerable period; but as conveying a general view of his religious or theological opinions, will state the following facts. Some eight or ten years prior to his death, in conversing with him upon this subject, the writer took occasion to refer, in terms of approbation, to the sermons and writings generally of Dr. W. E. Channing; and, finding he was considerably interested in the statement I made of the opinions held by that author, I proposed to present him (Lincoln) a copy of Channing's entire works, which I soon after did. Subsequently the contents of these volumes, together with the writings of Theodore Parker, furnished him, as he informed me, by his friend and law partner, William H. Herndon, became naturally the topics of conversation with us; and, though far from believing there was an entire harmony of views on his part with either of those authors, yet they were generally much admired and approved by him.

"No religious views with him seemed to find any favor except of the practical and rationalistic order; and if, from my recollections on this subject, I was called upon to designate an author whose views most nearly represented Mr. Lincoln's on this subject, I would say that author was Theodore Parker."

The last witness to testify before this case is submitted to the reader is no less a person than Mrs. Lincoln herself. In a statement made at a time and under circumstances detailed in a subsequent chapter she said this: "Mr. Lincoln had no faith and no hope in the usual acceptation of those words. He never joined a Church; but still, as I believe, he was a religious man by nature. He first seemed to think about the subject when our boy Willie died, and then more than ever about the time he went to Gettysburg; but it was a kind of poetry in his nature, and he was never a technical Christian."

No man had a stronger or firmer faith in Providence—God —than Mr. Lincoln, but the continued use by him late in life of the word God must not be interpreted to mean that he believed in a personal God. In 1854 he asked me to erase the word God from a speech which I had written and read to him for criticism because my language indicated a personal God, whereas he insisted no such personality ever existed.

My own testimony, however, in regard to Mr. Lincoln's religious views may perhaps invite discussion. The world has always insisted on making an orthodox Christian of him, and to analyze his sayings or sound his beliefs is but to break the idol. It only remains to say that, whether orthodox or not, he believed in God and immortality; and even if he questioned the existence of future eternal punishment he hoped to find a rest from trouble and a heaven beyond the grave. If at any time in his life he was skeptical of the divine origin of the Bible he ought not for that reason to be condemned; for he accepted the practical precepts of that great book as binding alike upon his head and his conscience. The benevolence of his impulses, the seriousness of his convictions, and the nobility of his character are evidences unimpeachable that his soul was ever filled with the exalted purity and sublime faith of natural religion.

11

1858-1860

The result of the campaign of 1858 wrought more disaster to Lincoln's finances than to his political prospects. The loss of over six months from his business, and the expenses of the canvass, made a severe drain on his personal income. He was anxious to get back to the law once more and earn a little ready money. A letter written about this time to his friend Norman B. Judd, Chairman of the Republican State Committee, will serve to throw some light on the situation he found himself in. "I have been on expenses so long, without earning anything," he says, "that I am absolutely without money now for even household expenses. Still, if you can put in $250 for me towards discharging the debt of the committee, I will allow it when you and I settle the private matter between us. This, with what I have already paid, with an outstanding note of mine, will exceed my subscription of $500. This, too, is exclusive of my ordinary expenses during the campaign, all of which, being added to my loss of time and business, bears pretty heavily upon one no better off than I am. But as I had the post of honor, it is not for me to be over-nice." At the time this letter was written his property consisted of the house and lot on which he lived, a few law books and some household furniture. He owned a small tract of land in Iowa which yielded him nothing, and the annual income from his law practice did not exceed $3,000; yet the party's committee in Chicago were dunning their late standard-bearer, who, besides the chagrin of his defeat, his own expenses, and the sacrifice of his time, was asked to aid in meeting the general expenses of the campaign. At this day one is a little surprised that some of the generous and wealthy members of the party in Chicago or elsewhere did not come forward and volunteer their aid. But they did not, and whether Lincoln felt in his heart the injustice of this treatment or not, he went straight ahead in his own path and said nothing about it.

Political business being off his hands, he now conceived the idea of entering the lecture field. He began preparations in the usual way by noting down ideas on stray pieces of paper, which found a lodgment inside his hat, and finally brought forth in connected form a lecture on "Inventions." He recounted the wonderful improvements in machinery, the arts, and sciences. Now and then he indulged in a humorous paragraph, and witticisms were freely sprinkled throughout the lecture. During the winter he delivered it at several towns in the central part of the State, but it was so commonplace, and met with such indifferent success, that he soon dropped it altogether. The effort met with the disapproval of his friends, and he himself was filled with disgust. If his address in 1852, over the death of Clay, proved that he was no eulogist, then this last effort demonstrated that he was no lecturer. Invitations to deliver the lecture—prompted no doubt by the advertisement given him in the contest with Douglas—came in very freely; but beyond the three attempts named, he declined them all. "Press of business in the courts" afforded him a convenient excuse, and he retired from the field.

During the fall of 1859 invitations to take part in the canvass came from over half-a-dozen States where elections were to be held. Douglas, fresh from the Senate, had gone to Ohio, and thither in September Lincoln, in response to the demands of party friends everywhere, followed. He delivered telling and impressive speeches at Cincinnati and Columbus, following Douglas at both places. He made such a favorable impression among his Ohio friends that, after a glorious Republican victory, the State committee asked the privilege of publishing his speeches, along with those of Douglas, to be used and distributed as a campaign document. This request he especially appreciated, because after some effort he had failed to induce any publisher in Springfield to undertake the enterprise, thus proving anew that "a prophet is not without honor, save in his own country."

In December he visited Kansas, speaking at Atchison, Troy, Leavenworth, and other towns near the border. His speeches there served to extend his reputation still further westward. Though his arguments were repetitions of the doctrine laid down in the contest with Douglas, yet they were new to the majority of his Kansas hearers and were enthusiastically approved.

By the close of the year he was back again in the dingy law office in Springfield.

The opening of the year 1860 found Mr. Lincoln's name freely mentioned in connection with the Republican nomination for the Presidency. To be classed with Seward, Chase, McLean, and other celebrities was enough to stimulate any Illinois lawyer's pride; but in Mr. Lincoln's case, if it had any such effect, he was most artful in concealing it. Now and then some ardent friend, an editor, for example, would run his name up to the masthead, but in all cases he discouraged the attempt. "In regard to the matter you spoke of," he answered one man who proposed his name, "I beg that you will not give it further mention. Seriously, I do not think I am fit for the Presidency."

The first effort in his behalf as a Presidential aspirant was the action taken by his friends at a meeting held in the State House early in 1860, in the rooms of O. M. Hatch, then Secretary of State. Besides Hatch there were present Norman B. Judd, chairman of the Republican State Committee, Ebenezer Peck, Jackson Grimshaw, and others of equal prominence in the party. "We all expressed a personal preference for Mr. Lincoln," relates one who was a participant in the meeting, "as the Illinois candidate for the Presidency, and asked him if his name might be used at once in connection with the nomination and election. With his characteristic modesty he doubted whether he could get the nomination even if he wished it, and asked until the next morning to answer us whether his name might be announced. Late the next day he authorized us, if we thought proper to do so, to place him in the field." To the question from Mr. Grimshaw whether, if the nomination for President could not be obtained, he would accept the post of Vice-President, he answered that he would not; that his name having been used for the office of President, he would not permit it to be used for any other office, however honorable it might be. This meeting was preliminary to the Decatur convention, and was also the first concerted action in his behalf on the part of his friends.

In the preceding October he came rushing into the office one morning, with the letter from New York City, inviting him to deliver a lecture there, and asked my advice and that of other

friends as to the subject and character of his address. We all recommended a speech on the political situation. Remembering his
poor success as a lecturer himself, he adopted our suggestions.
He accepted the invitation of the New York committee, at the
same time notifying them that his speech would deal entirely
with political questions, and fixing a day late in February as the
most convenient time. Meanwhile he spent the intervening time
in careful preparation. He searched through the dusty volumes
of congressional proceedings in the State library, and dug deeply
into political history. He was painstaking and thorough in the
study of his subject, but when at last he left for New York we
had many misgivings—and he not a few himself—of his success
in the great metropolis. What effect the unpretentious Western
lawyer would have on the wealthy and fashionable society of the
great city could only be conjectured. A description of the meeting at Cooper Institute, a list of the names of the prominent men
and women present, or an account of Lincoln in the delivery of
the address would be needless repetitions of well-known history.[1] It only remains to say that his speech was devoid of all rhetorical imagery, with a marked suppression of the pyrotechnics
of stump oratory. It was constructed with a view to accuracy of
statement, simplicity of language, and unity of thought. In some
respects like a lawyer's brief, it was logical, temperate in tone,
powerful—irresistibly driving conviction home to men's reasons
and their souls. No former effort in the line of speech-making
had cost Lincoln so much time and thought as this one. It is said
by one of his biographers, that those afterwards engaged in getting out the speech as a campaign document were three weeks in
verifying the statements and finding the historical records

---

[1]On his return home Lincoln told me that for once in his life he was greatly
abashed over his personal appearance. The new suit of clothes which he
donned on his arrival in New York were ill-fitting garments, and showed the
creases made while packed in the valise; and for a long time after he began his
speech and before he became "warmed up" he imagined that the audience noticed the contrast between his Western clothes and the neat-fitting suits of Mr.
Bryant and others who sat on the platform. The collar of his coat on the right
side had an unpleasant way of flying up whenever he raised his arm to gesticulate. He imagined the audience noticed that also. After the meeting closed, the
newspaper reporters called for slips of his speech. This amused him, because he
had no idea what slips were, and besides, didn't suppose the newspapers cared
to print his speech verbatim.

referred to and consulted by him. This is probably a little over-stated as to time, but unquestionably the work of verification and reference was in any event a very labored and extended one. (Mr. Lincoln obtained most of the facts of his Cooper Institute speech from Eliott's "Debates on the Federal Constitution." There were six volumes, which he gave to me when he went to Washington in 1861.) The day following the Cooper Institute meeting, the leading New York dailies published the speech in full, and made favorable editorial mention of it and of the speak-er as well. It was plain now that Lincoln had captured the me-tropolis. From New York he traveled to New England to visit his son Robert, who was attending college. In answer to the many calls and invitations which showered on him, he spoke at various places in Connecticut, Rhode Island, and New Hampshire. In all these places he not only left deep impressions of his ability, but he convinced New England of his intense ear-nestness in the great cause. The newspapers treated him with no little consideration. One paper characterized his speech as one of "great fairness," delivered with "great apparent candor and wonderful interest. For the first half hour his opponents would agree with every word he uttered; and from that point he would lead them off little by little until it seemed as if he had got them all into his fold. He is far from prepossessing in personal appear-ance, and his voice is disagreeable; and yet he wins your atten-tion from the start. He indulges in no flowers of rhetoric, no elo-quent passages. . . . He displays more shrewdness, more knowl-edge of the masses of mankind than any public speaker we have heard since Long Jim Wilson left for California."

Lincoln's return to Springfield after his dazzling success in the East was the signal for earnest congratulations on the part of his friends. Seward was the great man of the day, but Lincoln had demonstrated to the satisfaction of his friends that he was tall enough and strong enough to measure swords with the Auburn statesman. His triumph in New York and New England had shown that the idea of a house divided against itself induced as strong cooperation and hearty support in prevention of a great wrong in the East as the famous "irrepressible conflict" attracted warriors to Seward's standard in the Mississippi valley. It was apparent now to Lincoln that the Presidential nomination was

within his reach. He began gradually to lose his interest in the
law and to trim his political sails at the same time. His recent
success had stimulated his self-confidence to unwonted proportions. He wrote to influential party workers everywhere. I know
the idea prevails that Lincoln sat still in his chair in Springfield,
and that one of those unlooked-for tides in human affairs came
along and cast the nomination into his lap; but any man who
has had experience in such things knows that great political
prizes are not obtained in that way. The truth is, Lincoln was as
vigilant as he was ambitious, and there is no denying the fact
that he understood the situation perfectly from the start. In the
management of his own interests he was obliged to rely almost
entirely on his own resources. He had no money with which to
maintain a political bureau, and he lacked any kind of personal
organization whatever. Seward had all these things, and, behind
them all, a brilliant record in the United States Senate with
which to dazzle his followers. But with all his prestige and experience the latter was no more adroit and no more untiring in
pursuit of his ambition than the man who had just delivered the
Cooper Institute speech. A letter written by Lincoln about this
time to a friend in Kansas serves to illustrate his methods, and
measures the extent of his ambition. The letter is dated March
10, and is now in my possession. For obvious reasons I withhold
the friend's name. "As to your kind wishes for myself," writes
Lincoln, "allow me to say I cannot enter the ring on the money
basis—first, because in the main it is wrong; and secondly, I
have not and cannot get the money. I say in the main the use of
money is wrong; but for certain objects in a political contest the
use of some is both right and indispensable. With me, as with
yourself, this long struggle has been one of great pecuniary loss.
I now distinctly say this: 'If you shall be appointed a delegate to
Chicago I will furnish one hundred dollars to bear the expenses
of the trip.' " There is enough in this letter to show that Lincoln
was not only determined in his political ambition, but intensely
practical as well. His eye was constantly fastened on Seward,
who had already freely exercised the rights of leadership in the
party. All other competitors he dropped out of the problem. In
the middle of April he again writes his Kansas friend: "Reaching
home last night I found yours of the 7th. You know I was

recently in New England. Some of the acquaintances I made while there write me since the election that the close vote in Connecticut and the quasi-defeat in Rhode Island are a drawback upon the prospects of Governor Seward; and Trumbull writes Dubois to the same effect. Do not mention this as coming from me. Both these States are safe enough in the fall." But, while Seward may have lost ground near his home, he was acquiring strength in the West. He had invaded the very territory Lincoln was intending to retain by virtue of his course in the contest with Douglas. Lincoln's friend in Kansas, instead of securing that delegation for him, had suffered the Seward men to outgeneral him, and the prospects were by no means flattering. "I see by the dispatches," writes Lincoln, in a burst of surprise, "that, since you wrote, Kansas has appointed delegates and instructed for Seward. Don't stir them up to anger, but come along to the convention and I will do as I said about expenses." Whether the friend ever accepted Lincoln's generous offer I do not know,[2] but it may not be without interest to state that within ten days after the latter's inauguration he appointed him to a Federal office with comfortable salary attached, and even asked for his preferences as to other contemplated appointments in his own State. "You will start for Kansas before I see you again"; he wrote, "and when I saw you a moment this morning I forgot to ask you about some of the Kansas appointments, which I intended to do. If you care much about them you can write, as I think I shall not make the appointments just yet."

In the rapid, stirring scenes that crowd upon each other from this time forward the individuality of Lincoln is easily lost sight of. He was so thoroughly interwoven in the issues before the people of Illinois that he had become a part of them. Among his colleagues at the bar he was no longer looked upon as the circuit court lawyer of earlier days. To them it seemed as if the nation were about to lay its claim upon him. His tall form enlarged, un-

[2]This case illustrates quite forcibly Lincoln's weakness in dealing with individuals. This man I know had written Lincoln, promising to bring the Kansas delegation to Chicago for him if he would only pay his expenses. Lincoln was weak enough to make the promise, and yet such was his faith in the man that he appointed him to an important judicial position and gave him great prominence in other ways. What President or candidate for President would dare do such a thing now?

til, to use a figurative expression, he could no longer pass
through the door of our dingy office. Reference has already been
made to the envy of his rivals at the bar, and the jealousy of his
political contemporaries. Very few indeed were free from the
degrading passion; but it made no difference in Lincoln's treatment of them. He was as generous and deferred to them as much
as ever. The first public movement by the Illinois people in his
interest was the action of the State convention, which met at
Decatur on the 9th and 10th of May. It was at this convention
that Lincoln's friend and cousin, John Hanks, brought in the two
historic rails which both had made in the Sangamon bottom in
1830, and which served the double purpose of electrifying the Illinois people and kindling the fire of enthusiasm that was destined to sweep over the nation. In the words of an ardent Lincoln delegate, "These rails were to represent the issue in the
coming contest between labor free and labor slave; between
democracy and aristocracy. Little did I think," continues our
jubilant and effusive friend, "of the mighty consequences of this
little incident; little did I think that the tall, and angular, and
bony rail-splitter who stood in girlish diffidence bowing with
awkward grace would fill the chair once filled by Washington,
and that his name would echo in chants of praise along the cor-
ridor of all coming time." A week later the hosts were gathered
for the great convention in Chicago. David Davis had rented
rooms in the Tremont House and opened up "Lincoln's
headquarters." I was not a delegate, but belonged to the contingent which had Lincoln's interests in charge. Judge Logan was
the Springfield delegate, and to him Lincoln had given a letter
authorizing the withdrawal of his name whenever his friends
deemed such action necessary or proper. Davis was the active
man, and had the business management in charge. If any negotiations were made, he made them. The convention was held in a
monster building called the Wigwam. No one who has ever attempted a description of it has overdrawn its enthusiasm and exciting scenes. Amid all the din and confusion, the curbstone con-
tentions, the promiscuous wrangling of delegates, the deafening
roar of the assembled hosts, the contest narrowed down to a
neck-and-neck race between the brilliant statesman of Auburn
and the less pretentious, but manly rail-splitter from the San-

gamon bottoms. With the proceedings of the convention the world is already well familiar. On the first ballot Seward led, but was closely followed by Lincoln; on the second Lincoln gained amazingly; on the third the race was an even one until the dramatic change by Carter, of Ohio, when Lincoln, swinging loose, swept grandly to the front. The cannon planted on the roof of the Wigwam belched forth a boom across the Illinois prairies. The sound was taken up and reverberated from Maine to California. With the nomination of Hannibal Hamlin, of Maine, the convention adjourned. The delegates—victorious and vanquished alike—turned their steps homeward, and the great campaign of 1860 had begun. The day before the nomination the editor of the Springfield *Journal* arrived in Chicago with a copy of the Missouri *Democrat*, in which Lincoln had marked three passages referring to Seward's position on the slavery question. On the margin of the paper he had written in pencil, "I agree with Seward in his 'Irrepressible Conflict,' but I do not endorse his 'Higher Law' doctrine." Then he added in words underscored: "Make no contracts that will bind me." This paper was brought into the room where Davis, Judd, Logan, and I were gathered, and was read to us. But Lincoln was down in Springfield, some distance away from Chicago, and could therefore not appreciate the gravity of the situation; at least so Davis argued, and, viewing it in that light, the latter went ahead with his negotiations. What the consequences of these deals were will appear later on. The news of his nomination found Lincoln at Springfield in the office of the *Journal*. Naturally enough he was nervous, restless, and laboring under more or less suppressed excitement. He had been tossing ball—a pastime frequently indulged in by the lawyers of that day, and had played a few games of billiards to keep down, as another has expressed it, "the unnatural excitement that threatened to possess him." When the telegram containing the result of the last ballot came in, although apparently calm and undisturbed, a close observer could have detected in the compressed lip and serious countenance evidences of deep and unusual emotion. As the balloting progressed he had gone to the office of the *Journal*, and was sitting in a large arm-chair there when the news of his nomination came. What a line of scenes, stretching from the barren glade in

Kentucky to the jubilant and enthusiastic throng in the Wigwam
at Chicago, must have broken in upon his vision as he hastened
from the newspaper office to "tell a little woman down the street
the news!" In the evening his friends and neighbors called to
congratulate him. He thanked them feelingly and shook them
each by the hand.

A day later the committee from the convention, with George
Ashmun, of Massachusetts, at its head, called, and delivered formal notice of his nomination. This meeting took place at his
house. His response was couched in polite and dignified language, and many of the committee, who now met him for the
first time, departed with an improved impression of the new
standard-bearer. A few days later he wrote his official letter of
acceptance, in which he warmly endorsed the resolutions of the
convention. His actions and utterances so far had begun to dissipate the erroneous notion prevalent in some of the more
remote Eastern States, that he was more of a backwoods boor
than a gentleman; but with the arrival of the campaign in dead
earnest, people paid less attention to the candidates and more to
the great issues at stake. Briefly stated, the Republican platform
was a declaration that "the new dogma, that the Constitution
carries slavery into all the Territories, is a dangerous political
heresy, revolutionary in tendency and subversive of the peace
and harmony of the country; that the normal condition of all the
Territories is that of freedom; that neither Congress, the Territorial Legislature, nor any individual can give legal existence to
slavery in any Territory; that the opening of the slave trade
would be a crime against humanity." Resolutions favoring a
homestead law, river and harbor improvements, and the Pacific
railroad were also included in the platform. With these the
Republicans, as a lawyer would say, went to the country. The
campaign which followed was one with few parallels in American history. There was not only the customary exultation and
enthusiasm over candidates, but there was patient listening and
hard thinking among the masses. The slavery question, it was
felt, must soon be decided. Threats of disunion were the texts of
many a campaign speech in the South: in fact, as has since been
shown, a deep laid conspiracy to overthrow the Union was then
forming, and was only awaiting the election of a Republican
President to show its hideous head. The Democratic party was

struggling under the demoralizing effects of a split, in which even the Buchanan administration had taken sides. Douglas, the nominee of one wing, in his desperation had entered into the canvass himself, making speeches with all the power and elo- quence at his command. The Republicans, cheered over the pros- pect, had joined hands with the Abolitionists, and both were marching to victory under the inspiration of Lincoln's sentiment, that "the further spread of slavery should be arrested, and it should be placed where the public mind shall rest in the belief of its ultimate extinction."

As the canvass advanced and waxed warm I tendered my ser- vices and made a number of speeches in the central part of the State. I remember, in the midst of a speech at Petersburg, and just as I was approaching an oratorical climax, a man out of breath came rushing up to me and thrust a message into my hand. I was somewhat frustrated and greatly alarmed, fearing it might contain news of some accident in my family; but great was my relief when I read it, which I did aloud. It was a message from Lincoln, telling me to be of good cheer, that Ohio, Pennsyl- vania, and Indiana had gone Republican.[3]

These were then October States, and this was the first gun for the great cause. It created so much demonstration, such a burst of enthusiasm and confusion, that the crowd forgot they had any speaker; they ran yelling and hurrahing out of the hall, and I never succeeded in finishing the speech.

As soon as officially notified of his nomination Mr. Lincoln moved his headquarters from our office to a room in the State House building, and there, with his secretary, John G. Nicolay, he spent the busy and exciting days of his campaign. Of course he attended to no law business, but still he loved to come to our office of evenings, and spend an hour with a few choice friends in a friendly privacy which was denied him at his public

---

[3]The handwriting of the note was a little tremulous, showing that Lincoln was excited and nervous when he wrote it. Following is a copy of the original MS.:

"Springfield, Ill., October 10, 1860.
    "Dear William: I cannot give you details, but it is entirely certain that Penn- sylvania and Indiana have gone Republican very largely. Pennsylvania 25,000, and Indiana 5,000 to 10,000. Ohio of course is safe.
                                                    "Yours as ever,
                                                        "A. Lincoln."

quarters. These were among the last meetings we had with Lincoln as our friend and fellow at the bar; and they are also the most delightful recollections any of us have retained of him.[4]

At last the turmoil and excitement and fatigue of the campaign were over: the enthusiastic political workers threw aside their campaign uniforms, the boys blew out their torches, and the voter approached the polls with his ballot. On the morning of election day I stepped in to see Mr. Lincoln, and was surprised to learn that he did not intend to cast his vote. I knew of course that he did so because of a feeling that the candidate for a Presidential office ought not to vote for his own electors; but when I suggested the plan of cutting off the Presidential electors and voting for the State officers, he was struck with the idea, and at last consented. His appearance at the polls, accompanied by Ward Lamon, the lamented young Ellsworth, and myself, was the occasion of no little surprise because of the general impression which prevailed that he did not intend to vote. The crowd around the polls opened a gap as the distinguished voter approached, and some even removed their hats as he deposited his ticket and announced in a subdued voice his name, "Abraham Lincoln."

The election was held on the 6th of November. The result showed a popular vote of 1,857,610 for Lincoln; 1,291,574 for Douglas; 850,022 for Breckenridge; and 646,124 for Bell. In the electoral college Lincoln received 180 votes, Breckenridge 72, Bell 39, and Douglas 12. Mr. Lincoln having now been elected, there remained, before taking up the reins of government, the details of his departure from Springfield, and the selection of a cabinet.

[4]One of what Lincoln regarded as the remarkable features of his canvass for President was the attitude of some of his neighbors in Springfield. A poll of the voters had been made in a little book and given to him. On running over the names he found that the greater part of the clergy of the city—in fact all but three—were against him. This depressed him somewhat, and he called in Dr. Newton Bateman, who as Superintendent of Public Instruction occupied the room adjoining his own in the State House, and whom he habitually addressed as "Mr. Schoolmaster." He commented bitterly on the attitude of the preachers and many of their followers, who, pretending to be believers in the Bible and God-fearing Christians, yet by their votes demonstrated that they cared not whether slavery was voted up or down. "God cares and humanity cares," he reflected, "and if they do not they surely have not read their Bible aright."

12

President-Elect

The election over, Mr. Lincoln scarcely had time to take a breath until another campaign and one equally trying, so far as a test of his constitution and nerves are concerned, as the one through which he had just passed, opened up before him. I refer to the siege of the cabinetmakers and officeseekers. It proved to be a severe and protracted strain and one from which there seemed to be no relief, as the President-elect of this renowned democratic Government is by custom and precedent expected to meet and listen to everybody who calls to see him. "Individuals, deputations, and delegations," says one of Mr. Lincoln's biographers, "from all quarters pressed in upon him in a manner that might have killed a man of less robust constitution. The hotels of Springfield were filled with gentlemen who came with light baggage and heavy schemes. The party had never been in office. A clean sweep of the 'ins' was expected, and all the 'outs' were patriotically anxious to take the vacant places. It was a party that had never fed; and it was vigorously hungry. Mr. Lincoln and Artemus Ward saw a great deal of fun in it; and in all human probability it was the fun alone that enabled Mr. Lincoln to bear it."

A newspaper correspondent who had been sent down from Chicago to "write up" Mr. Lincoln soon after his nomination, was kind enough several years ago to furnish me with an account of his visit. As some of his reminiscences are more or less interesting, I take the liberty of inserting a portion of his letter. "A what-not in the corner of the room," he relates, "was laden with various kinds of shells. Taking one in my hand, I said, 'This, I suppose, is called a Trocus by the geologist or naturalist.' Mr. Lincoln paused a moment as if reflecting and then replied, 'I do not know, for I never studied either geology or natural history.' I then took to examining the few pictures that hung on the walls, and was paying more than ordinary attention to one that hung above the sofa. He was immediately at my left and pointing to it said, 'That picture gives a very fair representation of my homely face.' . . . The time for my departure nearing,

I made the usual apologies and started to go. 'You cannot get out
of town before a quarter past eleven,' remonstrated Mr. Lincoln,
'and you may as well stay a little longer.' Under pretence of
some unfinished matters down town, however, I very reluctantly
withdrew from the mansion. 'Well,' said Mr. Lincoln, as we
passed into the hall, 'suppose you come over to the State House
before you start for Chicago.' After a moment's deliberation I
promised to do so. Mr. Lincoln, following without his hat, and
continuing the conversation, shook hands across the gate, saying, 'Now, come over.' I wended my way to my hotel, and after a
brief period was in his office at the State House. Resuming conversation, he said, 'If the man comes with the key before you go,
I want to give you a book.' I certainly hoped the man *would*
come with the key. Some conversation had taken place at the
house on which his book treated—but I had forgotten this—and
soon Mr. Lincoln absented himself for perhaps two minutes and
returned with a copy of the debates between himself and Judge
Douglas. He placed the book on his knee, as he sat on two legs
of his chair, and wrote on the flyleaf, 'J. S. Bliss, from A. Lincoln.' Besides this he marked a complete paragraph near the
middle of the book. While sitting in the position described little
Willie, his son, came in and begged his father for twenty-five
cents. 'My son,' said the father, 'what do you want with twenty-
five cents?' 'I want it to buy candy with,' cried the boy. 'I cannot
give you twenty-five cents, my son, but will give you five cents,'
at the same time putting his thumb and finger into his vest
pocket and taking therefrom five cents in silver, which he placed
upon the desk for the boy. But this did not reach Willie's expectations; he scorned the pile, and turning away clambered downstairs and through the spacious halls of the Capitol, leaving
behind him his five cents and a distinct reverberation of sound.
Mr. Lincoln turned to me and said, 'He will be back after that in
a few minutes.' 'Why do you think so?' said I. 'Because, as soon
as he finds I will give him no more he will come and get it.'
After the matter had been nearly forgotten and conversation had
turned in an entirely different channel, Willie came cautiously in
behind my chair and that of his father, picked up the specie, and
went away without saying a word."[1]

[1]This paragraph was a footnote in the original edition.

His own election of course disposed of any claims Illinois might have had to any further representation in the cabinet, but it afforded Mr. Lincoln no relief from the argumentative interviews and pressing claims of the endless list of ambitious statesmen in the thirty-two other states, who swarmed into Springfield from every point of the compass. He told each one of them a story, and even if he failed to put their names on his slate they went away without knowing that fact, and never forgot the visit. He had a way of pretending to assure his visitor that in the choice of his advisers he was "free to act as his judgment dictated," although David Davis, acting as his manager at the Chicago convention, had negotiated with the Indiana and Pennsylvania delegations, and assigned places in the cabinet to Simon Cameron and Caleb Smith, besides making other "arrangements" which Mr. Lincoln was expected to ratify. Of this he was undoubtedly aware, although in answer to a letter from Joshua R. Giddings, of Ohio, congratulating him on his nomination, he said, "It is indeed most grateful to my feelings that the responsible position assigned me comes without conditions." Out of regard to the dignity of the exalted station he was about to occupy, he was not as free in discussing the matter of his probable appointments with some of his personal friends as they had believed he would be. In one or two instances, I remember, the latter were offended at his seeming disregard of the claims of old friendship. My advice was not asked for on such grave subjects, nor had I any right or reason to believe it would be; hence I never felt slighted or offended. On some occasions in our office, when Mr. Lincoln had come across from the State House for a rest or a chat with me, he would relate now and then some circumstance—generally an amusing one—connected with the settlement of the cabinet problem, but it was said in such a way that one would not have felt free to interrogate him about his plans. Soon after his election I received from my friend Joseph Medill, of Chicago, a letter which argued strongly against the appointment of Simon Cameron to a place in the cabinet, and which the writer desired I should bring to Mr. Lincoln's attention. I awaited a favorable opportunity, and one evening when we were alone in our office I gave it to him. It was an eloquent protest against the appointment of a corrupt and debased man, and coming from the source it did—the writer being one of Lincoln's best newspaper supporters—made a deep impression on him. Lincoln read it over several times, but refrained from expressing any opinion. He did say, however, that he felt himself under no promise or obligation to appoint anyone; that if his friends made any agreements for him they did so over his expressed direction and without his knowledge. At another time he said that he wanted to give the South, by way of placation, a place in his cabinet, that a fair division of the country entitled the Southern States to a reasonable representation there, and if not interfered with he would make such a distribution as would satisfy all persons interested. He named three persons who would be acceptable to him. They were Botts, of Virginia; Stephens, of Georgia; and Maynard, of Tennessee. He apprehended no such grave danger to the Union as the mass of people supposed would result from the Southern threats, and said he could not in his heart believe that the South designed the overthrow of the Government. This is the extent of my conversation about the cabinet. Thurlow Weed, the veteran in journalism and politics, came out from New York and spent several days with Lincoln. He was not only the representative of Senator Seward, but rendered the President-elect signal service in the formation of his cabinet. In his autobiography Mr. Weed relates numerous incidents of this visit. He was one day opposing the claims of Montgomery Blair who aspired to a cabinet appointment, when Mr. Lincoln inquired of Weed whom he would recommend. "Henry Winter Davis," was the response. "David Davis, I see, has been posting you up on this question," retorted Lincoln. "He has Davis on the brain. I think Maryland must be a good State to move from." The President then told a story of a witness in court in a neighboring county, who on being asked his age replied, "Sixty." Being satisfied he was much older the question was repeated, and on receiving the same answer, the court admonished the witness, saying, "The court knows you to be much older than sixty." "Oh, I understand now," was the rejoinder; "you're thinking of those ten years I spent on the eastern shore of Maryland; that was so much time lost and don't count."

Before departing for Washington Mr. Lincoln went to Chicago for a few days' stay, and there by previous arrangement met his old friend, Joshua F. Speed. Both were accompanied by their wives, and while the latter were out shopping the two husbands repaired to Speed's room at the hotel. "For an hour or more," relates Speed, "we lived over again the scenes of other days. Finally Lincoln threw himself on the bed, and fixing his eyes on a spot in the ceiling asked me this question, 'Speed, what is your pecuniary condition? are you rich or poor?' I answered, addressing him by his new title, 'Mr. President, I think I can anticipate what you are going to say. I'll speak candidly to you on the subject. My pecuniary condition is satisfactory to me now; you would perhaps call it good. I do not think you have within your gift any office I could afford to take.' Mr. Lincoln then proposed to make Guthrie, of Kentucky, Secretary of War, but did not want to write to him—asked me to feel of him. I did as requested, but the Kentucky statesman declined on the ground of his advanced age, and consequent physical inability to fill the position. He gave substantial assurance of his loyal sentiments, however, and insisted that the Union should be preserved at all hazards."

Late in January Mr. Lincoln informed me that he was ready to begin the preparation of his inaugural address. He had, aside from his law books and the few gilded volumes that ornamented the centre-table in his parlor at home, comparatively no library. He never seemed to care to own or collect books. On the other hand I had a very respectable collection, and was adding to it every day. To my library Lincoln very frequently had access. When, therefore, he began on his inaugural speech he told me what works he intended to consult. I looked for a long list, but when he went over it I was greatly surprised. He asked me to furnish him with Henry Clay's great speech delivered in 1850; Andrew Jackson's proclamation against Nullification; and a copy of the Constitution. He afterwards called for Webster's reply to Hayne, a speech which he read when he lived at New Salem, and which he always regarded as the grandest specimen of American oratory. With these few "volumes," and no further sources of reference, he locked himself up in a room upstairs over a store across the street from the State House, and there, cut off from all communication and intrusion, he prepared the address. Though composed amid the unromantic surroundings of a dingy, dusty, and neglected back room, the speech has become a memorable document. Posterity will assign to it a high rank among historical utterances; and it will ever bear comparison with the efforts of Washington, Jefferson, Adams, or any that preceded its delivery from the steps of the national Capitol.

After Mr. Lincoln's rise to national prominence, and especially since his death, I have often been asked if I did not write this or that paper for him; if I did not prepare or help prepare some of his speeches. I know that other and abler friends of Lincoln have been asked the same question. To people who made such inquiries I always responded, "You don't understand Mr. Lincoln. No man ever asked less aid than he; his confidence in his own ability to meet the requirements of every hour was so marked that his friends never thought of tendering their aid, and therefore no one could share his responsibilities. I never wrote a line for him; he never asked me to. I was never conscious of having exerted any influence over him. He often called out my views on some philosophical question, simply because I was a fond student of philosophy, and conceding that I had given the subject more attention than he; he often asked as to the use of a word or the turn of a sentence, but if I volunteered to recommend or even suggest a change of language which involved a change of sentiment I found him the most inflexible man I have ever seen."

One more duty—an act of filial devotion—remained to be done before Abraham Lincoln could announce his readiness to depart for the city of Washington—a place from which it was unfortunately decreed he should never return. In the first week of February he slipped quietly away from Springfield and rode to Farmington in Coles County, where his aged step-mother was still living. Here, in the little country village, he met also the surviving members of the Hanks and Johnston families. He visited the grave of his father, old Thomas Lincoln, which had been unmarked and neglected for almost a decade, and left directions that a suitable stone should be placed there to mark the spot. Retracing his steps in the direction of Springfield he stopped over night in the town of Charleston, where he made a brief address, recalling many of his boyhood exploits, in the public hall. In the audience were many persons who had known him first as the stalwart young oxdriver when his father's family drove into Illinois from southern Indiana. One man had brought with him a horse which the President-elect, in the earlier days of his law practice, had recovered for him in a replevin suit; another one was able to recite from personal recollection the thrilling details of the famous wrestling match between Lincoln the flatboatman in 1830 and Daniel Needham; and all had some reminiscence of his early manhood to relate. The separation from his stepmother was particularly touching. The parting, when the good old woman, with tears streaming down her cheeks, gave him a mother's benediction, expressing the fear that his life might be taken by his enemies, will never be forgotten by those who witnessed it. Deeply impressed by this farewell scene Mr. Lincoln reluctantly withdrew from the circle of warm friends who crowded around him, and, filled with gloomy forebodings of the future, returned to Springfield. The great questions of state having been pretty well settled in his own mind, and a few days yet remaining before his final departure, his neighbors and old friends called to take leave of him and pay their "best respects." Many of these callers were from New Salem, where he had made his start in life, and each one had some pleasant or amusing incident of earlier days to call up when they met. Hannah Armstrong, who had "foxed" his trousers with buckskin in the days when he served as surveyor under John Calhoun, and whose son Lincoln had afterwards acquitted in the trial for murder at Beardstown, gave positive evidence of the interest she took in his continued rise in the world. She bade him good-bye, but was filled with a presentiment that she would never see him alive again. "Hannah," he said, jovially, "if they do kill me I shall never die again."

Early in February the last item of preparation for the journey to Washington had been made. Mr. Lincoln had disposed of his household goods and furniture to a neighbor, had rented his house; and as these constituted all the property he owned in Illinois there was no further occasion for concern on that score. In the afternoon of his last day in Springfield he came down to our office to examine some papers and confer with me about certain legal matters in which he still felt some interest. On several previous occasions he had told me he was coming over to the office "to have a long talk with me," as he expressed it. We ran over the books and arranged for the completion of all unsettled and unfinished matters. In some cases he had certain requests to make—certain lines of procedure he wished me to observe. After these things were all disposed of he crossed to the opposite side of the room and threw himself down on the old office sofa, which, after many years of service, had been moved against the wall for support. He lay for some moments, his face towards the ceiling, without either of us speaking. Presently he inquired, "Billy"—he always called me by that name—"how long have we been together?" "Over sixteen years," I answered. "We've never had a cross word during all that time, have we?" to which I returned a vehement, "No, indeed we have not." He then recalled some incidents of his early practice and took great pleasure in delineating the ludicrous features of many a lawsuit on the circuit. It was at this last interview in Springfield that he told me of the efforts that had been made by other lawyers to supplant me in the partnership with him. He insisted that such men were weak creatures, who, to use his own language, "hoped to secure a law practice by hanging to his coattail." I never saw him in a more cheerful mood. He gathered a bundle of books and papers he wished to take with him and started to go; but before leaving he made the strange request that the sign-board which swung on its rusty hinges at the foot of the stairway should remain. "Let it hang there undisturbed,"[2] he said, with a significant lowering of his voice. "Give our clients to understand that the election of a President makes no change in the firm of Lincoln and Herndon. If I live I'm coming back some time, and then we'll go right on practicing law as if nothing had ever hap-

[2] In answer to the many inquiries made of me, I will say here that during this last interview Mr. Lincoln, for the first time, brought up the subject of an office under his administration. He asked me if I desired an appointment at his hands, and, if so, what I wanted. I answered that I had no desire for a Federal office, that I was then holding the office of Bank Commissioner under appointment of Governor Bissell, and that if he would request my retention in office by Yates, the incoming Governor, I should be satisfied. He made the necessary recommendation, and Governor Yates complied. I was present at the meeting between Yates and Lincoln, and I remember that the former, when Lincoln urged my claims for retention in office, asked Lincoln to appoint their mutual friend A. Y. Ellis postmaster at Springfield. I do not remember whether Lincoln promised to do so or not, but Ellis was never appointed.

pened." He lingered for a moment as if to take a last look at the old quarters, and then passed through the door into the narrow hallway. I accompanied him downstairs. On the way he spoke of the unpleasant features surrounding the Presidential office. "I am sick of office-holding already," he complained, "and I shudder when I think of the tasks that are still ahead." He said the sorrow of parting from his old associates was deeper than most persons would imagine, but it was more marked in his case because of the feeling which had become irrepressible that he would never return alive. I argued against the thought, characterizing it as an illusory notion not in harmony or keeping with the popular ideal of a President. "But it is in keeping with my philosophy," was his quick retort. Our conversation was frequently broken in upon by the interruptions of passers-by, who, each in succession, seemed desirous of claiming his attention. At length he broke away from them all. Grasping my hand warmly and with a fervent "Good-bye," he disappeared down the street, and never came back to the office again.

On the morning following this last interview, the 11th day of February, the Presidential party repaired to the railway station, where the train which was to convey them to Washington awaited the ceremony of departure. The day was a stormy one, with dense clouds hanging heavily overhead. A goodly throng of Springfield people had gathered to see the distinguished party safely off. After the latter had entered the car the people closed about it until the President appeared on the rear platform. He stood for a moment as if to suppress evidences of his emotion, and removing his hat made the following brief but dignified and touching address:

Friends: No one who has never been placed in a like position can understand my feelings at this hour, nor the oppressive sadness I feel at this parting. For more than a quarter of a century I have lived among you, and during all that time I have received nothing but kindness at your hands. Here I have lived from my youth until now I am an old man. Here the most sacred ties of earth were assumed. Here all my children were born; and here one of them lies buried. To you, dear friends, I owe all that I have, all that I am. All the strange, checkered past seems to crowd now upon my mind. Today I leave you. I go to assume a task more difficult than that which devolved upon Washington. Unless the great God who assisted him shall be with and aid me, I must fail; but if the same omniscient mind and almighty arm that directed and protected him shall guide and support me I shall not fail—I shall succeed. Let us all pray that the God of our fathers may not forsake us now. To him I commend you all. Permit me to ask that with equal sincerity and faith you will invoke his wisdom and guidance for me. With these words I must leave you, for how long I know not. Friends, one and all, I must now bid you an affectionate farewell.